*The Shape of Fate:
From Classical Philosophy
to Astrological Practice*

THE SHAPE OF FATE:
FROM CLASSICAL PHILOSOPHY
TO ASTROLOGICAL PRACTICE

Bernadette Brady

SOPHIA CENTRE PRESS
Ceredigion, Wales
2025

The Shape of Fate: From Classical Philosophy to Astrological Practice
Bernadette Brady

© Sophia Centre Press 2025

First published in 2025.

All rights reserved. No part of this publication may be reproduced
or utilised in any form or by any means, electronic or mechanical,
including photocopying, recording, or by any information storage
and retrieval system, without permission in writing from the Publishers.

Sophia Centre Press
University of Wales Trinity Saint David
Ceredigion, Wales SA48 7ED, United Kingdom.
www.sophiacentrepress.com

Typeset by Daniela Puia
Cover design: Jenn Zahrt

ISBN: 9781907767173

Publisher's Cataloging-in-Publication
(Provided by Cassidy Cataloguing Services, Inc.)

Names: Brady, Bernadette, 1950- author.
Title: The shape of fate : from classical philosophy to astrological practice / Bernadette Brady.
Description: Ceredigion, Wales : Sophia Centre Press, 2025. | Includes bibliographical references and index.
Identifiers: ISBN: 9781907767173 (paperback) | 9781907767487 (ebook)
Subjects: LCSH: Determinism (Philosophy) | Free will and determinism--Philosophy. | Fate and fatalism. | Astrology--Philosophy.
Classification: LCC: B105.D47 B73 2025 | DDC: 123--dc23

Printed by Lightning Source.

To the time when this book was just a dream

CONTENTS

ACKNOWLEDGEMENTS	ix
INTRODUCTION - THE MODERN ENIGMA OF FATE	1
CHAPTER ONE - FATE: ITS WESTERN ROOTS	7
Fate in Ancient Egypt and Assyria	7
Fate in the Greek archaic and early classical tradition	11
CHAPTER TWO - FATE IN CLASSICAL PHILOSOPHY	15
Plato: moral responsibility and fate	15
Aristotle's mortal soul and contingency	18
The Stoics – fate and divine harmony	20
Cicero – against universal fate	22
Living with fate – the astrologers	25
Theories of fate	29
CHAPTER THREE - THE THREADS OF FATE IN THE MEDIEVAL PERIOD	33
Augustine and divine providence	33
Calcidius – fate and contingents	35
Early Arabic views of fate	38
A Jewish perspective – hierarchical fate	41
Fate – the division of body and soul	42
Fate for the working astrologer	45
CHAPTER FOUR - THE EARLY MODERN AND FREE WILL	49
René Descartes – free will is true	49
Baruch de Spinoza – free will is false.	51
The Early Modern – living with fate	55
Galileo and astrology	55
Jean-Baptiste Morin	57
William Lilly – fate casting	58
CHAPTER FIVE - THE DILEMMA OF DETERMINISM	63
The World Machine and determinism	63
Incompatibilism – free will is false	66
Incompatibilism – universal determinism is false	68
Compatibilism – free will and determinism are both true	70
Problems with determinism	71
CHAPTER SIX - ASTROLOGY FROM WITHOUT AND WITHIN	75
Definitions of astrology	75
Criticisms of astrology	78
Researching beliefs of astrologers	83

Chapter Seven - Asking about Fate — 87
- Who are the astrologers — 88
- The astrologers and their theories of fate — 89
- Secular or non-secular astrology — 93
- Fate as pattern and telos — 94
- Prediction and fate — 96
- Astrology, authoritarianism and moral responsibility — 99

Chapter Eight - Notes in a Bottle — 103
- Echoes of ancient theories of fate — 104
- Cicero's hard incompatibilism — 104
- Plato and the freedom of the soul — 106
- Stoicism and Spinozian thinking – fate and acceptance — 108
- Stoic time and cycles — 112
- Calcidius's theory of fate — 116
- Fate as an illusion — 117
- Living as an astrologer in a sympathetic cosmos — 118

Chapter Nine - Conversations about Fate — 123
- Fate as the order of the world — 123
- Fate and the soul — 127
- Fate, soul and the horoscope — 130
- Fate, time, and the horoscope — 133
- Fate and reason — 135
- Living with fate — 137
- Fate-Casting — 140

Chapter Ten - A Topography of Fate — 145
- Fate, a different ontology — 146
- Fate as story — 149
- Fate and astrology — 150

Appendix — 155
- The Questionnaire — 155

Notes — 163
References — 185
Index — 203

ACKNOWLEDGEMENTS

This work has been a part of my life for nearly 30 years. It began its formal scholarly journey in 2008 with my PhD research, which was guided and supported by my supervisor, Nick Campion. Fourteen years later, he encouraged me to turn the work into this volume. Thus, without Nick Campion's support, as well as his untiring efforts in offering suggestions and comments on the manuscript, this book would not have come into existence. My thanks also go to the one thousand and more grassroots astrologers from the global community of astrologers who opened their arms to this research and often shared with me their years of thought on fate.

Additionally, I would like to extend my gratitude to the professional astrologers who have opened their doors to allow me to quiz them about fate. They are Brian Clark, Stephanie Johnson and Gillian Helfgott from Australia, Faye Cossar and Karen Hamaker-Zondag from Netherlands, Darby Costello, Barbara Dunn, Roy Gillet, Liz Greene, Clare Martin, Melanie Reinhardt, Christeen Skinner, Sue Tompkins and Sue Ward from the UK, Ben Dykes, Carolyn Egan, Demetra George, Dorain Greenbaum, Robert Hand, and Alan Oken, from the US and Rod Suskin from South Africa. All of them were instrumental in helping my research reveal the nature of fate. Finally, I would like to acknowledge the unwavering support of my life partner, Darrelyn Gunzburg, who had to endure all the ups and downs that any research journey entails. Without all this support from these people, this book would not now be resting in your hands.

INTRODUCTION

THE MODERN ENIGMA OF FATE

Fate lives in the margins of modern Western culture. It can be found in English usage as a common term but is assumed to be a relic from a far earlier time. It is echoed in popular expressions such as 'he met his fate', meaning a life cut short, or 'it is in the hands of fate' when an outcome is beyond human control, or 'don't tempt fate' when one does not want to upset an outcome, as if one may 'jinx it' through over-expectation, or to 'tempt fate' by taking a foolish risk. There is also the 'fickle finger of fate', or a 'twist of fate', an expression used to capture an encounter with a powerful event that shapes one's life path. These everyday expressions reveal a popular concept of fate that appears to be random and changeable.

Fate is also seen as unknowable and possibly capricious. Sarah Broadie commented on the experience of fate, suggesting that it felt like it had 'an agency concerning which… all we know, is that it has a certain purpose and is clever and foreknowing and powerful enough to carry out this intention no matter what'.[1] While Robert Solomon offered another view of fate as being an 'otherness' where 'fate provides something by way of "hands" in which we can place ourselves whether or not we have the confidence in their goodness'.[2] Indeed, as implied by both Broadie and Solomon, fate is a powerful personal force that can shape one's life, and they write of the phenomenon of the encounter, a sense of its agency, of being held in hands that are informed and decisive.

Anthony Giddens, writing on self-identity, also offered a comment on fate:

> Fateful moments are times when events come together in such a way that an individual stands, as it were, at a crossroads in his existence; or where a person learns of information with fateful consequences.[3]

For Giddens, fate is a marker of change, the awareness of encountering a non-reversible shift that transforms the life path. Giddens, however, focused on the actual moment of the encounter, the shock — whether good or bad — of one's life changing in an instant. Giddens viewed fate not from the phenomenological perspective, as Broadie and Solomon did; nevertheless, all these arguments imply a certain inevitability to fate's nature.

This inevitable nature of fate is also a theme in modern Arabic culture. Dalya Cohen-Mor, an independent scholar of Arabic and Islamic studies, considered it as a superior power that shapes people's lives and thus allows them to adjust more easily to difficult circumstances. She argued that within the Arabic world, it enabled acceptance of difficulties and 'fulfils a basic human need for order and harmony'.[4] She found that despite significant changes since the birth of Islam, in modern-day Arabic culture, the belief in fate 'has retained its vitality and continues to function as a viable cultural force'.[5] This version of fate is trusted because it is in God's hands.

These views all link fate to inevitability, a position promoted by modern philosophical arguments that view fate as a form of early causal determinism. Causal determinism, considered later in Chapter Five, is the argument that the future is the result of the past and the laws of nature. Since one cannot change the past or the laws of nature, then the future is fixed and inevitable.[6] Fatalism, however, is not a simple extension of fate; it is the belief that no matter what action one takes, one cannot alter a future event.[7] Pascal Massie pointed out that fatalism is a belief that '…what will be will be no matter what causal path brings it about'.[8] Hence, fatalism does not contain any antecedent causes (which is causal determinism) and thus does not imply the future is embedded in the past.[9] There is also the idea of destiny (discussed in greater detail in Chapter One), which appears to be a softer version of fate or fatalism. It tends to be used when an outcome is positive; one is destined to achieve or encounter an inevitable event in the future. Richard Bargdill, coming from a psychological background, noted that destiny has a destination embedded in its use, whereas fate is linked to the written or spoken word; you learn your fate, but you encounter your destiny.[10]

Solomon commented that 'Today, both concepts [fate and fatalism] tend to be the target of widespread philosophical disdain'.[11] This disdain arises because, in Western culture, a belief in this definition of fate is often viewed as a form of flawed thinking, that accepting the inevitability of one's life seems to deny the freedom of the will. As complex as this form of thinking is in philosophical debates, considered later in Chapter Five, in popular thinking, accepting inevitability in one's life is viewed as flawed. According to Nicola Gess, it is 'primitive thinking'. Gess explored early twentieth-century German culture and defined primitive thought as a distinct mode of thinking characterised by magical, mythical, mystical, or prelogical approaches to understanding and living in the world, a world 'whereby mere coincidences appear to be matters of fate'.[12] For

Gess, this mode of thinking was characteristic of indigenous cultures, children, the mentally ill, and those generally categorised as 'the other'.[13] Gess's argument suggests that only a minority held this mindset.

However, in 2019, Stuart Vyse, writing on superstition, noted that although science has become the dominant standard for viewing the world, making it easier to draw a line between rational thinking and superstition, he mused that many people crossed these lines every day, although he argued it was impossible to know how widespread this line-crossing was.[14] Some research indicates that this figure could be quite high. For example, in 1994, Gillian Bennett researched belief in predestined events amongst residents of a northern UK city. She interviewed 120 people who were visiting a podiatry (foot-treatment) clinic and found that, 'Running like a thread through many of my informants' conversations was the concept of predestination with its passive-compliant corollary, complete acceptance…'.[15] Bennett's group tended to view the future as already ordained and adopted an attitude of acceptance. Bennett commented that they were 'submitting to their fate' but also drawing comfort from the knowledge that there is a plan, even if they had no idea of the nature of the plan. Bennett's work suggested the presence of theological fatalism, which is the acceptance of God's providence, but with the tool of prayer used in the face of an inevitable outcome to ask God to alter the laws of nature, thereby changing the future. Granted, this is a sample of just 120 people, but these northern English individuals represent the common folk, drawn together by problems with their feet, not, as Gess assumed, children, indigenous people, or the mentally ill, thus not part of Gess's notion of alterity or otherness.

Eugene Subbotsky established similar conclusions to Bennett from a different sample. He worked with university students to explore belief in magical thinking. He found that 18% of his admittedly small sample of 30 undergraduates accepted the efficacy of a magical spell. However, significantly, this shifted to 60% if there was a chance that the individual could injure their hand if they ignored the warning of the spell.[16] He concluded that magical thinking was evident in modern educated adults. A 2017 OnePoll.com survey also supported Subbotsky's findings. It focused on superstitious beliefs and found that around half of the British population described themselves as superstitious. In an article on 13 October 2017 by Grant Bailey in the British newspaper *The Mirror*, the commissioner of the survey, Tatton-Brown, was quoted stating:

> Even in modern times, with the power of science and technology at our backs, with less mystery in the world than ever before, it is hard to shake the feeling that invisible forces hold some sway over our lives.[17]

Superstitions are a version of fate. However, they are a fate which is malleable and limited. They are a belief that an individual's actions can change a future outcome deemed to be outside of one's control; They are a belief in that self-agency can alter the future. A particular action will encourage fate to produce a positive result, while, in the case of a jinx (an action believed to bring bad luck), one must take care to avoid damaging a potential future outcome.[18] Some football fans, for instance, believe that they must perform rituals on match days, such as eating certain foods, wearing particular clothes, sitting in the same stadium seat, and so on, to ensure that they aid their team's victory.[19] Such actions are a collective moral duty conducted for the good of the whole. Indeed, superstitions are widespread within the sporting world among both athletes and their supporters.[20] Superstitions, however, are limited in that they tend to focus only on an exact outcome, such as a sporting event or, for example, a job interview. Nevertheless, their presence in popular culture suggests an everyday fate, one that is limited, frequently encountered, and sensitive to human agency.

Fate itself, however is generally deemed to be an all-prevailing cosmological force, holding greater influence than a single superstition. Also, unlike superstition, the causal-determinist version of fate does challenge the notion of free will. In 2006, Jeremy Burrus and Neil Roese researched the belief in inevitable fate with a group of University of Illinois undergraduates. They defined fate as: 'Fate means that an event was meant to be, that is, predetermined by prior unseen forces'.[21] They found inconsistencies in how the students thought about fate and free will. The students balanced the tension between fate and free will by believing in self-agency. Burrus and Roese found that 'Most (75%) did indeed believe in fate, [defined as inevitability] but …85% further believed it possible for events to be decided jointly by both fate and individual action'.[22] The students revealed the error in Burrus and Roese's definition of fate. Intellectually, they accepted the standard definition of inevitable fate, but in their lived experience, they believed that if a future event held importance for them, they could change the outcome.

The ethnographic studies, such as Burrus and Roese's research, as well as the presence of superstitions in popular culture and Subbotsky's work with university students, to cite just a few cases, all indicate that the definition of fate as inevitable is not sustainable. Nevertheless, rather than challenging the entrenched view of fate as inevitable, it is simpler for researchers to dismiss their evidence. To encapsulate their ethnographies as being flawed or to consider the participants as having a 'primitive mind' or as confused young people or mentally ill. Those suffering from what the twentieth-century Swiss psychiatrist, Eugen Bleuler, labelled as those who built a world on the 'delusion of references'.[23]

But such dismissal means the more profound questions about fate are ignored. Such questions as to why it has been a part of human history since the dawn of literature and what purpose does it serve? Also, the more difficult question is, what is fate? Is it real or an illusion?

This work focuses on these questions. I aimed to research the historical discourse on fate through the perspectives of two groups that have grappled with its meaning: philosophers and astrologers. Philosophers have a long-documented debate on the notion of free will, first in the face of fate and then later in the face of determinism. Astrologers also have a long literary tradition on the problems of living with fate. Astrology requires the practitioner to accept that the movement of the heavens has an influence on or significance for one's life that places fate at the heart of the individual life. In that regard, astrologers have written about their experiences of living with fate from the neo-Assyrian period in Mesopotamia in the eighth century BCE right through to today. As such, their literature represents an exploration of various versions of fate spanning three thousand years. In 2012, Nicholas Campion, researching astrological beliefs, cited Gallup poll data claiming that about 25% of the adult populations of the UK, US, and France subscribed to astrology and made the point that astrology 'has millions of fans, a number of vociferous opponents, and is a familiar part of popular culture'.[24] With this level of support, astrology is a cultural carrier of fate, for better or for worse, in modern popular culture.

This book begins by exploring the Western roots of fate, the ancient Egyptian literature from the third and second millennium BCE and also that of the Mesopotamians of the Bronze Age period. Chapter Two then turns to the voices from the classical period, of both the key philosophers and astrologers. This point in time marks the period when fate became the centre of philosophical discourse, laying the foundation for later Western thought. Chapter Three follows two parallel perspectives, philosophy and astrology, into the medieval period. Chapter Four addresses the early modern period, while Chapter Five considers contemporary philosophical views on determinism and the struggle and slow separation between fate and determinism evident in the work of astrological authors. Chapter Six examines the connection between astrology and fate, as well as the growing tension with its critics, who equate fate with determinism. Chapters Seven, Eight and Nine, present my ethnographic research into the lifestyles of modern-day astrologers who live with the idea of fate. This group consisted of over 1000 astrologers from 40 different countries. Chapter Ten considers the nature of fate as a human phenomenon that exists beyond the boundaries of astrological beliefs.

CHAPTER ONE

FATE: ITS WESTERN ROOTS

Debates concerning the nature of fate have a long history and are situated at the intersection of cosmology, theology, ethics, and individual experience. From the earliest written sources, the concept of fate exhibits a range of meanings and implications, reflecting evolving understandings of the human condition and the nature of the cosmos. This chapter examines key developments in ancient conceptions of fate, beginning with early Egyptian and Mesopotamian traditions in which fate was conceived as a divine decree—an expression of cosmic order governed by the will of the gods. Later, during the Hellenistic period, a systematic philosophical engagement with the concept of fate emerged. Thinkers of this era developed frameworks that sought to reconcile human agency with the will of the gods. This resulted in distinct approaches, such as Plato's emphasis on the role of the individual soul and the Stoic view of fate as a rational, deterministic principle guiding the universe as a whole. The chapter also considers how these abstract theories intersected with the lived experiences of astrologers, whose interpretations of celestial movements provided practical insights into the manifestations of fate in daily life.

By tracing these varying perspectives, the chapter aims to show the ancient world's diverse attempts to understand the nature of personal freedom existing within a divinely ordered cosmos.

Fate in Ancient Egypt and Assyria

For the ancient Egyptians, fate was closely tied to the length of one's life. During the 5th dynasty of the Old Kingdom (2495–2345 BCE), the 'Instructions of Ptahhotep' have Ptahhotep presenting a long list of instructions to his son, who is about to take over his role as the king's Vizier (the highest government official). The instructions focused on living according to *maat*, a divine concept which encompasses truth, justice, and order.[1] Ptahhotep warned his son not to take action against those who angered him. Miriam Lichtheim's translation reads, 'His time does not fail to come. One does not escape what is fated'—suggesting that his enemy will eventually die, and in death, he would have to face his fate.[2] Drawing on this example, May Ahmed Hosny argued that fate, at this time, was 'inescapable and related to death'.[3] But also related to this theme of death is the idea of judgment.

By the New Kingdom (late second millennium BCE), fate was personified into a male deity named Shai. His guise varied, but his name, Shai, refers to 'what is decreed', with the decrees coming from the gods or of his own making.[4] Along with Shai there were two goddesses, Renenet (the goddess of nourishment) and Meskhenet (the goddess of childbirth), also linked to fate. These two joined Shai, with Shai and Renenet predicting birth and death while Meskhenet predicted the child's social position.[5] The New Kingdom Papyrus of Ani, composed a thousand years after the 'Instructions of Ptahhotep', is a copy of the 'Book of Going Forth by Day', and depicts a scene of the weighing of Ani's heart against the *maat*-feather of truth. The scene contains Shai, Renenet and Meskhenet, along with the soul (*Ba*) of Ana (see Fig.1). The text reads:

> Thoth's declaration to the Great Ennead in the presence of Osiris : "Hear ye in very truth this statement; I have judged the heart of this Osiris [i.e., Ani], his soul standing as witness for him. His deeds are true upon the great balance; no evil has been found in him ...Great Ennead's proclamation to Thoth: "This utterance of yours is true. The Osiris, king's scribe Ani, justified, is without evil. We have nothing to accuse him of."[6]

The scene shows both the fate given at birth and the fate of death (Shai, Renenet and Meskhenet). They stand in the presence of Ani's *Ba* and both Ani and his wife Tutu await the outcome of the judgment. The heart is weighed against *maat* (truth and justice) and judged by the gods of Egypt, displayed along the top register. Thoth records the results of the judgment, and if the deceased fails, then the monster Ammut awaits to devour him and deny him an afterlife. Dorian Greenbaum argued that such scenes are evidence of the notion that 'what has been decreed at the beginning of life can change to some extent though the actual living of that life, and how the person deals with what they have been given'.[7] The ritual of the weighing of the heart upon death is, therefore, a process of judging how the deceased has lived with his birth-given fate. Only after considering his life journey could his final fate be determined, the fate of his afterlife. If the New Kingdom Egyptian view of fate was fixed and inevitable, then there would be no reason for the ritual of the weighing of the heart. Ani was given a fate, but it was his duty to live with that fate as best he could in terms of following truth and justice. If he manages to do that, then he gains an afterlife; his fate is in his hands. As Jan Assmann commented, the fate of the soul's afterlife 'determined the earthly conduct of the individual'.[8]

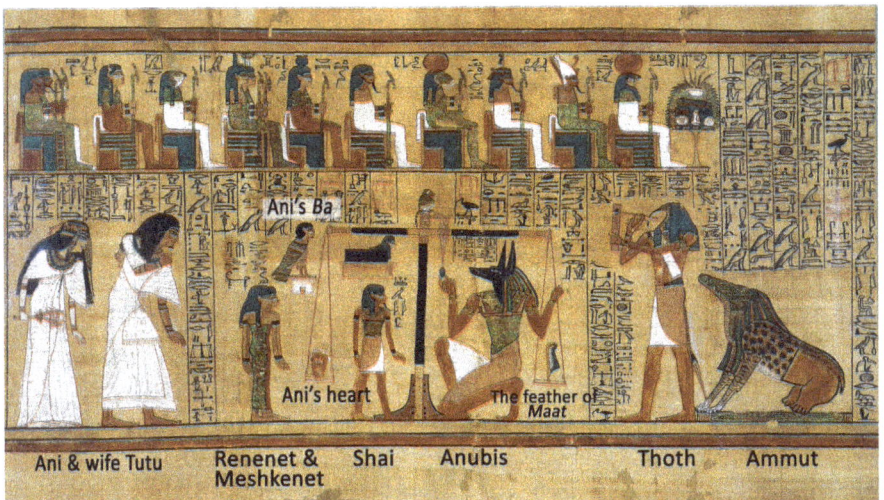

Figure 1: A section of the Papyrus Ani. The Weighing of the Heart of Ani, 18th dynasty. On the left, Ani and his wife Tutu watch the weighing scene with Renenet, Meshkenet and Shai. Thoth stands on the right. British Museum Image: © Trustees of the British Museum.

Along with Renenet, Meshkenet and Shai, fate was also personified as the Seven Hathors. These functioned alongside or in parallel with the above three deities; they were a collective force frequently present at the birth of the child and who also allocated the individual's fate. In the case of the 18th dynasty 'Tale of the Doomed Prince' there is a story about the interplay between fate and agency. In the tale, a childless king petitions the gods for a son. The gods grant his request, and at the prince's birth, the seven Hathors appear to pronounce his fate: he is fated to die by crocodile, snake, or dog. In response, the king attempts to shield his son from these threats. However, upon reaching maturity, the prince questions the purpose of his constrained existence, declaring, 'To what purpose is my sitting here? I am committed to Fate. Let me go, that I may act according to my heart, until the god does what is in his heart'.[9] The prince departs and experiences a period of joy by hunting, fishing and falling in love. The ending of the tale is fragmentary, so the conclusion is unknown. However, the underlying message remains evident: even if fate is preordained, it does not negate the possibility of living a full and meaningful life.

Finally, for the ancient Egyptians, fate was divinely ordained but could be influenced through rituals, prayers, and magic. Magic, known as *Heka*, was a legitimate and divine tool which was a part of *maat* (cosmic order). It was every individual's right to use it to shape or direct their own fate. From the Coffin Texts of the Middle Kingdom (c. 2000 BCE) is Spell 261: 'I am he who created *ḥeka* for the Ennead and I am he who gave it to the people so that they might be strong through it'. *Heka* was, according to Edward Karshner, a powerful force that could be used to control one's life.[10] It was a magic power that could manipulate the natural and supernatural worlds. Importantly, *Heka* was available to anyone with the skill to use it.[11] Hence, for the ancient Egyptians, fate was only inevitable if one lacked the skills and knowledge to control it. The use of the intellect could alleviate one's fate, a concept that reemerged a thousand or so years later in the work of Plato, discussed in the next chapter.

Contemporary with Egyptian culture of the first millennium BCE was that of the Akkadians, who emerged in Mesopotamia around 2300 BCE. The older Sumerian word for fate was 'nam-tar', a destiny decided, and the Akkadian word was *šīmtu*, to determine.[12] Francesca Rochberg claimed that *šīmtu* expressed the idea that the gods decreed the nature, or lot, for every person, animal, plant and stone and that the omens contained in Akkadian literature 'could have been understood as things ordained by the gods to occur'.[13] The role of the gods was central to Akkadian fate; the Code of Hammurabi (composed c. 1755–1750 BCE) warned any future king who did not follow Hammurabi's laws that 'mighty Anum, the father of the gods, who proclaimed my reign, deprive him of the glory of sovereignty, may he break his sceptre, may he curse his fate!'[14] The gods created and controlled fate: it was a tool used to govern the universe and they could bestow a good or bad fate either at birth or upon request.[15]

In the Enūma Eliš (c. 1125 BC–1104 BCE), the Bronze Age Babylonian hero, Marduk, demands before fighting Tiamat and Kingu, 'If I indeed as your avenger, am to vanquish Tiamat and save your lives, set up the Assembly, proclaim supreme my destiny! …let my word, instead of you, determine the fates'.[16] Marduk is fighting Tiamat because she has given the 'Tablets of Destiny' to her consort Kingu and, with them, he controls the cosmic order and all fates.[17] In this regard, Marduk's request shows that humans or other gods could ask the gods to allocate a new fate.[18]

By the time of the Assyrians, in the early first millennium BCE, the movement of the heavens was viewed as a stone surface —a surface that could be used for writing the gods' messages, much like a scribe would inscribe on clay.[19] This heavenly writing, the movement of the planets against the stars, became the decree of the gods, which could be studied to understand the divine messages, viewed as omens of worldly events.[20] Nevertheless, they believed that these laws or decrees could be manipulated. In a planetary omen from c. 650 BCE the king's death was predicted by the heavenly writing, Yet, fate could be managed.

The omen was read to be about the nation-state rather than the person of the king. The Assyrian priest, discussing the omen, wrote:

> As [regards the su]bstitute king about whom [the king, my lord, wrote to me]: Let him sit for a 100 days; (only) [after] he has completed the 100 days, [he should go to his fate].[21]

The Assyrian view of fate was that it needed to be fulfilled, but how this was achieved could be managed. A substitute king could be installed, who would then become the subject of the omen, and the original king would retake the throne once the omen had been fulfilled. This strategy ensured minimum impact on the kingdom while at the same time providing an avenue for the expression of fate. Although this is an example of managing fate, Campion argued that it is debatable whether the Mesopotamians possessed a theoretical concept of fate.[22]

Fate in the Greek archaic and early classical tradition

For the Greeks, fate was personified in the *Moirai*, three goddesses who managed or produced fate. First cited in the eighth century BCE by Hesiod in his *Theogony*, he claimed that they were created by the entity of Night,

> Also she bore the Destinies [Moirai] and the ruthless, avenging Fates, Clotho and Lachesis and Atropos, who give men at their birth both evil and good to have.[23]

Homer also named the *Moirai* in his work. Recorded in the eighth century BCE, he used both Necessity and the *Moirai* in his epic work of the *Iliad*. At the time of the Trojan War, the wife of Priam, king of Troy, while grieving for the death of her son Hector, tried to stop the king from taking revenge for their son's death. She reminded her husband that the *Moirai* had spun Hector's fate at his birth. Samuel Butler's translation reads,

> Let us then weep Hector from afar here in our own house, for when I gave him birth the threads of overruling fate were spun for him that dogs should eat his flesh far from his parents…[24]

Hector's fate was set by Necessity. For Homer, Necessity was a universal force which sought balance to maintain cosmic order and was, unlike the Mesopotamian view, beyond the control of the gods. Homer wrote of it in his description of the death of Hector:

> ... when they reached the Spring for the fourth time, the Father [Zeus] held out his golden scales, and putting sentence of death in either pan, on one side for Achilles, on the other for horse-taming Hector, he raised the balance by the middle of the beam. The beam came down on Hector's side, spelling his doom. He was a dead man.[25]

With these scales in mind, Simone Weil argued that Homer's Necessity had a ruthless universality. The inevitable escalation of rage, inherent in the nature of war, led the characters to become enslaved to the power of Necessity.[26] Weil argued that 'geometrical rigour' was a part of Homer's idea of Necessity: it was a force that constantly redressed itself with no regard for humanity as it sought perfection or balance.[27] Hector's fate was written at his birth and found its expression through the cauldron of war, where the redressing actions of Necessity became the vehicle which delivered his fate.

Some 500 years later, a different view of fate was portrayed in the play *Oedipus Rex*, written by the Greek tragedian Sophocles (c. 496–406 BCE). A key theme in the play was fate, which, at the time, was viewed as a personalised decree of the divine.[28] In Sophocles' play, Apollo, through the Oracle of Delphi, declares that Oedipus's fate was to kill his father and marry his mother. Oedipus retells the Oracle's prediction:

> His voice flashed other answers, things of woe,
> Terror, and desolation. I must know
> my mother's body and beget thereon
> a race no mortal eye durst look upon,
> and spill in murder mine own father's blood.[29]

Seeking to avoid the prophecy, Oedipus flees to another country, choosing never to see his parents again. He cried out:

> Suffer not this, oh suffer not this sin.
> To be, that e'er I look on such a day!
> Out of all vision of mankind away
> To darkness let me fall ere such a fate
> Touch me, so unclear and so desolate![30]

However, Oedipus is unaware of his true parents and, in error, flees to their location. There, he unknowingly fights with his father and kills him. In retribution, he has to marry his father's wife, who is his mother, thereby fulfilling the fate prophesied by Apollo.

The importance of this play is that Sophocles did not accept that fate mitigated Oedipus's moral responsibility for his actions. Instead, he held his protagonist to account, and upon fulfilling his fate, Oedipus lamented his actions and, in self-inflicted punishment, blinded himself. He took personal responsibility for his actions and, unlike the characters swept up in the battle in Homer's *Iliad*, Oedipus recognised his lack of awareness. He acknowledged his initial lack of judgment in killing the 'old man' on the road, his biological father, and his further lack of awareness of the prophecy when confronted with the required marriage to his victim's widow, his biological mother. He blinded himself in punishment, symbolising his blindness to his actions, for he and he alone was the instrument of his fate.

This is the difference between Homer's Necessity and the *Moirai* and Sophocles' view of fate. Homer's heroes, such as Hector, were not expected to use their reason, whereas Sophocles' character, Oedipus, was. Eric Dodds argued that the gods did not predict that Oedipus would pursue the truth, only that he would commit the crimes.[31] Sophocles' play suggests that human reason is the source of moral responsibility, and fate cannot, or should not, override moral responsibility. This argument is a philosophical question that is still vigorously debated today. Fellow Athenian Plato (c. 428–347 BCE) was a young man when Sophocles' play was performed in Athens, and it requires little speculation to assume that he was aware of its theme.

This chapter has considered fate in the Egyptian, Mesopotamian and early Greek traditions. In all of these, fate is portrayed as part of a divinely instituted order, administered by gods or divine figures such as Shai, Renenet, and Meskhenet, as well as the Seven Hathors, or through cosmic instruments like the Tablets of Destiny. While these systems portrayed fate as originating from divine decree, they also accommodated the possibility of human response—whether through ritual or petition to the gods (Mesopotamian fate) or magical practice such as *heka* (Egyptian fate). It is evident that in both Egypt and Mesopotamia, fate was fixed in principle but flexible in practice.

The early Greek tradition introduced further nuance. Homer's depiction of the *Moirai* and Necessity emphasises an impersonal cosmic order, indifferent to human will, where Hector follows blind reactions to the rage of war to fall victim to his fate. Five hundred years later, in contrast to the inevitability of Hector's fate, Sophocles posed a new perspective. In his play *Oedipus Rex*, he portrayed fate as being subject to moral responsibility; the inevitability of fate did not negate Oedipus's actions. For Sophocles, moral responsibility was an expression of the human will, which he viewed as free. The idea of freedom had been hinted at by the Egyptian and Mesopotamian literature but dismissed in the Homeric model. However, Sophocles made it a centre piece of his thinking—fate and free will could coexist. Sophocles' emphasis on human awareness and moral accountability anticipated later philosophical concerns—particularly those of Plato and the Stoics, considered in the next chapter—regarding the role of reason in negotiating the terms of one's fate.

CHAPTER TWO

FATE IN CLASSICAL PHILOSOPHY

The Classical period, approximately the fifth to fourth centuries BCE in Greece and extending into the Roman era, constitutes a formative epoch in the development of philosophical doctrines concerning fate, necessity, and human agency. During this time, a range of intellectual traditions emerged, each holding distinct positions on the nature of fate and human freedom. These doctrines exerted influence on subsequent theological and philosophical discourses, including those of late antiquity and early modern Europe. This chapter examines these foundational developments and subsequently explores how contemporary astrologers conceptualised the role of astrology in relation to the experience of living under fate.

Plato: moral responsibility and fate

The potential influence of Sophocles' play *Oedipus Rex* on Plato's thinking can be seen in how he assigned moral responsibility to a central role of the human soul. Plato argued that the soul, using its divine nature, could free itself from the influence of both Necessity and the *Moirai* (the Fates). For Plato, the origin of the human soul was the World Soul, located at the centre of a divine and ordered cosmos.[1] Plato viewed the divine as both transcendent and immanent—both external and separate from the material world—but at the same time embedded in 'the minutest constituents of the universe'.[2] The divine World Soul was motionless and 'unmoved', while at the same time, it provided the motion for all other parts of the cosmos.[3] The World Soul was the source of the human soul, which, by moving into the world of matter at the time of birth, became separated from the World Soul.[4] The human soul, however, was immortal, and it needed to eventually return to the stars, its divine place of origin. Plato wrote of the Demiurge, the artisan-like agent of the divine, assigning each soul to a star and,

> If they mastered their emotions, their lives would be just, whereas if they were mastered by them, they would be unjust. And if a person lived a good life throughout the due course of his time, he would, at the end, return to his dwelling place in his companion star, to live a life of happiness that agreed with his character.[5]

Hence, when the soul existed in the material world, it could achieve its return to the divine by using reason to master the body's emotions. Plato wrote of the individual soul:

> He [the soul] would have no rest from these toilsome transformations [reincarnations] until he had dragged that massive accretion of fire-water-air-earth into conformity with the revolution of the Same and uniform within him, and so subdued that turbulent, irrational mass by means of reason. This would return him to his original condition of excellence.[6]

Plato's philosophy contrasts with Homer's Necessity, cited earlier, but is in accord with Sophocles' views on Oedipus's struggle with his fate, as Plato considered that reason could overcome both Necessity and the *Moirai*.[7] In this way, Plato developed a dualist doctrine that viewed the mind (reason) and the body as composed of different substances.[8] As human reason was free of and not composed of matter, it was therefore not subject to the laws of Fate and Necessity. Building on this dualist philosophy, Plato proposed two orders of existence: *Being* and *Becoming*. *Being*, which belonged to the divine, was unchanging, eternal and unmoving, while the lower realm, *Becoming*, was where all things passed in and out of existence, forever changing, as in the realm of matter.[9] Within this hierarchy, the physical body was a lower-status partner to the individual soul, serving as a necessary yet temporary physical vehicle for the divine soul. Plato wrote that the body '…confuses the soul and does not allow it to acquire truth and wisdom…' and added that '… because as long as we have a body and our soul is fused with such an evil we shall never adequately attain what we desire…'[10]

The refinement of the human soul happened in two ways: firstly, through the soul's use of reason to resist the physical desires of its current mortal body, and secondly, in its divine state after death it was able to use its developed wisdom to choose the nature of its next incarnation.[11] Plato described this moment of choice in the *Myth of Er*. The myth is the story of a soldier named Er, who dies in battle and returns to life to recount his experiences in the afterlife. He described how souls chose their next lives by being told that 'Your daemon or guardian spirit will not be assigned to you by lot; you will choose him'.[12] The three *Moirai* were present in the dream, with Lachesis presenting each soul with choices of possible future lives. Clotho then turn the Spindle of Necessity to confirm the fate and bind it to the soul, while Atropos made the thread irreversible.[13] Once the lots, the future lives, were chosen, the souls were pointedly told, 'The responsibility lies with the one who makes the choice; the god has none'.[14] Hence, Plato argued that each person is responsible for their fate. Richard Onians argued that Plato's use of the threads and the spinning of the *Moirai* was a 'binding process on the part of the powers determining man's fate'.[15] This binding to one's fate implied that the fate was personal; substitutions, as in the Mesopotamian model cited earlier, could not alter it. Plato also cited the goddess Anankē (Necessity). She was the mother of the three *Moirai* and enthroned at the centre of the cosmos.

Anankē held on her knee the revolving Spindle of Necessity.[16] The *Moirai* operated the spindle, but Anankē was the axis of their work—she, with the spindle, ensured the cosmos ran according to immutable laws. Anankē denoted natural law, the rational structure of reality, or cause and effect—the consequence of earlier actions and the force that produced events based on the nature of the world.[17] The spindle itself was the rotation of the heavens, the movement of the stars around the fixed still centre of the pole and the planetary orbits.[18] Plato thus echoed the Mesopotamian view that fate comes from the heavens, for he viewed the human soul, along with its fate, as being born onto the Earth through celestial movements. An individual's fate, the workings of the *Moirai*, was subject to the laws of Necessity, and Plato linked these to the rotation of the heavens.

The Platonic notion of the human soul was a soul that had to live within the universal laws of matter—Necessity or Anankē—but was altered by its actions over its many lifetimes. The cosmic purpose of the union of the material body with the immortal soul was to allow for the refinement of the soul so it can reunite with the World Soul.[19] Plato hinted that this journey of personal soul refinement had a larger purpose, 'You forget that creation is not for your benefit: *you* exist for the sake of the universe'[20] Nevertheless, his focus was on the soul's journey. He wrote in *Phaedrus*, '…any who have led their lives with justice will change to a better fate, and any who have led theirs with injustice, to a worse one'.[21] Ihan Dilman described this view of the soul as being governed by 'moral determinism', as it was the soul's past actions which dictated their future lives.[22] Hence, individuals lived in two worlds: the divine, free of Necessity, and the material ruled by Necessity. How a person's immortal soul, which belonged to the divine, managed this union over many lifetimes shaped their fate.

This dualism provided a place for free will. Free will resided with the soul (reason) hence the individual's life choices, whether they used their reason or let their emotions govern them, would alter their fate, their future lives. However, the individual was not free in the modern sense, as they were limited in the choices they could make. There was an element of coercion in that one had to choose to live a morally responsible life. Failing to live such a life influenced the quality of the next life. The doctrine of reincarnation served as a key component of this theological view, as it made each individual accountable for their current life and their future lives. Hence, the individual's quest to unite with the divine lay entirely in the individual's hands.

Plato's views laid the foundation for the dualist approach to fate, which persists to this day in both philosophy as well as astrological thinking.

Aristotle's mortal soul and contingency

Plato's student, Aristotle (384–322 BCE), developed a different cosmology from that of his teacher. He disagreed with Plato's dualism of body and soul, as well as the divine status of the soul. He also resisted the mythologising of what he deemed to be natural causes. In *Metaphysics*, Aristotle presented a model of the solar system with the Earth residing at the centre of a series of fifty-five interconnected spheres.[23] The main spheres were those of the fixed stars, followed by the individual planetary spheres and that of the moon; under all of these spheres was the Earth. A divine being, the divine 'unmoved mover', existed outside the spheres, and drove the entire system, this was the primary source of all motion. Aristotle considered the unmoved mover method of motion 'as something loved'. That is not as a cause and effect action but instead as a desire that draws things to it, like a magnet drawing object to itself. However, this was not a physical force but instead as a final cause,(telos), a divine force that draws all things toward it.[24] Additionally, in *De Caelo* (On the Heavens), Aristotle confirmed that not only was the prime mover responsive to love but that each of the planets moving in its sphere was also the seat of a divine essence. In speaking of ancient writers, he commented, 'they thought that in speaking of the upper bodies they were treating of bodies which were earthlike and had weight, when they posited for the heaven the constraint of a living being'.[25]

In *Meteorologica,* Aristotle linked this movement of the heavens, these living stars, to the cause of all things on Earth, 'It is the motion of the stars that is the cause of all generation and destruction'.[26] Hence, the living stars, through the eternal movement initiated by the love of the unmoved mover, were responsible for all movement on the Earth. This movement led to changes in the four elements which existed in all things. Aristotle spoke of the impact of this movement on a person as 'at one time white, and at another black, and warm and cold, and bad and good'.[27] On the foundation of these elements, Aristotle built a theory of causation. This theory consisted of four components: the material cause (the substance contained in the object), the formal cause (how this substance was arranged), the efficient or moving cause (its movement) and the final cause, which was its purpose (that for which it was designed).[28] Aristotle applied his causal theory to the natural sciences and, since humanity was part of the natural world, also to human behaviour.²⁹ Thus, the natural world was the source of all influences on human behaviour, physical and emotional.

Aristotle placed the soul within this cosmology by viewing it as the life force inherent in all living things, whether plant or animal. As the life force, the soul was mortal and did not exist after death, for 'Since the soul is the actuality of the body, it does not exist without the body. Therefore, the soul that is the form of a natural body cannot exist after death in the same way'.³⁰ In contrast, the intellect was less clearly defined, as Aristotle considered that the intellect was, on the one hand, contained in matter but, on the other, not made of matter and could, therefore, be immortal.³¹ However, being contained in matter, it was moved by matter. Aristotle generally held a monist position—a belief that the body and soul are of the same material and subject to the same laws, and that there was only one world.³² Nevertheless, from that position, he also maintained a division within that one world, the eternal, unchanging motion of the heavens and the corruptible and changing sublunar realm.³³ It was an ordered hierarchical system with the top of the hierarchy being God, the primary cause; the planetary spheres and their movements provided additional secondary causes. These primary and secondary causes produced temporary disturbances in all earthly objects below the moon by mixing the elements. Aristotle taught that the elements—fire, earth, air, and water—in the sublunar world were individually drawn to their proper place, that each element sought its natural habitat in the material world.³⁴ This was his view of perfection, an element in its proper place. He stated, 'The movement of natural bodies is towards a condition of being at rest in their own place; and being in that place is for them their nature perfected'.³⁵ For Aristotle, therefore, perfection could be found in the sublunar realm, fuelled by the natural motion of the elements rather than a divinely inspired desire.

Aristotle considered future events within the context of his theories on causation, specifically in how the future came into being. He used a future contingency puzzle, which explored the possibility of a sea battle, to illustrate his thinking on the nature of the future.³⁶ Aristotle challenged the concept of logical determinism, which posits that every future event must be necessary. For example, if it is necessary that there will be a sea battle tomorrow, then there will be a sea battle tomorrow, without fail. If it is necessary that there will not be a sea battle, then there will not be a sea battle. According to this logic, the result is that nothing is possible except what happens. However, Aristotle claimed that such future-tense statements are not necessarily true or false in the present tense. Instead, he argued for a contingent option, asserting that some truths are only conditionally true; their truth depends on what happens in the present, making them contingent.³⁷

Aristotle's cosmology dominated thinking until the seventeenth century. It also became a force within astrology through the work of the first century CE Greek astronomer and astrologer Claudius Ptolemy, who will be discussed later in this chapter.

The Stoics – fate and divine harmony

Susanne Bobzien defines stoic philosophy as a systematic philosophy. All the theories within it need to fit together to form a consistent whole.[38] The Stoics, like Plato and Aristotle, regarded the cosmos as a living entity. Diogenes, the third-century Greek biographer who wrote of Zeno of Citium (d. 263 BCE), the founder of the Stoa, stated that '… the entire cosmos too, being an animal … [is] alive and rational…'[39] This living creature was linked to all of its parts by *sumpatheia*, or sympathy.[40] Bobzien defined *sumpatheia* as the idea that 'in some sense everything in the universe emits some physical influence on everything else'.[41] The Stoic sympathetic cosmos was, according to Marcus Tullius Cicero (106 BCE–43 BCE), driven by the 'one divine and continuously connected *pneuma*'.[42] *Pneuma* was the ancient Greek word for breath, and Chrysippus, who became the third head of the Stoa in 232 BCE, considered *pneuma* to be the sustaining principle of the world.[43] *Pneuma* was divine intelligence manifested as breath, and it was the principle of internal coherence for all individual bodies, from stones to plants to animals. Because it permeated everything without interruption, it was the agent that made the world a single, coherent body.[44]

Stoic philosophy was, therefore, a form of monism, as the world consisted of only one substance.[45] This Stoic cosmos contrasted markedly from Plato's view. Plato's cosmos was divinely ordered and biased towards good, the will of the World Soul.[46] For Plato, the divine was both transcendent, existing beyond matter, and immanent, existing within matter; it was unmoving and the prime causal agent in the chain of causation. In Plato's scheme, the divine could never be subject to change—it was unmoved and not of the same substance as the world of matter. The Stoic view, however, was that there was *only* immanence; the divine was the matter of the world, it was in movement, and it was neutral. Additionally, as a moving, changing divine, it was in a state of creation.[47] Humans, as a part of the material world, had a moral responsibility to help produce harmony within the world of matter, as this was the pathway towards aiding the creation of the divine.[48]

Botros commented that Stoic cosmology included the idea of an immanent world, where nature, life, God, and the organic and inorganic worlds are combined in one sympathetic, connected relationship.[49] With soul and body, both held in the world of matter, the Stoic view of fate needed to contain human subjection to the world of matter and its laws while also embracing freedom. They approached this dilemma by viewing the two concepts as non-conflicting separate issues.[50] The first-century Greek Stoic philosopher Epictetus (55–135 CE) wrote of freedom as the ability to 'deal rightly with our impressions'.[51] These 'impressions' reveal the location of Stoic free will, that is, the freedom of mental agency. In Stoic cosmology, one cannot change external events in life, but one can choose one's mental attitude. To the Stoics, thoughts were separate from matter; hence, one was free to shape them as one wished. This freedom stood in stark contrast to any physical freedom compromised by tyranny or slavery. It was internal psychological freedom, freedom from being led by passions and desires.[52] Epictetus wrote:

> I must die. But must I die groaning? I must be imprisoned. But must I whine as well? I must suffer exile. Can anyone then hinder me from going with a smile, and good courage, and at peace? [53]

It should be noted at this point that the concept of free will did not come into classical philosophy until Epictetus's work, who used the phrase 'what is up to us'.[54] Here, Epictetus used Stoic thinking to define what is 'up to us' as the mind's internal reactions to external events.[55] Bobzien commented that Chrysippus did not use a word for freedom but instead talked of a notion described as 'not externally hindered, not necessitated'.[56] The actual term free will, according to Michael Frede, was not used until the third quarter of the second century when the Christian apologist Tatian, in his *Oratio and Graecos,* referred to *'eleutheria tēs prohaireseōs',* which Frede translates as 'the freedom of the will'.[57]

Stoic doctrine also viewed the transmigration of souls in a manner different from Plato. A.A. Long stated that 'The Stoics ... insist[ed] that the soul is corporeal'.[58] In other words, it was part of the physical body, not separate from it. With the soul being corporeal, the body and soul were reborn together, but only as a result of the rebirth of the entire world through the conflagration—the great cycle that saw the universe periodically consumed by fire, only to be remade afresh. After each conflagration, a person was reborn—body and soul—at the appointed time of his or her birth in the history of the world.[59] With this rebirth, one lived the same life as before, with the hope that in each life, one improved the harmony of one's mind. Reincarnation was thus linked to the periodic cosmic conflagration and not, as in Plato's view, with personal progress through varying lifetimes, driven by the pursuit of moral integrity.

Long and Sedley argued that the Stoic model of reincarnation led to the idea that time is cyclical, with the past embedded in the future just as the future is embedded in the past.⁶⁰ This notion of time as circular can lead to fatalism. In this regard, it is the same as the notion of destiny portrayed in Sophocles' play *Oedipus Rex*, where Oedipus cannot avoid his fate even though he holds himself responsible for the actions that he chooses to take. On one level, the endless repetition of a given life is fatalistic, as no present action will change the future outcome. However, the external worldly events that the individual endured on their endless journeys through lifetimes were not significant. Central to Stoic philosophy was the idea that the individual could use the freedom of their mind to grow in peace and harmony, with the ultimate goal of developing mental self-agency for the good of the divine.

The Roman author Aulus Gellius (125–c.180) commented that Chrysippus wrote,

> the order and reason and necessity of fate set in motion the general types and starting points of the causes, but each person's own will [or decisions] and the character of his mind govern the impulses of our thoughts and minds and our very actions.⁶¹

At the heart of Stoic philosophy was its view of an all-encompassing fate and the need to align it with moral responsibility. Stoic philosophy was grappling with what is known today as the philosophical problem of compatibilism, the belief that free will can exist in a deterministic world (discussed in Chapter Five). Bobzien argued that 'as a result, Stoic philosophy is extremely complex'. ⁶²

Stoic cosmology can be summarised as monist, in that all was contained in the one world – God, the material world, soul and body. With that established, the divine cosmos was in a state of creation, immanent in nature and influenced by and influencing all things within the cosmos. This cosmos was a sympathetic cosmos bound together by a divine breath. The fate, of one's life, was to be a part of the repeating great cycles of the conflagration. Personal freedom can be found within the world of matter through mental self-agency, allowing one to experience inner happiness regardless of external events. One's moral responsibility was not under coercion as in the Platonist model but lay in an altruistic desire for the individual to contribute to the creation of divine harmony.

Cicero – against universal fate

The Roman statesman Marcus Tullius Cicero (106–43 BCE), rejected the Stoic notion of a universal fate, which encouraged the development of mental self-agency. He presented an alternative approach. First, he accepted the Stoic idea that fate was the consequence of linear causation. He wrote that fate was 'an orderly succession of causes, wherein cause is linked to causes and each cause of itself produces an effect'.⁶³ Cicero spoke of the working of fate as,

> [t]hings which are to be do not suddenly spring into existence, but the evolution of time is like the unwinding of a cable: it creates nothing new and only unfolds each event in its order.⁶⁴

In the face of this inevitable fate, Cicero challenged Stoic monism. In *De Fato* Cicero critiqued the Stoic idea that fate was universal.

> For it does not follow that if differences in men's propensities are due to natural and antecedent causes, therefore our will and desires are also due to natural and antecedent causes; for it that were the case, we should have no freedom of the will at all.⁶⁵

Cicero argued that if fate was universal, then all motion was caused by a previous event, precedent causes. However, he claimed that such a proposition was intolerable.⁶⁶ He argued that some events could be predestined, 'but in other cases there can be some elements of chance'.⁶⁷ Chance is used here by Cicero as meaning an event considered to have no antecedent causes and thus impossible to foresee. Such events were deemed to happen by chance, luck, or accident and believed to occur randomly.⁶⁸ Cicero was referring to the older Greek notion of *Tyche*, that which happens by chance or a concept of a thing that happens by accident.⁶⁹ As Cicero claims, 'chance loves variation and abhors regularity'.⁷⁰ In the Roman period, *Tyche* became personified as the goddess Fortuna.⁷¹ It is due to his belief in the existence of *Tyche* that Cicero argued against universal fate. Apart from these arguments, he also pointed out that even if all events did have antecedent causes, 'it is nevertheless within our power to make the event turn out otherwise'.⁷² He supported this by arguing that the human mind was distinct from all other animals due to Reason and that Reason allowed humanity to achieve 'greatness of soul and a sense of superiority to worldly conditions'.⁷³ Cicero, like Plato before him, held a dualist position.

Cicero then criticised astrologers for claiming that, 'For the Chaldeans, [astrologers] according to their own statements, believe that a person's destiny [fate] is affected by the condition of the moon at the time of his birth'.⁷⁴ He asked the following questions concerning the viability of predictions based on the stars:

> On what law of nature do such prophecies depend? …[if prophecies] are controlled by some natural and immutable law such as regulates the movements of the stars, pray, can we conceive of anything happening

by accident, or chance? Surely nothing is so at variance with reason and stability as chance. Hence it seems to me that it is not in the power even of God himself to know what event is going to happen accidentally and by chance.[75]

Cicero was challenging two issues here. The first is the association of the Spindle of Necessity, the movement of the heavens, with human fate. Cicero dismissed the role of the heavens as a source or echo of fate and allocated the source of fate to a combination of time and antecedent causes. The second issue he challenged was the Stoic universalism of fate. Fate, for him, did not apply to humanity either in full or in part, because there was both the concept of chance and the ability of human reason to change the course of events.

Cicero redefined fate and then condemned it. He dismissed the idea that fate had a relationship to human agency, ignoring the arguments from antiquity of the Egyptians, who believed in magic to alter personal fate, and the Mesopotamians, who believed in beseeching the gods to decree a new fate. He also denied that fate had a purpose, as in Plato's balance between the *Moirai*, the Spindle of Necessity, and human agency, all of which were employed in shaping a future life, and he ignored fate's role in the development of mental self-agency as promoted by the Stoics.

Cicero's definition of fate is as an expression of closed time, the 'unwinding of a cable… unfolding', with all in order, dictated by time and previous events. He reduced fate to a form of necessity—which he viewed as solely a universal law of nature running its inevitable course. His definition changed fate from a hybrid of necessity and human agency to just necessity which he then split from human life. Consequently, Cicero stripped fate of its unique nature, tailor-made for each individual (either through the spindle or in some other manner). With the loss of fate's personal nature, it became meaningless, as it lost its purpose as a personal guide or wet stone for the development of moral responsibility; it also lost its relationship to any notions of the human soul.

Cicero's definition of fate has had a long-lasting influence, probably due to his writings serving as a primary source in the West for the study of Roman history and Latin literature. It is now a definition entrenched in mainstream thought. It is a hegemony of an argument to the point that even the possibility of a person holding a view of fate that is Platonic, Stoic, or alterable in any way, is inconceivable. For example, it is Cicero's definition of fate that Burrus and Roese assumed, cited in the Introduction. Their assumption that fate was simply necessity (determinism) caused considerable confusion for them when analysing their results. They assumed that there was only one fate, Cicero's version.

However, what they found was that their participants viewed fate differently, a hybrid of necessity and human agency. Unfortunately, because of the hegemony of Cicero's version of fate, Burrus and Roese did not understand that there were different kinds of fate, and thus did not explore their results any further.

Living with fate – the astrologers

In parallel with these philosophical views on fate, the lived experience of fate is expressed in Hellenistic writings on astrology. Modern historians sometimes define astrology in the classical period as a form of divination. David Potter remarked, 'Pride of place among the various forms of inductive divination available in the Roman world must go to astrology'.[76] Sarah Johnston also linked astrology to divination, grouping it with lecanomancy and haruspicy—scrying and interpreting animal entrails—because they were all practices that 'work by methods that are empirically unverifiable'.[77] David Pingree's pragmatic definition of astrology in this period did not view it as divination; instead, he defined it as '…the study of the impact of the celestial bodies — Moon, Sun, Mercury, Venus, Mars, Jupiter, Saturn, the fixed stars and sometimes the lunar nodes — upon the sublunar world'.[78]

In turning to definitions from astrological authors of that period, Claudius Ptolemy (c. 90–c. 168 CE), the first-century Alexandrian astronomer, geographer and astrologer, wrote a major astronomical text now known as the *Almagest* where he laid the foundations for finding the rate of precession, the slow rotation of the Earth's celestial axis. He also composed one of the central astrological works in Western history, the *Tetrabiblos*, which he regarded as his contribution to understanding the workings of the world of matter. Thus, his work combined the study of the heavens above with the influence of the heavens on the Earth below. To achieve this, he reformed astrology by embracing Aristotelian elements and Stoic concepts.[79] He compared the studies of astronomy and astrology when he wrote:

> The studies preliminary to the astronomical prognostication, O Syrus! are two: the one, first alike in order and in power, leads to the knowledge of the figurations of the Sun, the Moon, and the stars; and of their relative aspects to each other, and to the earth: the other takes into consideration the changes which their aspects create, by means of their natural properties, in objects under their influence.[80]

Campion noted that, due to Ptolemy's later influence within astronomy with his work *The Almagest*, his astrological work *Tetrabiblos* became 'one of the core texts of medieval and Renaissance astrology'.[81] Robert Hand commented that 'Ptolemy's *Tetrabiblos* is without doubt the single most influential book in all Western astrology'. Robert Scmidt wrote that its effect upon astrology is as great as Isaac Newton's *Principia* on Physics'.[82] Hence, Ptolemy's astrological philosophy has influenced astrological thinking for the last 2000 years, and his work became a carrier of Stoic views on fate into contemporary astrology practice.

Influenced by the Stoic tradition, Ptolemy, unlike Plato, did not invoke a divine entity. For Ptolemy, fate was a matter of personal engagement with the power that flowed from the heavens over the Earth: 'That a certain power, derived from the aethereal nature, is diffused over and pervades the whole atmosphere of the earth, is clearly evident to all men'.[83] The movement of both the fixed stars and the planets then altered this force:

> The stars likewise (as well the fixed stars as the planets), in performing their revolutions, produce many impressions on the Ambient. They cause heats, winds, and storms, to the influence of which earthly things are conformably subjected. And, further, the mutual configurations of all these heavenly bodies, by comingling the influence with which each is separately invested, produce a multiplicity of changes.[84]

Thus, change on Earth was the result of the movement of the heavenly spheres being translated to Earth, which, on the Earth, then produced the comingling of the Aristotelian elements, viewed by Ptolemy as consisting of the qualities of hot, cold, wet and dry. This comingling, in turn, produced 'mutual configurations' which resulted in 'a multiplicity of changes'.[85] Consequently, all things on Earth were subject to change, and the source of this change was the heavenly bodies. The fate of a person or country could be understood by studying and plotting the movement of the heavenly bodies but with the caveat that the cominglings were complex and, at times, difficult to understand.

Ptolemy also differed from Plato's view of character. Plato saw character as an attribute of the immortal soul. In contrast, Ptolemy suggested that character was made up of different causes: the attributes of both species and of parents; upbringing or personal history; the influence of the place of conception or birth; and finally, the state of the four qualities (hot, cold, wet and dry) as expressed in the ambient, or natural environment, at the time of birth.[86] The quality of a particular moment, the moment of birth, was revealed by the movement of the heavenly bodies in relation to the local horizon and the zodiac signs.[87] However, Ptolemy pointed out that, 'consequently, unless every one of these varieties be duly blended with the causes arising in the Ambient, the prejudgment of any event will doubtless be very incomplete'.[88] Hence, for Ptolemy, astrology by itself was not able to predict with certainty, as 'It is further to be remarked that man is subject, not only to events applicable to his own private and individual nature, but also to others arising from general causes'.[89] To explore all these causes the astrologer needed to create a horoscope for the moment of birth, a map of the zodiac signs and the planets as they were orientated for a particular moment in time and place. By examining this map, the Ambient generated from the heavens, a judgment could be made of both character and fate.

Ptolemy allocated the actual selection of the time of birth not to Plato's notion that the immortal soul chose its next lifetime but instead to Necessity itself. The 'seed', so planted at conception and shaped by the causal factors at that time, began a chain of events which resulted in birth. The birth time and thus the individual's horoscope were sympathetic to the Ambient conditions of the individual's conception:

> because nature, after completing the formation in the womb, always effects the birth in immediate obedience to some certain position of the Ambient corresponding and sympathising with the primary position which operated the incipient formation.[90]

Thus, the Ambient reflected in the horoscope for birth contained in its complexity the Ambient of the time of conception.

In Stoic terms, Ptolemy saw the purpose of astrology as providing information which helped cultivate the freedom of the mind. Previously, Epictetus had argued that seeking advice from a diviner could help one live according to fate and in greater harmony.[91] Ptolemy agreed; he considered that humanity lived in a complex interplay of causes, all ordered and interlinked in an Aristotelian sympathetic cosmos. Some of these causes were external to the individual, while others were the individual's internal reaction to external events—their temperament. In his Stoic/Aristotelian secular astrology, Ptolemy considered that the individual's only option was to gain control of the turbulence of his or her mind rather than influence the world around them. Thus, he considered the purpose of astrology was to enable the calm acceptance of the inevitable:

> if arriving [the event] unforeseen, [it] will either overwhelm the mind with terror or destroy its composer by sudden delight; if, however, such events should have been foreknown, the mind will have been previously prepared for their reception and will preserve an equable calmness,

> by having been accustomed to contemplate the approaching event as though it were present, so that, on its actual arrival, it will be sustained with tranquillity and constancy.[92]

For Ptolemy, the predictive tools of astrology were to be used in the Stoic tradition to prepare the mind and body for the future so that one's virtue would not be challenged.

Ptolemy, unlike Plato, did not resort to a divine concept to maintain humanity's ability to do 'what is up to us'. The *Tetrabiblos* contained neither warning of difficulties if one failed to make the spiritual return journey to the stars nor any warnings about what would happen if one succumbed to one's indicated fate. Ptolemy's Necessity was driven by a causal model based on the idea that all things were in motion within a sympathetic cosmology derived from Stoic and Aristotelian principles, where qualities were mixed by movement into multiple cominglings. Personal fate was one's unique 'slice' of these cominglings, and freedom was the human right and ability to reach for mental peace.

Ptolemy's younger contemporary Vettius Valens (b. 120, *fl* 145–170 CE) took a different approach. Valens was a native of Antioch who travelled widely in Egypt and it is logical to assume he knew of or may have even met Ptolemy. His view differed from Ptolemy's in that he, Valens, saw it as all-containing. Greenbaum pointed out that Valens considered that humans were made of three parts, 'the body furnished by the earth, the soul furnished by the moon and the mind furnished by the sun'. Gone were Ptolemy's different levels of causation, of the influence of parents, culture, place and so forth. Valens considered that the entire individual was under the influence of the luminaries and the planets, as governed by astrology. It was central to life, and he wrote, 'Without it [astrology] there neither is nor will be anything: its contains the foreknowledge of the beginning and the end'.[93]

Valens commented directly about fate in Book VI, chapter 9 of his work, *The Anthology Book*, where he, like Ptolemy, adopted a Stoic position by viewing a life lived in accord with fate as a perfect life:

> For no one is free; we all are slaves of fate and if we follow her voluntarily, we will live undisturbed and without grief as a whole, having trained our minds to be confident.[94]

And later in Book VII

> For the universe, whirling in a sphere and sending the emanations of the stars onto this globe, does nothing vainly or uselessly: every moment it

makes many things new in life, things which each person must abide patiently, some at one time, others at another, in order to fulfil the aims of fate.

Astrology was the centre of Valens' faith. His astrology held a divine fate that guided the direction of all events in accord with the 'starry vault of the heaven and by the twelve-fold circle, by the sun, the moon, and the five wandering stars by whole all of life is guided, and by Providence itself and Holy Fate'.[95] To walk with one's fate was to walk a divine path. For Valens, astrology was a divine gift filled with sacred, mysterious knowledge that needed to be protected from misuse.

For both Ptolemy and Valens, the role of astrology, and hence to know one's fate, was to help maintain the virtue of the mind and accept the inevitable—not in a futile manner but in the Stoic manner of taking personal internal mental action to help minimise the mental impact of a future inevitable events. Thus, futilism was avoided, for one could use the knowledge of one's fate to be mentally prepared. Both Ptolemy and Valens saw fate as unchangeable. However, Ptolemy took into account errors in astrological judgments as being caused by the inadequacies of the horoscope, so it could not be used as an inevitable instrument due to its limited representation of the cominglings. In comparison, Valens did not consider incorrect judgments and railed against charlatans who put the divine gift of God into disrepute. For him, fate was a form of divine providence, it filled all of life, and to follow one's fate was to walk with this divine gift.

Theories of fate

These different classical views on the nature of fate, as presented by Plato, the Stoics, Aristotle, and those of Ptolemy and Valens, all required slightly different ontological frameworks, or theories of existence, which Bobzien defined as the philosophical school's theory of fate.[96] My research shows that people today still hold various theories of fate, and a better understanding of these individual versions of fate can be gained by returning to this Classical topography of fate. This topography consists of four interrelated topics.

The nature of the cosmos

A theory of fate will contain at its centre a belief concerning the nature of the cosmos. Plato's view of fate was derived from his view of the cosmos as inherently good and a well-ordered, rational structure that reflected the goodness and rationality of its creator, the Demiurge.[97] In contrast, for the Stoics, the cosmos was fundamentally neutral, neither inherently good nor evil. It was ordered by divine reason or natural law and did not bestow moral judgments.[98] By accepting the neutral nature of the cosmos, Stoics strove to achieve tranquillity and resilience, recognising that the cosmos did not act with malice or benevolence but rather followed its rational order.

A sympathetic cosmos

Good, bad, or neutral, the cosmos must also be sympathetic. Fate requires a cosmos where everything is linked by a chain of correspondences bound by *sumpatheia*, the idea that all things are interconnected. The Stoic sympathetic cosmos was driven by the 'one divine and continuously connected *pneuma*', where pneuma is the divine breath that contained but also limited to the world of matter.[99] This Stoic *pneuma*, however, was only one form of the connecting agent in a sympathetic cosmos. Plato's cosmos was linked by the World Soul, an all-loving and knowing artisan being. It was the World Soul, therefore, that linked all things. Aristotle did not write of *sumpatheia,* but his world 'worked' by being a mechanical cosmos of fifty-five interconnected spheres which were powered by love.[100] These spheres drove the four elements, which constantly sought their proper places, which gave rise to human activity and thoughts.[101] For Aristotle, the interconnectedness (*sumpatheia*) was the ever-moving four elements.

The location of the Will

A theory of fate also requires a belief concerning the location of the human will/soul/mind/character. The Platonist model considered the soul to be divine and thus located it outside the world of matter. This was a dualist philosophy that allowed the individual to rise above the desires of the material world and, therefore, above one's fate. In contrast, the Stoics considered the soul to be fully a part of the physical cosmos, a monist philosophy, therefore under fate's influence. Different monist philosophies will have varying approaches to finding a place for moral responsibility in the face of fate.

A belief about the purpose of fate

Along with beliefs concerning the nature of the cosmos and the location of the soul or Will, a person's theory of fate will also suggest the purpose or role of fate. In Plato's model, the purpose of fate was to lead the soul back to the World Soul, whereas the Stoic model viewed fate as the pathway that enabled the individual to develop mental agency in order to help live in perfect harmony and contribute to the creation of the divine. For the astrologer, Valens, it was to accept God's providence.

These parameters form a matrix of beliefs that an individual must accept to acknowledge the existence of fate in their life, whether in the Classical period or today. Frede commented that, for the individual, some views about the world, no matter how incomplete or contradictory, are required for the individual to address questions about the nature of their free will.[102] Similarly, these four components of a theory of fate—the nature of the cosmos, the nature of sympathy, the location of the Will, and the purpose of fate—are beliefs that today, can be explored when questioning a person about their views on fate to help reveal the foundations of their beliefs.

In summary, by the end of the Classical period, fate was defined, with varying nuances, either by the dualist position of Plato, in which the soul could be separate from the body, or by the monist position of the Stoics, in which body and soul were one. In Plato's version, the will was free and needed to be used to cultivated a rational and virtuous lifestyle, where the person was motivated to do so to improve their next incarnation. His model was hierarchical, and one needed to rise above the lower levels, transcending bodily desires and fate. The Stoics took a more positive view of fate, accepting it by surrendering personal agency in the material world while controlling their mental state to maintain calmness. For the Stoics, one had a moral responsibility to contribute to cosmic harmony.

Aristotle focused on causality and challenged logical determinism (his sea battle argument) and instead argued for some events happening by chance, not requiring an antecedent cause.[103] He did not perceive a tension between free will and fate, as he adopted a dualist stance, viewing fate as non-universal. Cicero also adopted a dualist stance, claiming that universal fate was not valid as it would remove, *Tyche*, that is chance events, that happened without an antecedent cause. However, he also challenged the notion that the heavens bestowed fate, the Spindle of Necessity, and that fate was not a hybrid of human and cosmic forces. Instead, fate was solely the working of time and antecedent causes; in effect, he reduced fate to necessity. At this time, the astrology of the classical era, as typified by both Ptolemy and Valens, was informed by different theories of fate. Ptolemy reflected the Stoic view of fate. For him, the role of astrology was to aid mental calmness. In contrast, for Valens, astrology revealed God's plan for one's life, thereby helping one to cooperate with God and rejoice in the divine.

These different perspectives on fate permeate future philosophical debates on free will, astrological discussions on the role of astrology, and theological doctrines regarding the pathway to personal salvation.

CHAPTER THREE

THE THREADS OF FATE IN THE MEDIEVAL PERIOD

The Medieval period in Europe is generally considered to have begun with the fall of the Western Roman Empire in 476 CE.[1] At this time Christianity spread throughout Europe, underpinned by the theological writings of Saint Augustine.[2] It was not until the twelfth century that a significant wave of translations from Greek and Arabic into Latin introduced Western Europe to a broader intellectual tradition.[3] Foremost among these were the works of Aristotle. The reintroduction of Aristotelian cosmology sparked renewed theological and philosophical debates within Christianity, particularly concerning the nature of knowledge—whether it should be grounded in faith alone or could also be pursued through reason and empirical observation of the natural world.[4] This debate, in turn, prompted a deeper examination of the nature of human reason, its relationship to faith, and the concept of causation itself. At the heart of the issue was the question of whether God was the sole and direct cause of all events or whether Aristotle's cosmology—distinguishing between primary and secondary causes—provided a legitimate framework for understanding the workings of the world. This distinction gave rise to broader questions concerning human agency: should individuals passively accept divine providence, implying a denial of free will, or did human beings possess the capacity to act independently and shape the course of their lives within the structure of causality? This chapter explores how these theological and philosophical debates informed contemporary conceptions of fate and examines how astrologers of the period responded and adapted their practices accordingly.

Augustine and divine providence

Saint Augustine (354–430 CE) applied Christian principles to the ongoing debates on the nature of causation. He criticised Stoicism and replaced the Stoic sympathetic cosmos with a world governed by God's providence. According to Tim Hegedus, an early Christian motif was that 'humans were created upright in stature so as to contemplate the sky and fix their thoughts on heavenly things'.[5] Augustine was probably aware of this perspective as he encountered astrology and worked with it from his late teens to his early thirties.[6] However, his early engagement with astrology conflicted with his later twin objectives:

first, glorifying God, and second, removing any potential challenge to God's omnipotent power.[7] Accordingly, he reframed fate, detaching it from any connection to the stars and a chain of causes and made it instead an instrument of God's will:

> 'Fate'; a name given by some people not to the position of the stars but to a chain of causes dependent on God's will. There are those who use the name 'destiny' to refer not to the conjunction of stars at the moment of conception, or birth, or beginning, but to the connected series of causes which is responsible for anything that happens. ... For in fact they ascribe this orderly series, this chain of causes, to the will and power of the supreme God, who is believed, most rightly and truly, to know all things before they happen and who leaves nothing unordered.[8]

Fate was, therefore, removed from the stars and placed in God's hands. Augustine's logic was simple: 'It is beyond anything incredible that He should have willed the kingdoms of men, their dominations and their servitudes, to be outside the range of the laws of His providence'.[9] From this position, Augustine then argued that providence was not linked to classical necessity:

> Are men's wills under the sway of necessity? There is no need, then, to dread that 'necessity', through fear of which the Stoics took such pains to distinguish between the causes of things, withdrawing some of them from the sway of necessity, subjecting others to it, and classing our wills among the causes they wished to emancipate from necessity, for fear, I suppose, that they would not be free if subject to it... If, on the other hand, we define 'necessity' in the sense implied when we say that it is necessary a thing should be thus, or should happen thus, I see no reason to fear that this would rob us of free will.[10]

With this argument, Augustine downgraded necessity and dismissed the monism of the Stoic view in which all things in the world were part of a single order. Instead, like Plato, he adopted a dualist position, in which the human will was entirely free of physical constraints (his version of necessity), with the major caveat that it was still subject to God's providence: God made plans for people as He saw fit. Gerald Bonner argued that Augustine replaced fate and necessity with theological fatalism.[11] All things in all times are known by God who has a purpose, a divine plan. As Bonner pointed out, according to this view, if God knows all things, then He already knows which souls will reach the kingdom of heaven; these souls are predestined for salvation, while all other souls are condemned to eternal damnation, regardless of their actions, good or evil.[12] Augustine's cosmology was fuelled by theological fatalism, nothing one could do would influence the predestined fact that one was either saved or damned.

Having stated that humanity was subject to God's providence, Augustine also needed to dismiss the theory of reincarnation. In the Platonic model, reincarnation served as the soul's moral compass, with one's actions in this life influencing the quality of the next life. However, in the face of God's providence, this moral compass was removed. After all, where does moral responsibility lie if one was predestined either to be saved or damned? To solve this problem, Augustine argued that free will constitutes the individual's choice to accept God's plan freely. As simple as this may sound, it did not represent freedom of the will, for it was a choice made under coercion. Alan Hill pointed out that a lack of morally correct behaviour would result in damnation, which was itself pre-ordained by God's judgment.[13] One had to produce good works in the hope that God knew these actions and that because of these good works, one had been selected for salvation. Augustine's solution was, therefore, a delusion of freedom.

The concept of God's providence represented a break from the classical view of the divine heavens: God could now override any potential celestial influence. Mark Graubard commented that, 'Since the days of Democritus and Plato the writers of ancient Greece knew that the heavenly bodies were regarded as gods or as divine beings ever since oldest antiquity'.[14] Campion cited Augustine as a major figure in the attempt to, in his words, 'de-spiritualise the universe'.[15] He pointed out that, after Augustine, the stars no longer offered a path to salvation.[16] With the 'stars' downgraded, Augustine's notion of fate was, as cited earlier, 'a chain of causes' which emanated solely from God: the heavens were no longer required.

Calcidius – fate and contingents

A different view of fate was held by the fourth-century philosopher Calcidius, who placed Platonist views into Christian philosophy.[17] His translation of, and commentary on, part of Plato's *Timaeus*, up to chapter 53c, was the only extensive Platonic text known to the Latin West until the mid-fifteenth century.[18] He wrote the treatise 'On Fate', derived from his commentary on the *Timaeus*, and drew on another classical source, *De Fato*, attributed to Plutarch, on issues concerning providence and free will.[19]

As already noted, Platonic theories of fate included reincarnation as a mechanism for maintaining moral responsibility. However, with the rejection of reincarnation by Christian theologians, one's fate was no longer the result of choices made before birth. Furthermore, due to God's providence, the choices in one's current life would not influence one's future afterlife. Hence, Christian philosophers needed to revisit the question of personal moral responsibility. Calcidius attempted to present a solution to this problem. He cited Plato on virtue: '…virtue is independent and not subject to any necessity…' and then cited Moses, claiming that Moses told the story of the eating of the forbidden fruit from the Garden of Eden, and used this as evidence that humans, according to God, had the '…ability to abstain or not.'[20] Calcidius used these sources to make his case that God did not override the individual's moral compass, thereby restoring free will. Calcidius then explored God's providence, writing that,

> …the things within human power… can be divided into different stages, of all the things that were possible some were necessary and others were contingent.[21]

Pascal Massie defined this model of necessity as pertaining to that which is expected to happen: for example, all things that are born are expected to die. In contrast, things that may or may not happen were known as contingents.[22] Contingents were events that had no known causes, and as such, they are unexpected.[23] One of the sources of the idea of contingencies was Aristotle's theory of causation, discussed in Chapter Two. In brief, Aristotle viewed causation as consisting of four components: the material cause (the substance contained in the object), the formal cause (how this substance had been arranged), the efficient or moving cause (its movement), and the final cause which was its purpose (that for which it was designed).[24] Based on these four causes, he added the idea of voluntary and involuntary human actions.[25] Frede claimed that 'Aristotle seems to presuppose quite a large class of events which are not determined but which are 'open either way'; it is called the contingent… .'[26] Contingencies were linked to the Greek deity *Tyche*, as cited earlier, a personification of luck that produced events that lay outside the causal chain. It was in the idea of contingencies, also known later as particulars, that created the space for free will to exist.

Calcidius took the theological step of stating that God knew things that were necessary but not those that were contingent. He wrote: 'God does not know the nature of what is contingent in such a way as that which is certain and bound by necessity'.[27] Hence, God knew things by their nature, and the nature of contingencies was that they were required to be random. God chose not to know them, as it would be against their nature, that is, being random, to be known.[28]

Humanity was subject to necessity and its causal chain of fate. However, Calcidius argued that humanity could also be the originator of a new causal chain: a contingent event, once freely created, then produced its own causal chain. Hence, by the laws of necessity, these actions had consequences, and it was these consequences that imposed a moral responsibility on the instigator. Calcidius wrote:

> Now the preceding merit [fate] which can take one of two directions is caused by a motion of our mind and a judgment and an agreement and desire or avoidance, things put within our power, because these things as well as their contraries are for us to choose. So in this ordinance of things and according to a most ancient law some things are said to result from a preceding decision and are in our power; what comes after them, however, is the result, bound by necessity.[29]

The ideas contained in Calcidius's writings conform to what Robert Kane defines as a form of libertarianism, a belief that the causal chain can be altered or begin with the action of the individual who thus becomes 'the prime mover unmoved',[30] Roderick Chisholm also defined this libertarian principle as immanent causation, a cause initiated with the self, self-agency.[31] Having established a place for free will in his cosmology, Calcidius suggested that humanity would need guidance to avoid inadvertently creating a chain of adverse events, a negative fate. Calcidius's solution was to use astrology as the instrument of this guidance. He wrote,

> ...the astrologer will correctly and rationally try to catch the right moment to undertake an act according to the favourable position of stars and constellations so that if this will happen [an action taken], that will be the result [the resultant causal chain].[32]

The theory of fate proposed by Calcidius protected the autonomy of the self and maintained the notion of moral responsibility. Fate existed within the heavens, but it was also created by human action independent of any predetermined law, but once created it was compelling. This concept of fate resembled the ripples spreading across a pond after a stone was thrown in—for once an action occurred, necessity unfolded its inevitable consequences.

Given that the power to shape fate lay in human hands, Calcidius saw the pursuit of reason as essential—reason directed toward understanding the world, including the cosmic paths of the planets, rather than toward the purification of the soul. In this view, the capacity to engage with fate depended on knowledge and was thus independent of moral character or the condition of the soul. By taking this position, Calcidius asserted a limitation on divine knowledge—a boundary God voluntarily imposed upon Himself: the self-limitation of not knowing the precise nature or outcome of contingent events.

Bobzien referred to the idea of contingencies in the Middle Platonist writings as 'hypothetical fate' and states, 'Plato's formerly "pre-natal" choice of a life is presented as including the choice of individual *actions* in one's life, and it has become dependent on the soul whether or not to *act*'.[33] Bobzien pointed out the significance of this distinction:

> ... the importance of the introduction of individual choices lies in the fact that it is in their choices that people manifest themselves as rational or moral beings: my choices, since determined by nothing but myself, reflect who I am. This is why I am morally responsible for what I choose. It is in order to ensure this, that choices have been exempted from the predetermination by fate.[34]

Bobzien highlighted that the concept of an individual's action producing fate was a new theme within the middle Platonist literature. She argued that this concept, which allowed humanity to freely choose, effectively changed the philosophical landscape, ending the debates on 'causal universal determinism' within antiquity.[35]

Calcidius's reflections on fate remain relevant in popular culture, where superstitions and jinxes—discussed in the Introduction—express a belief in self-agency. A person may fear that a particular action could unintentionally trigger a chain of events that jeopardises a desired outcome, effectively creating a hostile fate. Conversely, carrying a lucky object is seen as an action taken to help attract a favourable fate into one's life. Calcidius's version of fate is still represented in some forms of astrology, discussed in later chapters.

Early Arabic views of fate

Philosophical arguments on causation also existed in the Islamic world. The Persian philosopher Ibn-Sīnā, known in the West as Avicenna (c. 980–1037), supported a God concerned with universals rather than particulars (contingencies), with God knowing of particulars only in a universal way. That is to say that God chose to know that particulars existed but only as a generic concept. For Avicenna, there was a fine theological distinction concerning the nature of universal knowledge as distinct to God's knowledge of particulars. In *The Metaphysics of the Book of Healing*, Avicenna discusses God's knowledge as being intellectual, of the mind, and not existing in the temporal world and consequently,

> In another respect, it is not possible that He would apprehend intellectually these changeables with the changes [they undergo] (inasmuch as they are changeable) in a temporal, individualised manner. For it is not possible that at one instance in a temporal [act] of intellectual apprehension He would apprehend them as existing, not nonexistting, and at another instance [in a state of] nothingness, nonexistting.[36]

By introducing the concept of 'particulars,' Avicenna made space for human free will within the sublunar realm. These particulars arose from an Aristotelian cosmology, where primary causes interacted with secondary causes.[37] The motion of the celestial spheres influenced the sublunary world through the mingling of the four elements, thereby generating the particulars. Avicenna took this idea further and formulating a cosmic psychology—comprising intellect, soul, and body—for each celestial sphere, thus linking the cosmic order to divine providence.[38] In this way, the secondary causation of the heavenly spheres, which gave rise to particulars, was ultimately traced back to God. Human free will, then, was understood as an extension of divine will.

Aristotle's cosmology and Avicenna's views were not universally accepted. From as early as the ninth century, critics within the Ash'arite school of Sunni Islam rejected the notion of causality, asserting that God alone was the cause of all events and denied the existence of secondary causes.[39] This doctrine was later reinforced by Abu Hamid al-Ghazālī (1058–1111), who, in his critique of Avicenna's philosophy, argued that Avicenna's God knew only universals, not individual persons or their specific actions.[40] Al-Ghazālī further challenged the principle of causation by condemning the works of Plato and Aristotle in his seminal text *The Incoherence of the Philosophers*, where he articulated a position later known as Islamic occasionalism. He maintained that God was the sole agent behind all occurrences, leaving no room for independent causation.[41] Al-Ghazālī's rationale was theological: if humans could effect change through secondary causes, this would undermine the possibility of miracles, where God and God alone, altered the causal chain.[42] By asserting God as the only cause of all things, the doctrine supported a worldview grounded in absolute predestination—since God knew all, all was preordained.[43]

The development of Arabic astrology—comprising the corpus of astrological texts written in Arabic within an Islamic cultural context—was shaped both by advances in Arabic mathematics and by the rejection of Aristotle's theory of secondary causes with its complex system of cominglings. Within this intellectual framework, occasionalism fostered a new approach to astrology among Islamic scholars. Since God's will was now regarded as the sole cause of all events, astrology was reinterpreted as a means of accessing direct knowledge of divine intention at the individual level.[44] As a result, astrologers began to pursue a more systematic and quantifiable analysis of the natal horoscope, seeking consistency and repeatability in their delineations. Through the application of arithmetic, the horoscope could be examined in a reductionist and methodical manner. This new development appeared in the astrology of Omar of Tiberias ('Umar ibn al-Farrukhan al-Tabari), who died around 816 CE. In his astrology, he used a technique known as *al-mubtazz*, which in Latin is referred to as almutens. This technique involved assigning quantitative values to the qualities of planets based on their positions within the horoscope and the zodiac.[45] These numerical scores could then be arithmetically manipulated, allowing the overall influence of a planet in a horoscope to be reduced to a single value—effectively grading its efficacy. This method introduced a level of consistency in interpretation, both between astrologers and across different horoscopes. Such consistency could then, hopefully, lead to a guarantee of empirical prediction in the sublunar world—that is, in human affairs. For, with no secondary causation, the horoscope was a direct link to God's will. Indeed, the Persian astrologer Abū Ma'shar (787–886) showed sympathy for the Ash'arite doctrine of occasionalism when he responded to a criticism of astrology that planets indicated universal things but not particular things such as the lives of individuals. Abū Ma'shar refuted this criticism by stating:

> 1. Genus, species, the four elements and coming-to-be and passing-away are found in every individual. 2. The planets indicate the genus, species, the four elements and coming-to-be and passing-away. 3. Therefore, the planets indicate separate individuals.[46]

Thus, for Abū Ma'shar, when a planet indicated a universal, it also revealed the individual and the particulars.[47] This was reflected in Abū Ma'shar's views on predictability when he wrote:

> …although men have free choice and can deliberate and ask advice, their decisions are still determined by the stars, which have indications for their animal and rational souls as well as over their bodies.[48]

For Abū Ma'shar, God knew of the particulars of an individual life, which could be defined and thus pursued within the horoscope. According to Roger French, with this new form of Arabic mathematical astrology 'came the notion that celestial causes were linked to mundane effects in a necessary way, which implied that once the planetary rulers were known, prediction was guaranteed'.[49] However, as with the cosmology of Augustine, the location of free will was questionable. The Persian astrologer Omar of Tiberias, cited earlier, wrote after almost every astrological prognosis in his work on nativities the words 'if God wills':

> But if one of the four [rulers] does not aspect this [the degree of the new moon] as we have said, it will be nullified, if God wills. [50]

The one caveat was that predictions could be made, but God could change his mind.

A Jewish perspective – hierarchical fate

The Jewish biblical scholar, astrologer and philosopher Rabbi Abraham Ibn Ezra (1089/1092–1164/1167) produced a different view of providence. He was born in Tudela, Spain, under Muslim rule, and spent the first fifty years of his life there, receiving an education in Arabic scientific thought and Jewish theology. He later travelled through Italy, France, and England, during which he wrote prolifically, producing biblical commentaries as well as covering other fields of learning, including astrology.[51] In his astrological books, he presented his views on fate, which appear to bridge the Islamic belief that God was the sole cause of an individual's fate with later Christian ideas that distinguished between the notions of universals and particulars. He replaced the idea of a single fate that emanated directly from God with a hierarchical form of fate. The first layer of this hierarchy was that of the nativity of the nation to which one belonged. This was deemed the most influential. Thus, if one was born an Israelite, regardless of one's horoscope, one could never become a king, as the national chart was for a nation in exile.[52] The other layers, in descending order, were one's race, the decisions of the country to go to war or not, matters of plague, one's family background, the horoscope of the nation's leader, the laws of nature and, finally, the individual. Within this model, the individual could reach for wisdom and exert an influence on fate by using the knowledge of astrology to mitigate the impact of a perceived future event. Reason was, then, the way of appealing to, or appeasing, God's will. Ibn Ezra wrote if 'one who has faith in God with all his heart God will turn things around and change circumstance to save him from every harm [indicated] in his nativity'.[53] In this way, the individual's fate—reflected in their horoscope—maintained a direct connection to God. However, while the chart could be consulted for guidance, it was always understood to hold a subordinate place within the greater hierarchy of fates. In total, Ibn Ezra wrote nineteen treatises on Greek and Arabic astrology in Hebrew and was the primary source of astrological literature for the Jewish diaspora in the Middle Ages. Additionally, shortly after his death, his work was translated into Latin and other emerging European languages.[54]

Ibn Ezra's work promoted a limited form of Platonic dualism, in which the human soul could be free of the many layers of fate, but only by following God. This feat could be aided by adopting an ascetic lifestyle. Deliverance from fate extended beyond death as salvation was achieved by intellectual betterment, which, upon death, enabled the soul to join the angels and live forever by ascending to the upper world.[55] Thus, for Ibn-Ezra, the role of astrology was to alleviate the workings of fate and assist in pursuing one's salvation.

Fate – the division of body and soul

The wave of translations in the twelfth century had a transformative impact on medieval European thought, ushering in a new era of intellectual development often referred to as the 'Twelfth-Century Renaissance'.[56] Through the systematic translation of Greek and Arabic texts into Latin—particularly works by Aristotle, Ptolemy, and Islamic thinkers such as Avicenna and Abū Ma'shar—European scholars gained access to advanced knowledge in philosophy, astronomy/astrology, medicine, and the natural sciences. This influx challenged and expanded the existing theological frameworks of the Latin West, prompting a re-evaluation of the relationship between reason and faith. Until this period, Christian theology was primarily shaped by Augustinian thought, which emphasised the value of divine revelation over human reason and the absolute sovereignty of God.[57] It also embraced the Platonist cosmology of the dual worlds, that of the perfect motion of the heavens and the corruptible and changing unknowable sublunar realm.[58]

The work of Abū Ma'shar was filtering through Europe at this time. His *The Great Introduction to Astrology* was translated into Latin twice: first in 1133 and then in 1140, and revealed to Western scholars the usefulness of astrology in medicine.[59] Campion noted that Arabic astrology 'held out [to the Christian world] the seductive prospect of control over a natural world which was otherwise chaotic and threatening'.[60] This form of control lay in the promise of predictability within the sublunar realm—a promise that appealed to physicians, who adopted it as a diagnostic tool despite it contradicting Plato's cosmology that sublunar predictability was not possible. Consequently, the work of the physicians began to be deemed heretical.[61]

Thomas Aquinas (c. 1225–1274) presented a solution to this tension between medicine and theology. He adapted Aristotle's natural philosophy and inserted it into Christianity.[62] He emphasised the significance of the natural world, encompassing the heavens and the role of celestial movements on human life. Patrick Curry observed that Aquinas 'legitimised the basis of astrology by granting the efficacy of Aristotle's descending spheres of celestial influence, but simultaneously delimited it by stressing the freedom of the will'.[63] This is evident when Aquinas addressed the significance of Aristotelian natural law and the role of the heavens by stating:

> Of course, acts of choice and movements of the will are controlled immediately by God. And human intellectual knowledge is ordered by God through the mediation of the angels. Whereas matters pertinent to bodily things, whether they are internal or external, when they come through the use of man, are governed by God by means of the angels and celestial bodies.[64]

Aquinas maintained the notion of free will by stating, '… whatever change might take place in our body as a result of the influence of a celestial body, it would not suffice to cause our choices'.[65] Aquinas accepted that the body could influence the mind in terms of health, age or desires, but one could override these desires. Patrick Quinn pointed out the Thomist soul was complex and able to function within both 'a temporal world of sensory experience, on the one hand, and the immaterial, eternal and intelligible realm of divine spiritual existence, on the other'.[66] Aquinas accepted the efficacy of the natural laws, required by astrology with its fate drawn by the heavenly movements, but he applied a dualist argument to the role of human life. The body was fated, now ruled by the Aristotelian elements mixed and co-mixed by the celestial spheres, but the soul was free.

Aquinas also challenged the certainty of the new Arabic astrology by stating that the planetary effect on the material world was evident but not exact; the effect was not inevitable. His logic was that if '…everything occurs by necessity, there is nothing fortuitous or by chance'.[67] In this case, 'chance' for Aquinas was similar to Calcidius's contingency, an event which 'escapes predictions' and is considered accidental and, according to Massie, is epistemologically irrelevant.[68] Thus, for Aquinas, the heavenly influence of fate on the material world had to allow for the unexpected. Additionally, he limited the role of fate in his *Summa Theologiae*, defining it as follows:

> ...fate is the ordering of second causes to effects foreseen by God. Whatever, therefore, is subject to second causes, is subject also to fate. But whatever is done immediately by God, since it is not subject to second causes, neither is it subject to fate; such are creation, the glorification of spiritual substances, and the like.[69]

Aquinas's fate was subservient to God's providence, but it was also limited, as it could not override events that happened by chance. He found within Christian theology a place for free will, which resided in the soul, while the movement of the heavens through Aristotle's comingling of the elements influenced the body. The practice of astrology, therefore, had a legitimate place in medicine and mundane life on Earth. Notably, by promoting the link between the body and the heavens, Aquinas's teachings allowed for the new medical astrology to be taught in Western Catholic Europe. As French explained, medicine thereafter became a rational Aristotelian science based on the practice of astrology.[70] Hence, Aquinas settled fate onto and into the body.

Aquinas, therefore, supported concurrentism, which posits that causality is shared between God and humans. Petr Dvořák discussed Aquinas's position on God and causality as,

> The middle stand taken by Aquinas, the most common among medieval scholastics usually termed concurrentism, stresses cooperation or "concurrence" of both causes, created and divine, in bringing about the effect of a secondary cause.[71]

He pointed out that at this time, debates around God's role in causation were 'a trichotomy: either causes alone [deism], God alone [occasionalism] or a cooperative model [concurrentism]'. It is by taking a concurrent position on the role of God that Aquinas accepted human self-agency, that is the ability to be a creator of a cause.

In summary, Aquinas addressed the complex relationship between celestial influence and human agency by integrating Aristotle's natural philosophy into Christian theology. He legitimised astrology by affirming the efficacy of celestial influences, particularly through Aristotle's model of descending spheres, while maintaining the primacy of free will. Aquinas argued that although heavenly bodies could affect the physical realm—including the human body—acts of will and intellect where free of these influences. This dualism allowed him to preserve human freedom in the soul while acknowledging bodily susceptibility to astrological forces. In *Summa Theologiae*, Aquinas defined fate as the operation of secondary causes under divine foresight, subordinated to God's providence and having no influence over fortuitous or chance events. His theological framework provided a legitimate role for astrology within medicine and daily life.

Fate for the working astrologer

The new Arabic astrology was adopted and altered by Western astrologers. One of the most prominent was Guido Bonatti (c. 1210–1290), who was born in Florence, or Forli, in northern Italy. He was employed by the political elite of his day, especially on military matters. He compiled a vast amount of astrological lore and added his unique contribution to the practice. Hand commented that Bonatti was possibly the most important astrologer in Europe of the High Middle Ages.[72] His fame was so noted that Dante Alighieri (c. 1265–1321) immortalised him in his *Divine Comedy* by placing him in Hell: the Eighth Circle, Fourth Ring, which was reserved for the Fortune Tellers and Diviners.[73]

Bonatti defined astrology, for which he used the word astronomy: 'Astronomy is the knowledge through which understanding is given not only of present things, but even of past and future things'.[74] Ignoring the complex philosophical arguments of his day, he took an Aristotelian, Ptolemaic approach to his astrology. He considered that the sublunar world was influenced by a multiplicity of planetary movements and the heat of the sun. This, in turn, churned the elements of fire, air, earth and water.[75] In his discussion on the role of astrology, he wrote, 'An unknown evil is not avoided, but a known one can be avoided, if it is known ahead of time, especially far ahead'.[76] He expanded this by arguing that,

> Foreknowledge of future things is useful in two ways. The first, because were a man to know ahead of time that some contrary thing ought to happen to him, he can properly diminish it or totally avoid it (or in part). Indeed [secondly] if the accident were useful, he to whom it should come will rejoice and be happy from the hour in which he knew he was going to achieve a matter which he strives for, ... which if he had not known that he ought to achieve it, ..he would be saddened and distressed in it, and fatigued.[77]

Bonatti's point was that this fatigue could cause him to lessen his efforts and thus reduce the potential benefit of the future event.

Bonatti saw the astrologer's role as one of foreseeing an individual's fate in order to enable proactive engagement with future outcomes. Through such foresight, one could act to avoid or mitigate undesirable outcomes, or alternatively, to encourage and support favourable ones. In this way, the active use of free will could shape the unfolding of fate. Bonatti employed the mathematical tools and algorithms of Arabic astrology to seek clear predictions from horoscopes; however, he did not adopt its philosophical aim of achieving exact predictions, as for him, the future was not fixed. Instead, his approach reflected a synthesis of Aquinian Christian doctrine and Calcidius's interpretation of fate, in which fate influences human life but does not determine it absolutely—events remain open to individual agency. For Bonatti, the value of astrology lay in its capacity to reveal future possibilities, thereby enabling the exercise of free will to intervene, redirect, or avert certain outcomes. His astrological practice embodies the vernacular understanding of fate in his time—acknowledging the influence of planetary cycles while affirming the individual's capacity for choice within that cosmic framework

To summarise, the concept of fate in the medieval period underwent various arguments based on two main themes concerning the nature of causation. The first of these was the split in causation between universals and contingencies. A universal was an event that occurred as a result of necessity and was expected to happen, while a contingency, also known as a particular, was an unexpected event that occurred by chance. Calcidius argued that fate existed within the heavens, but it was also created by human action independent of any predetermined law. Calcidian fate was compelling once it was created, and both humans and the movement of the celestial sphere were fate-creators. The second theme was the rise of divine providence by Augustine in Europe, while in the Islamic world the work of Abu Hamid al-Ghazālī established that God was the sole cause of all things. Both these theologies produced a fate that emanated directly from God, and prayer was one's only option for salvation. In contrast, the Jewish scholar Abraham Ibn Ezra created a variation on the model of God's providence, for although he saw God's providence as supreme, he did not accept that fate emanated only from God; instead, an individual's fate was limited or shaped through the workings of other fates, with the personal fate being the last in a line of hierarchical layers. The degree of agency—freedom to act—held by the individual was, for Ibn Ezra, restrained by their situation and the layers of fate above them.

By the twelfth century, tension grew in the West between the use of the new Arabic astrology in the practice of medicine and the Christian view that Plato's cosmology denied predictability in the sublunar realm. Theological breathing space was created by Aquinas, who introduced a mind-body dualism into Christianity, in which the body was subject to direct planetary influence, but the soul was not. This version of fate allowed it to govern the body and the material world but gave fate no dominion over the soul. At the same time, the military astrologer Bonatti took a pragmatic approach to fate. He used the horoscope as a map of one's fate, a map to inform one of the future so that it could then be avoided, diluted, or enhanced. For Bonati, fate only indicated a potential future, it was subject to human action. Thus, for him, his skill was to be able to read it and help his clients make use of that knowledge.

By the early modern period, beginning in the seventeenth century, the philosophical discussions on contingencies and necessity fell out of use. The causal arguments were replaced by the concept of determinism, free from theological debates and the problems of soul and fate. The astrologers, however, could not join in these discussions as they could not abandon fate, for fate was the fabric of the horoscope.

CHAPTER FOUR

THE EARLY MODERN AND FREE WILL

By the seventeenth century, philosophical debates had begun to shift away from traditional concerns with fate and divine causation, instead focusing on the nature of free will. Two key figures, René Descartes and Baruch Spinoza, exemplify opposing positions in this emerging discourse: Descartes upheld a dualist model in which human free will functioned independently of the physical world. At the same time, Spinoza rejected dualism entirely, advancing a vision of a deterministic universe governed by necessity. These divergent frameworks significantly influenced views of fate and human agency. This chapter explores the evolving relationship between free will and determinism in early modern philosophy and considers how these developments reshaped astrological understandings of fate.

René Descartes – free will is true

The French philosopher and mathematician René Descartes (1596–1650) is synonymous with the birth of the modern era in both science and philosophy.[1] The philosophy he founded is known as Cartesian, and he is considered a revolutionary in science for his development of the reductionist approach to the natural world.

Descartes' approach to physics began with his adoption of a deistic definition of God: God is indifferent and separate from the world of matter.[2] Descartes' deism was a notable departure from the earlier Medieval arguments concerning God and causation. Saint Augustine argued for occasionalism (God causes all things) in contrast to Saint Aquinas, who argued for concurrentism (causality is shared between God and humans). By adopting a deist view, Descartes made a substantial shift in arguments on causation, as it effectively removed God from any discussion on the subject. He did not deny God's existence but wrote of God as 'completely indifferent with respect to all things'. In talking of God's actions, he wrote 'although his actions were completely indifferent, they were also completely necessary'.[3]

By grounding his philosophical system in deism, he argued that God created the world as a perfectly ordered, mechanistic system governed by laws of nature. In this way, Descartes provided a metaphysical foundation for the idea that nature is rational and can be studied mathematically. Deism also allowed him to separate theology, which explained phenomena in terms of inherent purposes or divine interventions, from investigations into the rational world. For Descartes' deistic God was not continually interfering in the world but had designed it to run according to universal laws—like a clockmaker setting a clock in motion.[4] With the world as a machine, he saw matter as the passive component of this world. Descartes wrote:

> I recognise no matter in corporeal things apart from that which the geometers call quantity, and take as the object of their demonstrations, i.e. that to which every kind of *division, shape and motion* is applicable.[5]

Having argued that all of nature could be reduced to the concept of quantity, he then added a crucial caveat to his definition of nature: the realm of thought and mind were not included in the corporeal world.[6]

The world, for Descartes, was made of two distinct substances: the first was *res extensa*, the world of matter, which could be investigated through the reductionist approach, a method of approaching complex phenomena by breaking them down into simpler parts or more basic principles. The second was *res cogitans*, the world of thought, which was not subject to the laws of physics and which existed in every conscious mind.[7] Plato had previously advanced a body-soul duality in which the immortal soul was separate from the world of matter.[8] There were, though, as Broadie argued, fundamental differences between the dualism of Plato and that of Descartes. She claimed that this difference was found in 'Plato's acceptance and Descartes' rejection of the assumption that the soul (= intellect) is identical with what animates the body'.[9] She argued that, for Plato, the body was an instrument for the soul, which had 'a sort of limited omnipotence' and required a body to aid its return to the divine.[10] Broadie also pointed out that for Descartes, the mind—and in the example she discussed, she equated it with the soul—did not require the body: the 'mind and body are ontologically separable' with the mind able to exist independently.[11] She argued that Descartes saw a 'universal separability' between mind and body.[12] As C.E. Jarret wrote, for Descartes, the mind consisted of a substance whose whole essence was to think.[13] Hence, Descartes' famous argument of 'Cogito, ergo sum' (I think therefore I am) promoted universal separability, where the mind did not require membership of the material world.[14] This version of mind-body dualism was, for Descartes, an irresistible truth.[15]

Descartes' dualism then allowed him to assign humans a privileged place in the natural order. Unlike the rest of creation, which operated automatically according to physical laws, humans could think, reflect, and exercise free will. The mind was not subject to mechanical laws, and this capacity for rational thought made human beings capable of understanding the very laws that governed the universe. Thus, in Descartes' system, humans were not mere cogs in the machine but interpreters of it—endowed with the intellectual tools to investigate, understand, and even manipulate nature. As Weimin and Wei stated, freedom for Descartes 'belongs exclusively to the human soul'.[16] In this way, the human will was free and, as argued by Robert Rethy, was to be used to resemble God in action and thought.[17]

In 1984, Daniel Dennett commented on Descartes' dualist philosophy, when applied to the nature of free will, as having led philosophy on an interesting but '…wild goose chase…' for the last three centuries.[18] Notwithstanding such disdain, Manuel Vargas argued that dualist arguments had been reinforced by Western culture and Christianity for centuries. Descartes offered a simple solution to maintain freedom of the will in the face of a rational, scientific universe driven by the laws of nature; consequently, dualism is the dominant Western philosophical belief among non-philosophers.[19]

Baruch de Spinoza – free will is false.

Descartes' dualistic solution to the fate and free will problem was not accepted by his student, Baruch de Spinoza (1632–1677). Spinoza was dissatisfied with Cartesian physics and intentionally broke with the Cartesian view of the will as free.[20] The notion of self-control was, for Spinoza, not a matter of controlling the will, for as Ilham Dilman commented, Spinoza saw the will as subject to causation.[21] For Spinoza, the will was, therefore, not free; the very idea of free will was a misconception. Spinoza rejected Descartes' dualism, but he also dismissed the arguments of Plato and Aquinas. For Spinoza, the will was embedded *within* the framework of determinism. He argued that causes are required to produce any effect, writing that,

> …from a given determinate cause the effect follows necessarily; and conversely, if there is no determinate cause, it is impossible for an effect to follow.[22]

The will, in Spinoza's model, could not be free as it could only move by a determinate cause. With this limitation on the human will, Spinoza developed his thesis on determinism. Michael McKenna and Derk Pereboom define determinism as based on linear causation, where 'at any one time, only one future is physically possible'.[23] Determinism is also universal as it applies to all aspects of the natural order. As McKenna and Pereboom argued, even the number and length of the hairs on one's head, along with all of one's actions and thoughts, are the only possible options that can occur. Hence, Spinoza's arguments on determinism removed any potential for the will to be free. He considered that a person's perception of the freedom of their will was an illusion of ignorance:

> Men are mistaken in thinking themselves free; and this opinion depends on this alone, that they are conscious of their actions and ignorant of the causes by which they are determined. This, therefore, is their idea of liberty, that they should know no causes of their actions...[24]

Spinoza argued that a person who purely reacted to an emotion of hurt or anger lacked freedom and that their will was simply a response to the deterministic forces around them. Dilman expanded this point by stating that if a person has:

> ...only been a party to a transaction in which his role has been purely reactive and, therefore, passive, his reaction is the expression of a necessity that worked through him. In this respect he is like a puppet on a string. While he so reacts he is not himself.[25]

This type of reactivity, of being passive in the face of necessity, is what Simone Weil suggested was at the heart of Homer's *Iliad*, where the blind reaction of Homer's characters to the surrounding events swept them up in a deterministic momentum towards a final outcome. Hector was 'ignorant of the causes', thinking that he freely entered battle with Apollo, while in truth, he was simply reacting to the dictates of determinism.

Spinoza argued that the delusion of free will was to believe in the contingency of things, the unexpected nature of events that one could influence or control. This belief only occurred if the mind was passive; for Spinoza, reacting to impose one's will on external events revealed a lack of freedom.[26] His position on contingencies was opposite to that of Calcidius. Calcidius argued that the formation of contingent events was partly the result of the freely taken actions of individuals. He defined these contingent events as separate from God's providence. However, for Spinoza, such a claim was an illusion, a 'fictitious idea' that led to the construction of absurdities in philosophy 'which are not worthy of rational refutation'.[27] Freedom, for Spinoza, was the understanding and acceptance of the continual influence of emotions on the self.[28] Unlike the Stoics, who argued for the harmony of the mind, Spinoza considered that the mind could not be calmed, but one could move towards understanding one's mind.

Roger Scruton argued that this led Spinoza to the notion of mental determinism, where individuals were subject to internal 'chains that bind us', and he added that Spinoza believed that by 'gathering our chains into ourselves, and becoming conscious of their binding force, we also rid ourselves of them, and obtain the only freedom that we can or should desire'.[29] Thus, by being aware of one's reactions to the events of the external world, a form of freedom can be gained. However, this form of freedom was not a force of the will but rather an expression of a state of consciousness. Spinoza defined this as *conatus*, a sense of self, and the body as a form of mind where *conatus* flowed from our desire for the wellness of being. Hasana Sharp talked of the importance of *conatus* for Spinoza as the power for a being that '...preserves its integrity amidst infinitely many other beings...'[30] This Spinozian integrity is accepting the determinism of one's mind and body while maintaining a sense of individual self by seeking to understand and develop the self, *conatus*, to the fullest degree. For Spinoza, a person is self-determined when their actions are allowed to follow their nature, their *conatus*. If a person is unaware of the nature of their *conatus*, then they are unaware of their actions and are not self-determined; they have failed to understand their will.

Spinoza agreed with the Stoic concept of virtue. He saw happiness as the acceptance that one could *only* be self-determined concerning one's inner responses.[31] The inner happiness which resulted from such acceptance, in turn, constituted Spinoza's concept of virtue.[32] Firmin DeBrabander argued that Spinoza, drawing on Stoic moral theory, provided a form of ethical individualism that 'eschews external authority in ethical matters'.[33] In this regard, *conatus* for Spinoza was the idea of an inner self based on internal reflection rather than any external locus of control.

Spinoza considered there were two ways an individual could overcome the ignorance which produced the internal chains that bound them. The first, reminiscent of Plato, was by use of reason. Spinoza claimed that reason saw the world *sub specie aeternitatis* without reference to time. He wrote, 'In so far as the mind conceives a thing under the dictates of reason, it is affected equally, whether the idea be of a thing future, past, or present'.[34] He defended this argument by pointing out that reason was affected by its conception of things, as much by things in the past as those in the present and future. Therefore, as personal history and memories all existed in the present, they were timeless. Martin Lin noted that in this idea Spinoza does not mean eternity or time without end, but rather that he was referring to a form of 'atemporal timelessness'.[35] To this timelessness of reason, Spinoza added that our emotions and desires exist in the world of *specie durationis*—linear time—since our emotions and desires are subject to the flow of events, both internal and external.[36] Scruton commented that Spinoza considered that,

> ...freedom is not the release from necessity but the *consciousness* of necessity that comes when we manage to see the world *sub specie aeternitatis* — in a timelessness mode — and ourselves as bound by its immutable laws.[37]

Jarrett drew parallels between Plato, Aristotle, the Stoics, and Spinoza. He argued that 'His [Spinoza's] primary concern, like theirs, is with how it is best to live and his answer, in outline, is the same: in accordance with reason'.[38]

Spinoza's second concept to aid the release from ignorance was to use an instrument that existed in his idea of timelessness, *sub specie aeternitatis*, which allowed for a level of detachment.[39] Dilman argued that this detachment was not the same as indifference, as the ego needed a way to avoid reacting to the internal question of 'why has this happened to me?'[40] The individual thus requires a way to cultivate detachment in order to release their ego from the basic reactions of anger, blame, or feelings of rejection that the necessitated external events can catalyse. Scruton commented that, for Spinoza, the more we understand causality, the more we increase our understanding of it, so the more we are self-determined.[41] By recognising that emotions arise from natural causes, we can begin to transform passive emotions (which happen to us) into active ones (which we can understand and manage). In this way, Spinoza laid an early foundation for the psychological insight that understanding, not denial or resistance, leads to emotional health.

Spinoza's determinism also supported the Stoic view of an immanent world, a concept of reality in which the sacred, or the divine, is embedded within the material world itself rather than existing in a separate, transcendent realm. For determinism to be universal, it requires that the universe is self-contained, complete in itself, and immanent. Spinoza added to this argument by claiming that the substance of the universal had an infinite number of modes, of which humanity is only aware of two. One of these modes is thought (mind), and the other is extension (matter).[42] Spinoza considered that this idea was replicated throughout the whole of nature and that all physical objects had a mental correlate. Hence, an inorganic object like a stone could think.[43] In this way, all things contained mind and body, and all things were subject to determinism. Spinoza's naturalism and his Stoic immanent worldview led him to argue that humanity did not control nature but was instead dependent and embedded within it, a philosophy opposite to that of his teacher Descartes, who posited a split between the mind (or soul) and nature.

Spinoza's exploration of determinism and its implications for human life, as well as his reflections on consciousness, self-awareness, and the capacity for detachment by viewing the self through an instrument of *sub specie aeternitatis*, may appear to transcend discussions of fate. His approach to living within a deterministic framework, however, offers parallels for understanding how astrologers live with their concept of fate. Central to astrology is the horoscope, which functions as the medium through which fate is interpreted and integrated into the astrologer's life. For some astrologers, the horoscope assumes a Spinozian character, becoming a mirror of the self, viewed from a timeless perspective. In this way, the horoscope fosters a form of detachment that can circumvent the existential question—posed by Dilman—'Why has this happened to me?' Granted, this practice has emerged organically within the astrologers, stemming from their belief that the horoscope represents the self or, using Spinoza's term, *conatus*. This practice is revisited in later chapters.

Today, Spinoza's views on determinism and its role in human life are viewed as a form of 'hard incompatibilism', defined by Pereboom as the position that determinism is true and universal and hence incompatible with free will.[44] Spinoza presented both the philosophy of determinism and, more importantly, a methodology for living with it.

The Early Modern – living with fate

Three practicing astrologers who lived on the edge of the Medieval world were the astronomer and mathematician Galileo Galilei (1564–1642), who had an astrological practice, the astrologer Jean-Baptiste Morin (1583–1656), and the astrologer William Lilly (1602–1681). They each took a different approach to fate.

Galileo and astrology

Galileo's encounter with astrology likely began around 1582, when, at the age of 17, he became a student of medicine at the University of Pisa. In Pisa, he learnt, or consolidated, his astrology, as it formed a part of his medical training. Galileo did not complete his medical training but instead moved on to study mathematics. By 1589, at the age of 24, he was appointed Professor of Mathematics at Pisa. In 1592, he was appointed to the same position at the University of Padua, where he remained until 1610. According to Antonio Favaro and Dava Sobel, one of the duties of this chair was to teach astrology to medical students.⁴⁵ While holding the position of Professor of Mathematics at Padua, Galileo also undertook paid work as an astrologer. His daily account books show that he recorded income received for astrological readings.⁴⁶ His reputation as an astrologer was well known, and his services were called upon by the Grand Duchess Christina of Lorraine, who implored him to find the actual day of birth of the Duke by using astrology.⁴⁷ His genuine interest in astrology is evident in his long-standing correspondence with Ottavio Brenzoni, a professional astrologer in Verona with whom he discussed charts and sought astrological opinions over his eighteen years at Padua University.⁴⁸

Galileo's astrological notes and chart collection, *Astrologica nonnulla*, comprises some fifty pages of horoscopes and supporting astrological calculations in Galileo's hand. They form the first volume of the sixth part of Galileo's Manuscripts at the Biblioteca Nazionale in Florence.⁴⁹ In these papers Galileo did not comment on his views on fate and free will. However, in April 1604, Galileo was summoned and tried for being too fatalistic in his astrological forecasts for his clients. He was accused and found guilty not of practising astrology but rather that his astrology sought exact prediction in the sublunar realm. One of his servants had reported him, and the notes of the trial read:

> Q: [From the Inquisitor] You said before that in the nativities that this Galileo makes, he calls his predictions certain; this is heresy…
> A: [From the person bearing witness against Galileo] I know that he said that and that he calls his predictions from the nativities certain, but I am not aware that this has been declared heresy.⁵⁰

Galileo was found to be a heretic and charged with 'living as a heretic', but his position at Padua University probably protected him from further prosecution.⁵¹

The witness against Galileo claimed that he pursued certainty through astrology, which is evident in his papers, for Galileo employed the quantifiable style of Arabic astrology.⁵² His notes and horoscopes contain the quantification of planetary qualities in almuten tables, the Arabic astrological technique discussed in the previous chapter, which assigns a numerical value to a particular planet based on its horoscopic attributes. Additionally, Galileo used the concept of almutens to build *Dominus Geniturae* tables, a series of astrological axioms in which the quantified planets were added or subtracted from each other to determine which held the highest score. This highest scoring planet held the most significant astrological influence over the person's life. In his *Dominus Geniturae* tables, he experimented with different values and how to allocate values to a planet. For example, he strongly favoured direct (moving forward in the zodiac) or fast motion by a planet allocating it far a higher numerical value than slower or retrograde planets or even a planet in its correct zodiac sign (deemed in rulership) and the traditional way that astrology viewed the effectiveness of a planet.[53] This experimentation suggests that he regarded any failings in his predictions as a lack of clarity of the 'laws' of astrology. For Galileo, astrological fate was fixed and, like the laws of nature which he pursued, to perfect his astrological prediction was to perfect his astrological algorithms.

Galileo stood at the threshold between the medieval and modern worlds—a transitional era he helped to define. While his primary scientific focus was the study of motion, his astrological notes reveal a similar approach. His astrological techniques show a conceptual linkage between time, motion, and velocity. For Galileo, astrology was a practical tool for self-understanding, as well as for interpreting the lives of his daughters, friends, and clients. However, it is reasonable to infer that his mathematical mind carried elements of his astrological thinking into his physics, providing a mental space that allowed him to think beyond the prevailing intellectual frameworks of his time. He dared to seek certainty in nature.

Jean-Baptiste Morin

Jean-Baptiste Morin was a contemporary of Galileo who sought to reform astrology so it could fit into the emerging scientific views on causation. He was a mathematician, astronomer and astrologer, born in Villefranche-sur-Saône, France. Morin became one of the leading astrologers of his day, and his clients included the French king, Louis XIII. His major work, *Astrologia Gallica* (published posthumously in 1661), aimed to defend astrology against sceptics by proposing a more structured, causally-driven system.

He famously disagreed with the Copernican heliocentric solar system because if the Sun was the centre of the solar system, then the powers of the heavens could not flow downward to the Earth. Morin embedded himself in Aristotle's natural causality and sought to rationalise astrology through an empirical approach. He considered that the heavens, stars, and planets were both universal and particular causes, depending on their sphere of activity. He believed that a child chose his or her time of birth so that the heavenly 'imprint' of fate and character aligned with the child's nature already present in the womb.[54] The unborn infant's choice effectively, for Morin, softened the role of determinism and established a place for free will. He wrote:

> But the stars' indications so strongly incline or predispose the native that at least the inclination can be asserted with considerable certainty.

> And of the possible effects attendant upon such an inclination those which are not in the native's power will happen with the greatest certainty while those which depend on his own will have a more doubtful outcome.⁵⁵

In Morin's system the individual decides their own fate and apparently could use their will to influence a predicted difficult time lying in the future. However, Morin was unclear on this final point. For Morin, the source of fate was a physical force that radiated from the heavens. He required a geocentric circular solar system for this force to reach the Earth in an even manner. This cosmic force, to which each heavenly body contributed its unique quality or quantity, was mixed and altered by the accidental cause of the mundane parts of the horoscope; in other words, by the orientation of the planets and zodiac signs around the individual at birth.

Morin was a man clinging onto the old Aristotelian world as it crumbled around him. He strove to adjust astrology so that it would be in step with the new developments in physics and sought to fit astrology into a causal worldview. However, his causal model of astrology, which required a geocentric view of the solar system driven by some measurable causal elements that the planets imposed on the newborn infant, has struggled to find acceptance. He is an example of an astrologer seeking to gain acceptance in Descartes' new world order of causality.

William Lilly – fate casting

William Lilly was an English astrologer who ran a busy practice throughout the turbulent years of the English Civil War and the Restoration from the 1640s to 1670s. He engaged with a cross-section of the population of English society, from servants to the aristocracy.⁵⁶ Lilly also gained considerable fame through his correct predictions, notably that of the defeat of the Royalist forces at Naseby in 1645.⁵⁷

Lilly's predictions were derived from his practice of horary astrology. This is the branch of astrology that is used to answer a question by constructing a horoscope for the time and place of the question.⁵⁸ The premise of horary astrology is that the moment of an event—the asking of a question—contains the event's future and hence can be examined astrologically.

According to Lilly, a horoscope should be interpreted through a systematic method designed to yield consistent and reliable judgments. To support this approach, he established a set of rules for astrological interpretation. The objective was to understand how and when a matter would reach completion—

essentially, the outcome of an action already set in motion. A chart cast for the moment a question was posed was then analysed to determine a clear affirmative or negative response.[59] The practice of horary astrology by Lilly and his followers today is based in Calcidius's philosophy on fate and free will. To recap, Calcidius viewed humanity as being influenced by fate, yet simultaneously humanity were also fate creators. Calcidius argued that although one could act freely, that is, without any antecedent causes, it did involve taking a risk, for the new action would instigate a chain of fate. He suggested using astrology to gain guidance on the quality of the time and, hence, select the right time to take action to initiate the proper chain of fate.[60] This is also the remit of horary astrology. Lilly assumed the human will was free since the person chose the time to ask their question. The chosen time then resulted in a horoscope, which provided an unambiguous answer. Free will was maintained because, although one must accept the fate once it is cast, the individual initiated the action that led to the casting of the fate.

There are indications that Lilly thought that one could still alter a chosen fate. Curry pointed out that every extant portrait of Lilly shows him holding a horoscope bearing the words *'non congunt'*.[61] Literally, this means 'they (the planets) don't force'. Curry argued that this referred to the classical saying *Astra inclinant, sed non obligant*: the stars incline us, they do not bind us. Lilly taught his method to others, and his book *Christian Astrology* became a seminal work on the practice of horary astrology and is still studied by today's astrologers. In this regard, Lilly is a vehicle for the transmission of Calcidius's philosophy into contemporary culture.

Galileo, Morin, and Lilly all lived during the seventeenth-century Scientific Revolution; indeed, Galileo was a central figure of this revolution. During this period, the empirical sciences rose to prominence, displacing medieval science and natural philosophy based on Aristotelian principles.[62] Gary Deason commented on the new cosmology of seventeenth-century Europe as:

> The mechanical worldview rested on a single, fundamental assumption: *matter is passive*. It possesses no active internal forces. Nothing in matter compels it to develop or to move towards an ultimate goal. The matter of the seventeenth century possessed only the passive qualities of size, shape, and impenetrability.[63]

With matter redefined as passive, motion came to be understood in terms of external impacts rather than internal principles. This marked a departure from Aristotelian physics, in which matter was thought to possess intrinsic tendencies, such as the impulse to move toward its 'proper place'. Under the emerging mechanistic paradigm, which posited a universe filled with passive matter, all phenomena were held to be governed by antecedent causation; nothing could occur without a prior cause. This concept of matter as inert became foundational to the physics of Isaac Newton (1643–1727), who referred to it as the 'inactivity of matter'—a neutral substance capable of motion only when acted upon by an external force.[64] This passive view of matter was later contested in the twentieth century by Alfred North Whitehead (1861–1947), whose work is discussed in subsequent chapters. However, with matter lacking any initiating agency and the universe conceived as wholly driven by prior causes, the ancient notion of *sympathy*—the belief in a cosmos unified by hidden correspondences and resonances—was effectively abandoned. As a result, the essential precondition for fate—a sympathetic cosmology—was denied, leaving the concept of fate without an ontological foundation.

In summary, René Descartes held a dualistic worldview that separated the physical realm (*res extensa*) from the realm of thought (*res cogitans*). Descartes' dualism differed fundamentally from Plato's body-soul dualism, as he claimed that mind and body were ontologically separable—the mind could exist independently of the body. This separation extended to his view of the cosmos, which he saw as a mechanical system governed by impersonal laws. Unlike medieval theologians such as Augustine and Aquinas, who emphasised God's direct involvement in causation, Descartes embraced deism, seeing God as indifferent but necessary. For Descartes, freedom resided solely in the human soul, which was to use its will to emulate the divine in both action and thought.

In contrast, Baruch Spinoza rejected Descartes' dualism and the notion of free will, arguing instead for a fully deterministic universe where all thoughts and actions were based on previous causes. Free will, was, for Spinoza, an illusion born of ignorance of these causes. For him, true freedom lay not in choice but in understanding necessity and becoming aware of the internal and external forces shaping one's life. He introduced the concept of *conatus*—the individual's striving to persist and flourish—as a path to self-determination. Through reason and by viewing life from a timeless perspective (*sub specie aeternitatis*), one can achieve detachment from reactive emotions and live virtuously, echoing the principles of Stoic ethics. Spinoza's view parallels some astrological practices, where the horoscope becomes a mirror of the self, helping to integrate fate and life's events without imposing personal blame. His philosophy is now seen as hard incompatibilism—that determinism and free will are incompatible—yet he offered a way to live meaningfully within this framework.

Into this time of fundamental shifts in cosmology, Galileo was indifferent primarily to questions about fate as he assumed that his Arabic astrology could comply with the laws of nature, which was, of course, his focus. Morin, on the other hand, reshaped astrology, seeking to maintain its relevance in a cosmos driven by rational causation. He resisted abandoning Aristotle's celestial spheres, seeing the spheres as the driving force of his cosmology. Lilly seemed to ignore the new cosmology and adhered to a Platonist philosophy of a divine cosmos informed by Calcidius's view of fate, which blended fate and free will without conflict.

From this point onward, fate—excluded from the mechanical worldview—was relegated to popular culture as folk superstition or survived within the practice of astrology. The following chapter explores the challenges that the new cosmology posed to the concept of free will.

CHAPTER FIVE

THE DILEMMA OF DETERMINISM

By the early eighteenth century, and particularly after Spinoza's work, philosophical debates about fate began to shift toward a focus on determinism. This shift was rooted in the changing landscape of science and philosophy, catalysed by the Scientific Revolution of the seventeenth century. Adding to the change in perspective was the work of Isaac Newton (1643–1727), whose formulations of the laws of motion and gravitation were all grounded in calculus and differential equations. These provided the foundation for understanding the workings of the world, seeing it as a universe driven by cause and effect governed by consistent laws. As a result, the universe was viewed as a vast, predictable system—a 'world machine' in which every event followed inevitably from prior conditions. Every event was determined by the past. This is the worldview that supports universal determinism. However, determinism did not go unchallenged. Philosophers such as Immanuel Kant, Johann Wolfgang von Goethe, and Friedrich Schlegel raised objections to reducing living organisms and human consciousness to mere mechanical processes. These early critiques foreshadowed the philosophical dilemma of the tension between determinism and the notion of human free will.

This chapter examines the rise of universal determinism and its philosophical implications, highlighting the ongoing difficulty of reconciling causal necessity with human freedom. The arguments of the Scottish philosopher David Hume (1711–1776) are considered as they exemplify some of these philosophical difficulties. In doing so, this chapter aims to provide a later framework for understanding contemporary beliefs about fate and self-agency in a world shaped by the legacy of Newton's laws.

The World Machine and determinism

Newton defined matter as 'inactive'—a neutral substance incapable of initiating motion or change without the influence of an external force.[1] As such, matter, whether organic or inorganic, could not itself introduce causal agents into the environment. Every action, therefore, must be the result of a preceding cause. By systematically tracing these causes backwards, one ultimately arrives at the initial cause: the Big Bang, understood as the origin of the universe. As the first cause, the Big Bang is the singular agent behind all subsequent events, the source from which all actions unfold, and thereby the origin of linear time itself.[2] This concept bears resemblance to Saint Augustine's notion of divine providence and the occasionalism of Al-Ghazālī, as discussed earlier. However, unlike these theological frameworks, the Big Bang introduces no divine or metaphysical agency. It is the logical conclusion of a cosmology grounded in the passivity of matter, which, through its laws of nature, functions in a deterministic manner. As Fritjof Capra commented, the 'Newtonian world machine was seen as being completely causal and deterministic'.[3]

Determinism, supported by Newton's mathematics, became central in scientific thought to the point that any arguments which challenged determinism became an object of scorn. For example, François-Marie Arouet, known as Voltaire (1694–1778), one of the most influential philosophers of the eighteenth century, argued that if the large-scale structure of the universe is deterministic, the same laws must apply to the smallest details of life on Earth. He wrote, 'It would be very singular that all nature, all planets, should obey eternal laws, and that there should be a little animal, five feet high, who, in contempt of those laws, could act as he pleased, solely according to his caprice'.[4] Marquis Pierre Simon de Laplace (1749–1827), the French mathematician and astronomer, summarised this new view of the world by stating

> We may regard the present state of the universe as the effect of its past and the cause of its future. An intellect which at any given moment knew all of the forces that animate nature and the mutual positions of the beings that compose it, if this intellect were vast enough to submit the data to analysis, could condense into a single formula the movement of the greatest bodies of the universe and that of the lightest atom; for such an intellect nothing could be uncertain and the future just like the past would be present before its eyes.[5]

The universe was, therefore, viewed as a vast machine open to the discovery of its mechanisms.

There were challenges to determinism. Immanuel Kant (1724–1804) disagreed that all organisms can be reduced to the level of machines, suggesting that an organism 'cannot only be a machine, because a machine has only moving force; but an organism has an organising force… which cannot be explained by mechanical motion alone'.[6] Additionally, Johann Wolfgang von Goethe (1749–1832) and Friedrich von Schlegel (1772–1829) also resisted the mechanical approach and laid the foundations of a romantic philosophy, heavily influenced by Plato, that supported the notion of emergent principles of creation where self-organising forces were at play. However, it was the work of Charles Darwin (1809–1882), with his theory of evolution, that offered proof of the validity of the reductionist, mechanised worldview. As Edward Larson claimed, Darwin's theory attempted to show that complex organisms could evolve purely by the pressure of survival of the fittest, thereby removing the need for any natural self-organising elements.[7]

As determinism became established, debates shifted to the actual nature of determinism. According to Robert Bishop, writing in 2002, there were at that time over ninety varieties of determinism.[8] The version promoted by Laplace is known as Laplacian determinism, which holds that the past completely determines the future. This version of determinism tends to dominate popular thinking and philosophical debates.[9] William James (1842–1910) defined this version of determinism, also considered causal determinism, in 1896 as follows:

> It professes that those parts of the universe already laid down absolutely appoint and decree what the other parts shall be. The future has no ambiguous possibilities hidden in its womb: the part we call the present is compatible with only one totality. Any other future complement than the one fixed from eternity is impossible.[10]

Carl Hoefer, writing in 2010, did not define determinism but rather laid down what it required to be true:

> The *whole world* is *governed by* (or is *under the sway of*) determinism if and only if, given a specified *way things are at a time*, *t*, the way things go *thereafter* is *fixed* as a matter of *natural law*.[11]

Hoefer placed in italics the key elements of his argument. The 'whole world' implies that the whole universe has to be assumed to be governed by determinism; otherwise, an event outside the 'whole world' could interject an influence that previous events had not determined. Additionally, 'time' refers to a period before time began to prevent an event of a preceding time, '*t*', contributing to the 'otherwise' state of things. Accordingly, determinism applies to the entire future of the cosmos, one, as Hoefer added, defined by a Newtonian framework of space and time. The idea of universal determinism, as applied to the 'whole world' in Hoefer's argument, may seem doubtful at first. Yet, the laws of physics, the natural laws in Hoefer's list of determinism requirements, do support it. Universal determinism is required, for example, for Newton's laws of motion, the laws of thermodynamics, Kepler's laws of planetary motion, and Archimedes' principle. All these laws of nature require that determinism is universal and true.

This acceptance of the universal nature of determinism, however, has led to philosophical difficulties on the grounds that it contradicts the concept of free will: if the past determines all things, then there is no room for independent agency or individual free will. Philosophers continue, to this day, to produce different arguments to seek to resolve this question, known as the free will problem. The resulting philosophical arguments can be divided into various positions. Two of these positions are known as incompatibilism, which is the premise that free will and determinism are incompatible, and another is compatibilism, where the premise is that free will and determinism can coexist. The different nuances in these debates provide a framework for considering the diversity of beliefs in fate that exist today.

Incompatibilism – free will is false

The central argument of incompatibilism is that freedom, by any definition, is incompatible with the existence of determinism. Whether this is freedom of the mind, of the body, or of our actions and desires, determinism claims that the past determines everything that will happen in the future and, since we cannot change the past, we can have no control over the future. Hence, incompatibilists argue that determinism rules out any possibility of genuine control over our choices, actions, and mental states. Derk Pereboom took a hard incompatibilist position when he argued that determinism denied not only free will but also denied moral responsibility. He claimed that such a life 'without this sort of free will would not be devastating to our sense of meaning and purpose'.[12] He argued that one could still feel praiseworthy and experience a sense of achievement even if the actions that prompted these feelings were determined and, therefore, bound to occur, for he argued that:

> People typically do not become dispirited when they come to believe that success in a career depends very much on one's upbringing, opportunities in one's society, the assistance of colleagues, and good future. Realisations of this sort frequently give rise to a sense of thankfulness, and almost never, if at all, to dismay.[13]

Pereboom's argument appears to be similar to that of Spinoza (discussed in the previous chapter) in that there is happiness in ignorance.

It was, however, the Scottish philosopher David Hume (1711–1776) who offered a redefining of freedom in response to Spinoza's arguments. Hume was an incompatibilist as he accepted that determinism precluded free will. However, he redefined the notion of free will, similar to Spinoza's solution to living with determinism. Spinoza considered that most people's concept of freedom was based in ignorance of the influence of determinism on their minds. Hume agreed that any freedom we have lies in such ignorance.

Hume considered that an individual could have the illusion of freedom, particularly when unaware of any coercion. He called this the 'liberty of indifference'.[14] This was a liberty based in the illusion of autonomy.[15] It means to think that one is free to choose to do otherwise while free of any known coercion. To freely choose to stir one's tea clockwise or anticlockwise is a simplistic example of Hume's liberty of indifference. He argued that while all things are influenced by determinism, one could never know the entire prior cause of any personal action. Through this ignorance, one can perceive personal freedom. This perception of personal freedom led to a belief that one can undertake 'freely chosen' actions that reconfirm one's personal moral responsibility.[16] Robert Kane argued that Hume's liberty of indifference may be sufficient given that we are all products of our upbringing and social conditioning; thus, to pursue choices free from *any* coercion may be unrealistic.[17]

Hume considered that beliefs and our thoughts were instinctive and, as a product of determinism, were also irresistible.[18] For Hume, human beliefs were not formed by reason but rather by nature. Hume considered that even a belief in the divine was a product of nature. Don Garrett noted that Hume rejected the notion of God or supernatural beings, dismissed any dualist arguments (that there could be a soul independent of the body), and recognised the existence neither of miracles nor even undetermined acts of free will, 'endorsing instead a universal determinism requiring uniform laws that extend even to human belief and action'.[19] Hume wrote:

> …all our reasoning concerning causes and effects are derived from nothing but custom; and that belief is more properly an act of the sensitive, than of the cogitative part of our natures.[20]

For Hume the mind and reason were simply products of determinism. According to Donald Ainslie's interpretation of Hume, mental reflections and perceptions were the building blocks of personal identity, *not* reason.[21] Hume dismissed 'reason' as the vehicle for finding free will or self, which set him apart from Platonic and Stoic thought and thus, as Shaun Gallagher commented, Hume reduced the human soul, the supposed holder of reason, to just romantic fiction, something that was 'written by the imagination'.[22]

The thoughts of the mind, Hume considered, were the result of determinism and thus consisted of shifting and inconsistent beliefs formed partly by our history—the past—and partly by current circumstances. Hume's arguments challenged the very autonomy of the human mind. However, he argued that humanity may not have free will but still retained moral responsibility:

> … no human actions, where it [liberty] is wanting, are susceptible of any moral qualities, or can be the objects either of approbation or dislike. For as actions are objects of our moral sentiment, so far only as they are indications of the internal character, passions and affections it is impossible that they can give rise either to praise or blame, where they proceed not from these principles, but are derived altogether from external violence.[23]

Hume argued that if the world was not governed by determinism, then all events would be random and therefore, one's actions must also be random. Consequently, if one's actions could not be determined by one's 'internal character, passions and affections', then a person could not be held responsible for the random events they performed. Thus within Hume's arguments, moral responsibility required determinism, as personal moral responsibility came out of one's nature shaped by determinism rather than notions of free will.

In short, Hume argued that free will is a product of our imagination but is nevertheless an important one as it creates a place for the development of our moral responsibility. Moral responsibility, in turn, is how we make choices under the assumption that we have the freedom to choose.

Incompatibilism – universal determinism is false

A counterpoint to the tension between determinism and free will is to argue that determinism is not a universal phenomenon. Such arguments tend to be defined as libertarian: the belief that humans can act freely, as our actions are not always causally determined by factors beyond our control.[24] There are different forms of libertarianism, one of which was put forward in *De Rerum Natura* by the first-century BCE Greek Epicurean poet Titus Lucretius Carus. Lucretius expounded the theory that the world consists of indivisible units known as atoms, which combine to form all things. These atoms tend to move in a straight line. However, Lucretius introduced the notion of an occasional swerve in their path. Based on this random swerve, he claimed:

> If all motion is always one long chain, and new motion arises out of the old in order invariable, and if the first-beginnings do not make by swerving a beginning of motion such as to break the decrees of fate, that cause may not follow cause from infinity, whence comes this free will in living creatures all over the earth, whence I say is this will wrested from the fates by which we proceed whither pleasure leads each, swerving also our motions not at fixed times and fixed places, but just where our mind has taken us? For undoubtedly it is his own in each that begins these things, and from the will movements go rippling through the limbs.[25]

This swerve implied that humanity can engage in a moment of indeterministic action to produce an event from their will. This process creates a form of limited freedom in which determinism can, at times, be disrupted, allowing moments where the chain of causation does not solely dictate one's actions. Thus, determinism is not universal, and the inconsistencies in determinism can produce the possibility of freedom. This argument, based on Lucretius swerve, is defined as event-causal libertarianism.

There is also a version of libertarianism known as agent-causal, which gives a greater degree of freedom. Here, the agent is the cause of the event, as opposed to being merely involved in the sequence of events. A person can then be the originating cause of action. This style of libertarianism is reflective of the view of Calcidius cited earlier, in which humans can instigate new chains of fate through their actions.

Finally, there is also non-causal libertarianism, in which the role of determinism on human thought and will is denied. The human will is constructed of a substance which does not come under the influence of the chain of causation. Thus, the mind is not considered to function in the same manner described by the natural sciences. As McKenna and Pereboom commented, this allows for the insulation of the 'distinctively human features of reality from the natural scientific conception'.[26] This version of libertarianism corresponds to Plato's dualist worldview view in which human reason is linked to the divine and thus is free from the influence of fate. Humans are then solely responsible for their actions because they can use divine reason to make morally correct decisions.

In summary, within incompatibilism, there are different views on determinism's influence on free will. Free will can be denied, but we can have an illusion of freedom based on our ignorance. Alternatively, *universal* determinism can be denied, allowing us to possess limited free will. Or, determinism itself can be dismissed, allowing for a will that is truly free.

Compatibilism – free will and determinism are both true

In contrast to incompatibilism, compatibilism attempts to reconcile the idea of determinism with the notion of free will. Compatibilism does not take a stand on whether causal determinism is true but instead denies that it precludes some version of freedom. There are different approaches to the nature of the reconciliation between causal determinism and freedom. One of these returns to the concept that we all have moral responsibility but disagrees with Hume's 'liberty of indifference'. As Gary Watson pointed out, the freedom that Hume offered as the basis for maintaining moral responsibility is not one that most people would want to accept, as it is a freedom of illusion, a freedom born out of ignorance.[27] Harry Frankfurt proposed instead that people have second-order layers of desires above their instinctual desires. These second-order desires could be used to make choices based on one's value systems. Plato considered these choices to come from the use of divine reason. However, Frankfurt considered divine reason to be of a higher order, above such second-order desires.[28] A second-order desire was the use of the will to rise above a basic instinctual need. Frankfurt wrote, 'No animal other than man, however, appears to have the capacity for reflective self-evaluation that is manifested in the formation of second-order desires'.[29] Watson argued that our instinctual desires are formed by all that has gone before us, including our history, our genetics, our culture, our nation's history and, indeed, the entire chain of causation that constitutes determinism. Hence, Watson claimed that we cannot be free from our desires; instead, he argued that our value systems play a role, and we are free agents only when we do not allow our motivational desires to override our value systems.[30] That is, the use of the will to gain some control of our instinctual desires.

Watson's position implies that the locus of control of our behaviour is not wholly governed by determinism. Instead, we contain in some manner our own internal locus of control, which influences our choices and thus maintains moral responsibility. This idea was central to the theories of Immanuel Kant (1724–1804), who considered that the power of choice resided in the individual and was free of the 'necessitation of the impulses of sensibility'. Animal instincts were viewed as *arbitrium brutum*, but the human power of choice was *arbitrium sensitivum*, 'because sensibility does not render its action necessary, but in the human being there is a faculty of determining oneself from oneself, independently of necessitation by sensible impulses'.[31]

Overall, compatibilism attempts to reconcile the idea of determinism with the notion of free will by arguing that, even if all actions are determined, a person can still be said to have freely chosen them if they are the result of their will rising above their instinctual desires.

Daniel Dennett commented that the philosophical debates around free will have been ongoing for nearly 2000 years and that more has been written on free will than on any other philosophical topic of debate. Yet he pointed out that 'Any philosopher ought to feel at least a little embarrassed that with so much work so little progress has been made'.[32] Any progress made since the time of Newton and Spinoza has been largely hampered by the acceptance by philosophers of determinism as a universal thesis.

Problems with determinism

When Newton shaped the mechanical world with his laws of motion and differential equations, he pointed out that the limits of classical science were reached when trying to predict the movement of three planets moving around an object while influencing each other through gravity.[33] This became known as the Three Bodies problem, and it applies to any three bodies that influence each other, such as orbiting planets or three billiard balls colliding simultaneously on a billiard table after being spaced at 120° from one another. It was not until 1899 that the French mathematician Jules Henri Poincaré (1854–1912) solved the Three-Body problem by mathematically proving that there was no solution; the positions could only be estimated, not predicted.[34] Poincaré is now considered to be the grandfather of chaos theory, as his solution of 'no solution' was the beginning of the undoing of Newton's clockwork universe. Poincaré demonstrated that science cannot *know* everything. The paradigm of the ordered cosmos had encountered its limitations. Laplace's argument was finally, albeit slowly, banished.

Since that time there have been different voices raised against universal determinism. For example, Nancy Cartwright argued that it is a 'fundamentalism of physics' to believe that

> ...there is a tendency to believe that all facts must belong to one grand scheme and moreover that this is a scheme in which the facts ... have a special and privileged status.[35]

Cartwright suggested instead the idea of 'metaphysical nomological pluralism', which is the doctrine '...that nature is governed in different domains by different systems of laws not necessarily related to each other in any systematic or uniform way; by a patchwork of laws'.[36] She argued that the laws of physics are theoretical generalisations based on what should be the phenomenological laws of nature (that which can be observed) and that by this generalisation, they produce a false or incomplete picture.[37] Hoefer also listed a range of arguments against universal determinism, one of which is the assumption that the laws of physics *create* nature rather than simply *explain* nature.[38] He argued, in a similar way to Cartwright, for a determinism of parts, '...each part bears a determining—or partial-determining—relation to other parts, but in which no particular part [antecedent space or times] has a special, stronger determining role than any other'.[39]

More recently, in 2003, John Norton displayed another breakdown in universal determinism in what has become known as 'the dome'. He conducted a thought experiment in which a mass sits atop a frictionless dome in a gravitational field. The mass will remain motionless for a period of time but will then move spontaneously in an arbitrary direction that cannot be predicted. Thus, according to Norton, the dome manifests indeterminism in that it has a single past but can follow many different futures.[40]

Determinism, though, is essential for everyday life. If one repeats a physical action with the *same starting conditions,* one expects repeatable results. For example, to assume that a lightbulb will always work requires that you assume that there are no changes in the bulb, the building's fuses, or no power outage, and you can only do this by accepting some substantial *ceteris paribus* (all other things being equal) clauses; that is, the set of conditions which limit or ring-fencing the starting conditions for you to predict the outcome. This example is simple, but it shows why the whole set of possible circumstances must be known before determinism can be assured. Furthermore, if the light bulb is organic, it may resist the request to be turned on or off, and thus one may assume that the bulb is not governed solely by determinism, or one would require *ceteris paribus clauses* that contained the entire history of the universe to embrace the organic history of the bulb. This is both the strength and the weakness of the theory of determinism, as the entire history of the universe is unknowable and thus determinism cannot be 'tested'. However, as dominant as it is in defining the world, determinism struggles to be a useful tool when trying to understand dynamic organic systems. It is also silent on matters of quality of life, matters of fortune, misfortune, good, or evil and, as David Hodgson states, it, '...has no place and role for consciousness'.[41]

It is these issues with determinism that are the focus of Susan Wolf. She argued that the debates on determinism and its conflict with free will are irrelevant. She suggested instead that moral responsibility and one's depth of autonomy should be the centre of the argument, not freedom and determinism.[42] Wolf stated, 'Only this kind of freedom will be neither too much nor too little. For then, the agent is not so free as to be free from moral reasons, nor so unfree as to make these reasons ineffective'.[43] David Cockburn expanded Wolf's argument by suggesting that this question should not be about fitting moral responsibility into determinism (as David Hume had done) but rather one should see if '…there is room for determinism (and indeterminism) in the gaps left by responsibility'.[44]

Fitting determinism into the gaps left by moral responsibility is what Shaun Nichols' work unexpectedly highlighted. In 2006, he researched peoples' beliefs on the influence of determinism in their lives. He found that people considered the role of determinism to vary depending on the moral content of the situation.[45] Nichols was working within the field of experimental philosophy and used a survey instrument that employed a vignette technique to explore beliefs. A vignette technique involves presenting respondents with an imaginary situation featuring imaginary people, and then asking them to decide what the imaginary people should do.[46] Nichols' vignettes employed psychological duplicates, a thought experiment in which a person was asked to imagine having a twin who lives in another world and is identical to them, with an identical history. The survey then asked people varying questions concerning the actions of the twin and whether they would also act the same way. Nichols found that people accepted the idea of duplicating the action of the twin in minor situations. However, when the twin took morally questionable actions or actions that evoked strong emotions, the participants did not follow suit.

Nichols' research showed that participants believed that their lives were governed by determinism for minor events but rejected such beliefs for more morally questionable situations. Nichols labelled this inconsistency as 'folk intuition' as it disagreed with the accepted view within philosophy concerning determinism: an individual was expected to be consistent in their beliefs regardless of the situation. However, what his work showed, although he did not recognise this point, was that it supported the arguments made by Wolf and Cockburn. For Nichols' group, moral responsibility was being privileged over determinism. It may have been an illusion of freedom, of being able to assert one's moral responsibility; nevertheless, his research group revealed the 'gap' that Cockburn had suggested. Notwithstanding all of these challenges to the universal nature of determinism, Nichols preferred to label his group's thinking as 'folk intuitions' rather than rethinking the science-dominated position on determinism. Nichols' work is revisited in the next chapter, as I duplicated his work in my research with modern astrologers, examining their issues around moral responsibility in a life lived with fate.

In summary, once the cosmos came to be conceived as composed of passive matter governed by universal laws, it was effectively demystified—reimagined as a rational and ordered system subject to universal determinism. This mechanistic worldview, however, presented a challenge to the concept of free will. In response, philosophical debate has grappled with this problem for centuries. Broadly, the arguments are divided into three positions. The two incompatibilist positions are as follows: one rejects free will and affirms determinism, while the other, known as libertarianism, upholds free will by denying determinism. In contrast, the third position of compatibilism maintains that free will and determinism can coexist. Within the compatibilist arguments, some scholars question the universality of determinism, while others seek to redefine the nature of free will. A further line of inquiry focuses on determinism in organic and conscious systems, suggesting that in the case of human beings, determinism appears to be subject to moral responsibility, thereby challenging the universal credentials of determinism.

Back in the first century BCE the Roman Senator, Cicero, cited earlier, defined fate as,

> [t]hings which are to be do not suddenly spring into existence, but the evolution of time is like the unwinding of a cable: it creates nothing new and only unfolds each event in its order.[47]

Here, Cicero, without any notion of passive matter, produced a similar definition of fate as today's determinism. He reconciled this with his views on free will by adopting a position of non-causal libertarianism, that is, the role of determinism does not influence humanity. Cicero then ridiculed astrologers who believed that fate was a part of human life, as he considered that his philosophical position was the only solution to the free will dilemma.

However, the views of practising astrologers—past and present—reflect all the philosophical positions presented in this chapter; that is, all versions of incompatibilism and compatibilism, with the significant caveat that astrologers, by and large, do not accept the assumption that fate equals determinism. For astrologers, fate is negotiable and personal, whereas determinism is fixed and universal. The next chapter begins the investigation into the beliefs and practices of contemporary astrologers in how they live with fate.

CHAPTER SIX

ASTROLOGY FROM WITHOUT AND WITHIN

Astrology is a paradox. Since the time of Cicero in the first century BCE, it has been the subject of critique and ridicule. Its adherents are often portrayed as socially or intellectually marginalised—lacking formal education, social standing, or full integration into mainstream society. Yet, despite such persistent opposition, astrology has constituted a continuous cultural tradition maintained through both writing and practice for nearly three millennia.[1] From the earliest works of the Assyrian priest to the Hellenistic and Roman periods, it was adapted by Islamic scholars and later reintroduced to the West, along with Arabic mathematics and the astrolabe, where it became an integral part of medical practice in the Middle Ages. In the early modern period, it waxed and waned in both religious and academic institutions, and today it remains a vibrant part of popular culture.[2] Never absent, always there, astrology has not disappeared—however condemned or marginalised.

This paradox prompts several questions: What is astrology? What is the nature of its criticisms? And, perhaps most significantly, why has it endured across time? This chapter explores the first two questions through the lens of fate's role in society, while the third question is explored in the concluding section of this work.

Definitions of astrology

Today, there are many definitions of astrology, and they can be placed into different groups. Some definitions contain assumptions that astrology seeks to be one of the sciences. Philippa Waring's definition captured this concept when she stated:

> Astrology and fortune telling overlap the fields of superstition... What began with a natural veneration for the heavenly bodies primitive man saw above him, today has become a flourishing science [astronomy] — but the basic belief that their movements can affect people's lives remains unchanged.[3]

So, while Waring defined astrology as a natural veneration of the heavens which belongs to the primitive and hence superstitious chapter of human history, she acknowledges the historical union of astrology and astronomy, but focuses on the success of astronomy. Similarly, a definition of astrology in *Philip's Astronomy Dictionary* actually defines astrology in the context of science, stating that astrology is:

> A pseudo-science professing to assess people's personality traits and to predict events in their lives and future trends in general from aspects of the heavens, in particular the positions of the planets. Astrology is based on ideas which are scientifically unsound and which the great majority of rational people dismiss.[4]

Martin Ince, in the *Dictionary of Astronomy*, follows this line of thinking and defines astrology as:

> The ancient but still popular superstition for attempting to predict the future from celestial portents. Mocked by most (but not all) modern scientists, astrology separated from respectable astronomy in the 17th century as knowledge of the solar system grew, weakening the argument that the positions of the planets could affect our fortunes. Astrology is apparently immune to extinction despite scientific advance and the spread of education.[5]

Ince's definition, like Waring's and that of the *Philip's Astronomy Dictionary*, seek to understand astrology by comparing it with 'respectable' science and consequently considers astrology's robustness in popular culture as attributable to the failure of science to educate people.

In 1996, Geoffrey Dean, Ivan Kelly, and Arthur Mather offered a definition which was that 'Astrology is the study (generally nonscientific) of supposed relationships between the heavens and human affairs'.[6] They went on to challenge astrology on the basis that it was not a science. They summed up research into astrology as,

> ...the picture emerging from hundreds of studies is clear and consistent: astrology does not deliver factual truth, at least not truth commensurate with its claims. It contributes nothing to our knowledge of the world. Orthodox approaches are vastly better, which is why scientists and philosophers see astrology as unfruitful and (except for its historical and social implications) not worth serious study.[7]

Other definitions of astrology view it as a form of divination. Morris Jastrow, in *The Encyclopaedia Britannica* of 1910, defined astrology as, '...the ancient art or science of divining the fate and future of human beings from indications given by the positions of the stars (sun, moon and planets)'.[8] Jastrow's definition accepted that astrology may not be a science and acknowledged the role of fate within the subject, although he did not attempt to define the word fate. However, a definition of astrology as divination or a pseudo-science imposes restrictions upon any investigation into the nature of fate and/or determinism within astrology, the latter (science) requiring that astrology contains determinism, while the former (divination) imposes the need for a non-secular astrology based on the workings of the gods.

A different approach is to define astrology as magic. Lawrence Jerome linked astrology's late twentieth-century popularity to what he described as a general rise of interest in occultism.[9] George Hansen also associated astrology with a non-scientific discourse and saw it as belonging to the paranormal, arguing that, while non-rational discourses were marginalised, they were nevertheless still present within society.[10]

In turning to astrologers for their views, the seventeenth-century English astrologer William Lilly defined astrology as a divine force. He wrote of, '...this heavenly knowledge of the Stars, wherein the great and admirable works of the invisible and all-glorious God are so manifestly apparent'.[11] For Lilly, astrology was a gift from God. However, later twentieth-century definitions of astrology by astrologers differed significantly. The US astrologer and software developer Robert Hand saw astrology as a system of knowledge, writing that:

> Dane Rudhyar called astrology the algebra of life but I suggest it's much more like a taxonomy of life than an algebra. A taxonomy is a classification system. It classifies animals as reptiles or mammals, or humans as Aries or Taurus. If we could actually convert astrology into a symbolic algebra, into an algebra of quality, we would really have made a major advance in thought.[12]

Hand, with his background in computing, defined astrology as an expression of the natural world, using a zoological metaphor and suggesting it was a taxonomy of quality. At the same time, Michael R. Mayer who, in his book based on his PhD thesis on psychology and personality, wrote of astrology as 'One of the most intricate metaphoric/symbolic systems ever developed to speak of human personality… Here a language exists which transforms aspects of the universe into symbols to speak of personality'.[13] For Mayer, astrology was the language of the psyche while, for Hand, it is a taxonomy that can bring a greater understanding of the world.

These differing definitions, which vary from a type of science, a divine order, a style of taxonomy, the language of the psyche, divination, or a form of magic, can lead to confusion when astrology is discussed. Whether viewed in a sceptical, esoteric, or ethnographic light by non-astrologers or by those who describe themselves as astrologers, one needs to pay close attention to what a given individual thinks astrology is.

In 1999, Patrick Curry embraced this diversity of understanding in his definition of astrology within a wholly cultural framework. He defined astrology as '...the practice of relating the heavenly bodies to lives and events on earth, and the tradition that has thus been generated'.[14] Curry's definition can be accepted by practitioners and sceptics alike; however, where sceptics diverge from practitioners is in their definition of fate. Astrologers acknowledge a relationship between the movement of the heavenly bodies and their lives. This acknowledgement places fate, measurable and visible through planetary movements, firmly into their world. The sceptical view, since the work of Cicero, is that this fate is a form of classical determinism (necessity) and since the horoscope is the instrument that delivers this determinism, then it, the horoscope, can only describe one possible life—for determinism does not produce options, determinism produces one single certainty. Hence, this outsider's view of fate within astrology is that it creates an inevitable horoscope. Such a horoscope would impose a rigid authoritarian element on the life of the astrologer.

As difficult as this may sound, such inevitability fits into Derk Pereboom's definition of hard incompatibilism—to live with no free will and no moral responsibility.[15] Pereboom, as discussed in Chapter Five, argued that one could still find contentment in life with this position. This is also the position of the seventeenth-century philosopher Baruch de Spinoza (discussed in Chapter Four), who argued for a life that embraced hard incompatibilism. However, critics of astrology tend to overlook the philosophical discussions on determinism and free will, and believe that accepting any reality of hard incompatibilism in human life is a blight upon the freedom of the human spirit—collectively, without acknowledging it, zealously arguing for libertarianism.

Notwithstanding this philosophical argument on living with determinism, the majority of astrologers do not accept this sceptical definition of fate as a form of determinism.

Criticisms of astrology

The inevitable horoscope assumption is evident in the different arguments levelled at astrology. Having defined fate as determinism, Marcus Cicero challenged the viability of astrology by stating, 'And, again, the fact that men who were born at the very same instant, are unlike in character, career, and in destiny, makes it very clear that the time of birth has nothing to do in determining man's course in life'.[16] Cicero identified the astrological belief that the natal horoscope was an external image of the 'character' or self and that it revealed the life story of the individual. He then criticised astrologers by pointing out that the horoscope, based on his definition of fate, could only produce one possible life story. Future critics of astrology adopted Cicero's perspective.

For example, four hundred years after Cicero, Saint Augustine reproduced his argument when he wrote that the fact that time-twins for him this meant people born at the same date and time, have different lives is sufficient to show the fallacy of astrology.[17] Tim Hegedus noted that this was the 'argument of different destinies', and that it was a common feature of anti-astrology polemics.[18] Theodore Wedel and Lynn Thorndike both pointed out that the 'argument of different destinies' has been recycled and reused for centuries.[19] Hegedus also commented on the 'argument of common destinies'.[20] This was put forward by the third-century theologian Hippolytus (170–235) in his *Refutation* and by Saint Gregory of Nyssa (c. 335–after 394) in his *Poemata Arcana*.[21] This was the argument that two people may experience the same events in their lives, despite having very different horoscopes. Such examples come from the evidence that soldiers who had different horoscopes could all die in the same battle, or sailors could drown at the same time with the sinking of their vessel. Both these arguments, of 'different destinies' and 'common destinies', are grounded in Cicero's assumption that there can be only one possible life per horoscope—the inevitable horoscope argument.

Whether these arguments were or were not a valid criticism of fourth-century astrology is not relevant here. What is relevant is that these arguments have been maintained within the culture of anti-astrology polemics from one generation to the next, up to the present day, without critics considering the actual nature of fate. Additionally, as already noted, such a sweeping dismissal of fate (defined as determinism) in human life also reveals the critic's blindness to questioning their non-causal libertarian bias.

Other critics take a different approach and focus on the moral quality of the practitioner. Over the centuries, different *ad hominem* arguments have been directed at astrologers. Augustine had used a theological argument that astrology was an affront to God's ability to intervene in human lives, as well as tainting God's creation with the potential evil-doings of the stars. Augustine's arguments on the demonic nature of astrology are still invoked to this day when some Christians warn astrologers of the potential damnation of their souls.[22] However, by the seventeenth century, the damnation of the astrologer's soul had turned to ridicule. John Chamber (1564–1604) labelled astrologers 'figure-flingers' when in 1601 he challenged their mathematical ability to cast a horoscope for the completion of the building programme, which included the Wanden's Lodge and the FitzJames Arch at Merton College, Oxford.[23] However, it was in the twentieth century that the strongest *ad hominem* arguments emerged.

The German philosopher Theodor Adorno, writing in the 1950s, laid some of the blame for the holocaust at the feet of those who practised astrology. Adorno was concerned with the acceptance of Nazism by the German population before and during the second world war. To help with his investigation, he developed a scale to measure what he defined as an authoritarian personality type. Such a personality, he argued, fostered fascism. This scale, later known as the 'F-Scale', considered that low scorers were people who succumbed to authoritarianism and high scorers were those who sought authoritarian status: for Adorno, these were the two components of the authoritarian syndrome.[24] Through his research, Adorno linked superstition, including belief in astrology, as low scoring on his F-Scale and were thus traits in a population that could succumb to authoritarianism and hence lead to fascism.[25] He continued this work by conducting research using the astrological column written by Carroll Righter in the *Los Angeles Times*. He assessed this material over several years before concluding that astrological sun sign columns removed their readers' personal responsibility from their daily lives.[26] In his introduction to Adorno's work, Stephen Crook argued that, apart from the removal of free will, Adorno considered astrology was a promoter of authoritarian irrationalism within contemporary culture.[27] Adorno appeared to accept that astrologers and their followers lived by the dictates of the inevitable nature of their horoscopes, for he wrote that a person who used astrology was '…somewhat relieved of his responsibility'.[28] Thus, the person was moved into a state of believing that '…he has to obey some highly systematised orders without, however, any manifest interconnection between the system and himself'.[29]

For Adorno, the astrological column was a form of brainwashing, whereby its readers gradually accepted what Adorno considered a contradiction between the events of their daily lives and those forecasted in the column, eventually leading to the adoption of what he termed irrational authoritarianism.[30] Such behaviour scored low on his F-Scale, indicating the person could slip into accepting fascism. He summed up the consequences of living as an astrologer as follows:

> It is intrinsic to the astrological pattern itself: one believes he has to obey some highly systematised orders without, however, any manifest interconnection between the system and himself. In astrology as in compulsive neurosis, one has to keep very strictly to some rule command

or advice without ever being able to say why. It is just this 'blindness' of obedience which seems to be fused with the over-whelming and frightening power of the command. In as much as the stars as viewed in astrology form an intricate system of do's and don'ts, this system seems to be the projection of a compulsive system itself.[31]

Adorno's criticism of astrology was founded on two premises: the assumption of the inevitability of the horoscope as argued by Cicero; and his own personal attempt to understand the reasons for the acceptance of Nazism by the German population. Adorno's 'F-Scale' is now discredited and Adorno's anti-astrology arguments, proposing a link between astrology and fascism, have faded.[32] However, his claim that astrology is associated with issues of marginalisation and maladjusted personality disorders—based on the premise that its users accept the authoritarianism implications of the horoscope—still influences critics and researchers today.

Carrying Adorno's arguments forward, Robert Wuthnow conducted research in the US in the 1970s. He concluded that the people attracted to astrology were '…more poorly educated, the unemployed, non-whites, females, the unmarried, the overweight, the ill, and the lonely…'[33] He based his research on the assumption that astrology offered an alternative authoritarian system to religion. He concluded that,

> If it appeals to those whom modern society has left on the fringe, it may offer an alternative source of authority and reward, of comfort, just as churchly religion has been known to offer to socially marginal parishioners.[34]

Similarly, G.A. Tyson conducted research in the 1980s on people who consulted astrologers in South Africa. He wrote that:

> The independent variables used in the present study were all with one exception, ones which had previously been found to correlate with belief in astrology: viz. sex, age, marital status, education, religious affiliation, importance of religion, locus of control and a measure of maladjustment.[35]

He concluded that those who consulted astrologers were mainly women and thus astrology appealed to gullible people who were looking for a higher level of control to be imposed on their lives.[36] US academics Cary J. Nederman, a historian of science, and James Wray Goulding, a sociologist, adopted a similar position. In 1981 they wrote a paper commenting on Adorno's research and criticising the supposed beliefs that astrologers have in fate, writing :

> Take things as they are, since you are fated for them anyway… The importance of fate is not to be underestimated…. It is our star-determined fate, rather than our socio-economic status, which sets the pattern of our lives. Of course, in order to cloud any possible connection between the 'heavens' and the 'earth,' fate is interpreted as a cosmic throw of the dice. It is always the element of risk that determines one's fate.[37]

However, Nederman and Goulding did not define what they meant by the term 'fate', nor did they investigate how astrologers defined it.

In 1995 Richard Dawkins also drew on Adorno's arguments. He suggested that consumers of astrology are marginalised people who are preyed upon by maladjusted individuals. He wrote of people who use astrology to find a partner as:

> Lonely people, whose life might be transformed by a longed for compatible friendship, are deliberately encouraged, by their reading of astrological quacks in the newspapers, wantonly and pointlessly to throw away 11/12th of the available populations. This is not just silly, it is damaging, and the quacks concerned deserve our censure as strongly as their deluded victims deserve our pity.[38]

Later, in 1997, John Bauer and Martin Durant, both academics based in London, conducted research as to why people accepted astrological premises. Their work was based on the analysis of a British survey of 2009 people. They concluded that there was insufficient support for Adorno's hypothesis that astrologers sought an external locus of control; however, their research indicated that people who felt that they did not have control over their lives were drawn to astrology. They concluded, therefore, that, '…the fatalism element [in astrology] was confirmed'.[39]

Similarly, Adorno's views were central to the research conducted in 2004 by Michael Dambrun. His research questions were based around racism and he worked with French university students, collecting their views about Arabs living in France. Following Adorno's lead of looking for fascist-like tendencies, Dambrun drew a correlation between a belief in astrology and prejudice towards

Arabs, overweight people and women, suggesting that '…beliefs in astrology bias our perceptions and have some damaging consequences with regard to intergroup relations'.[40] Whether there could have been other social issues within the lives of the university students that contributed to these results or indeed whether the vehicle of a scale-based survey was sufficiently refined to justify these conclusions are concerns left unanswered.

Not seeking to support Adorno's hypothesis but still accepting Cicero's inevitable horoscope argument, in 1978 T.L. Brink from Notre Dame University in California conducted a study of the religious attitudes of 227 junior and senior students at a Catholic girls' high school to see if they believed in astrology, Catholicism, or reincarnation. Brink assumed these three beliefs to be mutually exclusive. For Brink, the omnipotence of God and the free will of man were views held to be inconsistent with a belief that fate was produced by the planets. Brink also assumed that '…astrology's fatalism is based upon blind impersonal forces [the solar system] and is substantially different to whatever fatalism reincarnationists attribute to the workings of karma'.[41] His results were inconclusive and he commented that his research did not support Adorno's and Wuthnow's marginalisation hypothesis.[42] However, when further considering his results, which did show a correlation between belief in astrology and belief in reincarnation, he concluded that his young research group were simply muddled in their thinking.[43] Being an outsider to astrology, Blink was not aware that reincarnation had been a strong theme within astrology since the early twentieth century, when it had absorbed theosophical teachings through the work of Alan Leo (1860–1917). Hence, its presence in the views of the 227 school juniors and seniors was not surprising.

Researching beliefs of astrologers

A different line of research was conducted in 1992 by the US academic Shoshanah Feher. Her work was on the more general beliefs held by astrologers. In 1989 she surveyed 383 people attending an astrology conference, the United Astrology Congress (UAC) in the US, and concluded that astrologers fell into two groups based on whether they considered astrology to be a spiritual practice or not. She defined these groups as New Age astrologers (non-secular, spiritual) and non-New Age astrologers (secular). She indicated that secular astrologers use astrology as a predictive tool, while non-secular astrologers use it for personal and spiritual growth.[44] The raw numbers in her reported results show that 42.3% of her sampled astrologers were secular and 57.7% were non-secular.[45] With the distinction between her two groups based on the astrologers' attitude to prediction, she assumed that the spiritual astrologers considered the influence of fate to be weaker or different in some manner—as they believed that it could not be used, or should not be used to predict a future event. In contrast, the non-New Age astrologers appeared to hold different views on fate as they did attempt to use it to make predictions. Feher's research, although not focused on fate, usefully demonstrated that there were varying views on the nature of fate and its role in their lives among astrologers.

In 1994 astrological associations in the US conducted their own survey, Project Focus, and received 657 responses.[46] The survey was focused on the education of astrologers and the legal position of the subject within the various states of the US. Of the 70 questions asked in the survey, two were associated with the role of fate in the astrologer's life. Of the 657 respondents, 74% stated that they used horoscopes to delineate personality, showing a belief in a link between the ordered heavens and an individual's character; 52% also stated that they sought to make predictions using astrology. The survey also revealed that 24% of the astrologers did not think that their lives contained any element of fate. These results showed a diversity of attitudes and definitions about fate amongst the astrologers.

Another survey, conducted by Campion for his doctoral research in 1999, questioned 159 astrologers at a UK conference and a further 152 at a US conference in 2002, making a total of 311 practitioners. His survey focused primarily on exploring astrology as a New Age phenomenon and also included several questions exploring the prevalence of fate in the beliefs held by astrologers. Of his 311 respondents, 66% agreed that astrology could make accurate predictions, and 87% agreed that, while the birth horoscope contains indicators of one's potential, how it was used or manifested was up to the individual.[47] Like the Project Focus survey, Campion's results reveal a high level of diversity regarding the understanding of, agreement with, or attitude towards fate within the UK and US astrological communities.

There has been further doctoral research conducted into the question of the role or place of astrology in contemporary society, but these have not included the role of fate as perceived by astrologers. Alison Bird's research in 2006 was focused on how astrologers learned astrology and she stated that, 'Astrology is the thinking woman's divination system of choice'.[48] Bird accepted that astrology was a form of divination but did not engage with fate. In the same year, Bridget Costello considered the practice of astrology and how astrologers used it, concluding that it was a moral discourse against the hegemony of science. She also ignored the question of fate.[49]

In summary, the personal views of the different etic researchers (i.e., non-astrologers) are evident when they offer a definition of astrology. They present it as a failed science and are unsure why modern education has not eradicated it; alternatively, they query the mental well-being of the practitioners. Convinced that believers of astrology are marginalised, the researchers seek to represent them as either confused or maladjusted individuals. In contrast, the emic (insider) researchers, such as Feher, Campion, Bird, and Costello encountered a multiplicity of views among different groups within the astrological community. In 2011, commenting on this finding, Campion and Greene wrote of an academic conference they organised:

> The conference title 'Astrologies', was designed to reflect the growing scholarly realisation that it is impossible to talk about astrology as a monolithic entity, unchanged since ancient times and the same from culture to culture.[50]

The common thread, however, for astrologers is that they all live with fate, a fate they view as imparted into their lives through their relationship with the heavens. Some may hold it as inevitable (a hard incompatibilist position), others may choose to disregard it (a libertarian position), while another group will seek to engage with it (a compatibilist position). All astrologers, however, have developed a lifestyle that in varying ways, lives with fate.

In closing, another context for considering the nature of astrology is the work of Duane Hamacher and Ray Norris. They work in the area of indigenous astronomy and have noted that indigenous astronomies serve their cultures by offering frameworks for explaining complex phenomena and fostering an understanding of the world. They contrast this with Western astronomy, which advances through reductionism, quantitative analysis, hypothesis testing, and the systematic rejection of outdated theories. In contrast they point out that indigenous astronomical traditions are holistic, integrating metaphysical and spiritual dimensions. Indigenous astronomers seek meaning through context—linking observation with lived experience—and do not discard older knowledge, even as new methods emerge. Their aim is not to establish universally provable truths but rather to sustain cultural continuity.[51]

Astrology, with its long-standing tradition, shares many features with the perspectives of Hamacher and Norris on indigenous astronomy. Like indigenous astronomers, the majority of astrologers do not pursue empirically provable truths; instead, they engage with the sky as part of a broader spiritual or holistic worldview. Additionally, within the practice of astrology, older techniques are not discarded; instead, they are preserved and continually integrated, as evidenced by the revival of classical and medieval astrological literature and practices in the late twentieth century. Astrology is also not evolutionary; it does not seek, like science, to build knowledge and improve from one discovery to the next. For astrologers, the sky serves as a source of meaning and guidance, forming an integral part of a way of life.[52] As such astrologers are the cultural carriers of classical fate in today's society.

Finally, by and large, astrologers do not recognise themselves in the modern-day criticisms of astrology because these critics view fate as determinism, the horoscope as inevitable and libertarianism as the only acceptable life philosophy. How the astrologers view fate and the lifestyle it produces is the subject of the following chapters.

CHAPTER SEVEN

ASKING ABOUT FATE

It is evident from the classical, medieval and early modern literature that astrology is associated with a belief in fate. Furthermore, there are untested assumptions about the nature of this fate. Between 2007 and 2010, I sought to test these assumptions by asking astrologers to share their views on the nature and purpose of fate and what they gain from incorporating it, in any format, into their lives. In my research, I engaged with grassroots astrologers—the individuals who were interested in astrology for their own use, the enthusiasts. To reach enthusiasts from different countries, I emailed a questionnaire to local organisations in the UK, the USA, Europe, South Africa, Australia, and New Zealand.

Additionally, I travelled to astrological conferences to manually gather responses. I eventually gathered 1,062 responses from over 40 different countries, along with thousands of words of additional text about people's thoughts on how they worked and lived with fate. These additional unsolicited comments are discussed in Chapter Eight. As the responses grew, it was apparent to me that astrologers wanted to share their views on fate.

I suspected that many astrologers would have classical threads within their views on fate. However, in considering the design of the questionnaire, these issues had to be approached indirectly. Astrologers might not be aware that they were using fate as defined by Calcidius, or as proposed by Plato, or promoted by the Stoic philosopher Epictetus, or even the practical and pragmatic fate incorporated into the astrology of Guido Bonatti in the thirteenth century. Additionally, I wanted to explore whether astrologers, knowingly or unknowingly, had any theories of fate, those complex sets of interlinked beliefs discussed by Bobzien and cited in Chapter Two, that support any ideas on fate.[1] With these aims in mind, the questionnaire needed to cover issues related to the soul, God, the role of prediction, and the relationship between fate and moral responsibility. Added to this was the problem of practice versus assumed belief. What an astrologer said they believed may not be the same as what drove their actions. Consequently, the questionnaire design phase underwent different pilot studies and focus groups before it reached its final version.

The resulting questionnaire, given in the appendix, represents my solution to these aims. The questionnaire was designed as an interconnected set of questions that allowed individual responses to be combined in ways to shed light on the concept of fate and its significance in the respondent's life. The results of this questionnaire are the focus of this chapter.

With my awareness of the diversity of views around fate that could be revealed, I placed at the top of the questionnaire a neutral definition of fate to act as a starting point for the respondents when addressing the different questions.

> A central tenet of astrology is that something is written at the moment of a birth or a moment in time and place, and some component of this moment has a bearing on the future. In this survey, this component, which astrology explores via horoscopes, is labelled the 'fate' of a person's life or the 'fate' contained in a moment in time.

Who are the astrologers

The astrologers in my research were predominantly female—they self-identified as 195 males and 868 females. The youngest was 20 years old, while the oldest was 90 years old. On average, they were in their mid-40s to early 60s. Another demographic question was about the length of time a person had studied astrology. My intention, which is discussed later in this chapter, was to ascertain if astrology shaped their views of fate. However, unexpectedly, another insight emerged. Fig. 1 shows the results for the length of time individual astrologers had studied astrology.

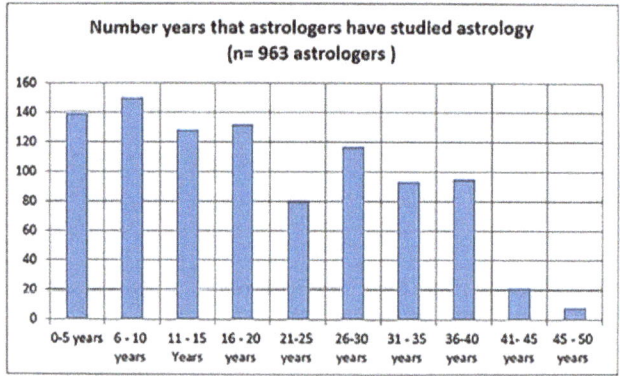

Figure 1: Number of years that an astrologer had studied astrology.

The number of astrologers who were new to astrology, involved between 0 to 5 years, and those who had studied astrology for 16 to 20 years was relatively even (see Fig.1). There was a drop in numbers from the 21-to-40-year-old groups. Still, by and large, this question reveals that once people took up astrology, they tended to remain interested in the subject. If the results showed a drop in numbers after a few years, then the 0-5-year group would capture those new astrologers but show a drop off in the next group of 6 to 10 years.

I also asked them how old they were when they started studying astrology, and their answers showed that the majority of people were in their early 20s to mid-30s when they began their studies. Given the large number of respondents, drawn from forty different countries, it is reasonable to generalise that, in the early twenty-first century, the contemporary astrologer is most commonly a woman who adopted astrology during young adulthood—a life stage often associated with marriage and child-rearing—and who, once engaged with the subject, sustained her interest throughout the rest of her life.

Additionally, combining the roughly consistent numbers which stretched across 'less than 5 years' to '36-40 years' shown in Fig.1 with the results of the age of people when they took up astrology, it is evident that since the mid-1960s (when the 36-40 years group would have begun studying astrology) the number of people taking up astrology has generally been maintained at a similar level to the present day, that is 2007/10. Hence, the popularity of astrology for the last 40 years has neither waxed nor waned; it has been constant. This result contradicts the varying arguments about the decline of astrology. Michelle Pfeffer challenged astrology's assumed decline in the second half of the twentieth century, claiming that it only appeared to decline in the '*learned* culture, particularly in universities' (Pfeffer's italics).[2] In 2009, Zheljana Peric lamented the decline of astrology and suggested that the modern disconnect with nature could be partly blamed on the decline of astrology in popular belief.[3] My fieldwork indicates that, at least since the mid-1960s, the practice of astrology has not declined in Western culture.

The astrologers and their theories of fate

The central theme of the questionnaire was focused on discovering if today's astrologers held theories of fate. To recap from Chapter Two, Bobzien argued that the nature of fate as viewed, for example, by Plato, the Stoics, and Aristotle, all required slightly different ontological frameworks, which she defined as a theory of fate.[4] A theory of fate, can be considered a set of interrelated beliefs concerning:

a) the nature of the cosmos (such as whether it is sympathetic and whether it is inherently good, neutral, or malefic).
b) the location of the human will (a belief in transcendent or immanent cosmos, which locates the will as free, dualism, or bound to the material world, monism).
c) The purpose and source of fate (God's plan or an expression of the natural world).

Two distinct sets of questions were used to explore some of the required components of a theory of fate. One set asked about the source of fate. I asked each astrologer to mark a Likert scale for these different statements concerning the source and purpose of fate.[5] In a Likert scale, answers are ranked on a scale, and I used a five-point scale ranging from 'strong disagreement' to 'strong agreement'.[6] The second set of questions asked the astrologer to mark a similar scale for six different statements concerning the purpose of fate.[7] To ensure a clear result, I only used the responses at the end of 'strongly agree', for both scales, thereby avoiding the weakness of a Likert scale, which is that the middle options can be used as a dumping ground for those with no opinion on the topic.[8] Only those astrologers who had selected a 'strongly agree' option for both sets of questions were tabulated, as they held a 'strongly agreed' opinion on both the source and purpose of fate. A total of 450 astrologers fulfilled these requirements.

Fig. 2 is a table of these results. There were forty-eight possible theories of fate to which the astrologers could subscribe. The columns in Fig.2 (labelled A to H), show opinions on the source of fate, while the rows (labelled 1 to 6) show the perceived purpose of fate. Each cell of the table contains the percentage (of the total number of 1062 astrologers sampled) and the number of times the cell received a 'strongly agree' opinion from an astrologer as a raw number. The totals for the rows and columns are the total number of astrologers who selected (strongly agree) a particular source of fate (columns) and the purpose of fate (rows). The totals show the sums for each row and column. An astrologer could select 'strongly agree' to more than one option; thus, the totals show the number of selections, not the number of individual astrologers. The four highest selected combinations are marked in blue, and are the cells C3, G3, C5, and G5, revealing four different theories of fate.

These four theories of fate can be divided into two groups. Two of these theories were shown in column C, with the source of fate being seen as a result of the soul's need for evolution. This suggested a distinctly Platonic theory of fate, centred within a divine cosmos and in which the individual desires to return to that divine essence. However, unlike Plato's model, the majority of these early

Purpose of Fate	Source of Fate								Total
	A God's Will	B Divine World	C Soul's Evolution	D One's Karma	E Determinism	F Family History	G Living Patterns	H Human Construct	
1 Work with God's plan	4.9% 52	8.6% 91	10.0% 106	5.9% 63	4.9% 52	5.0% 53	8.1% 86	2.6% 28	531
2 Help the soul transcend	1.0% 11	1.7% 18	3.0% 32	1.6% 17	1.4% 15	1.2% 13	1.8% 19	0.6% 6	131
3 To help reach full potential	5.4% 57	12.1% 128	23.8% 253	10.9% 116	8.7% 92	11.5% 122	15.6% 166	3.8% 40	974
4 To see what can/cannot happen	1.2% 13	1.6% 17	1.6% 17	0.9% 10	1.0% 11	0.9% 10	1.4% 15	0.4% 4	97
5 To live in harmony	4.2% 45	9.4% 100	12.3% 131	6.1% 65	6.6% 70	8.9% 94	13.0% 138	3.5% 37	680
6 To read an inevitable future	0.9% 10	1.5% 16	1.4% 15	1.0% 11	1.1% 12	1.0% 11	1.6% 17	0.3% 3	95
Total	188	370	554	282	252	303	441	118	

Figure 2: 'Strong Agreement'. This table shows the number of times a combination of the believed source of fate and the purpose of fate received a 'strongly agree' answer from an individual astrologer.

twenty-first-century astrologers (23.8%, cell C3) wanted to use their fate to help them achieve their full potential. In contrast, only 3% (cell C2) adopted Plato's model of transcending the material realm to join with the divine. This was a theory of fate driven by individualism, as fate was the result of the soul's journey to evolve to help it reach its full potential as indicated in the horoscope (Q. 4.1.3). It was, in nature, reflective of an Aristotelian philosophy, which advocated for perfection in this world, the material world, rather than Plato's divine sphere. In the late twentieth century, this model was promoted by the astrological author Dane Rudhyar, who used astrology to redefine the notion of self, portraying the horoscope as the seed of a person's potential.[9] Rudhyar's influence on astrology is discussed later in Chapter Eight.

The other theory of fate, shown in column C (cell C5), considered that fate was the soul's need to evolve; this evolution was achieved by living in harmony with the material world. This is the individualism of the soul's evolution (the source of fate) blended with the Stoic themes of the self-seeking to be a harmonious part of a larger whole—a holistic model focused on the natural or secular world. There was one other theory of fate shown in column C that 10% of the astrologers adopted and that was a theological fate. The source of fate was the journey of the individual's soul in its desire or attempt to work with God's plan. This is not necessarily a theological fatalism as the questionnaire did not ask about God's providence but did reflect a religious overtone to the astrologer's views on fate.

The other theories of fate that were supported were those in column G, which posits a fate created by living in a pattern. The total in column G showed that this option was the second-largest group—it was selected 441 times. This group considered that they lived in a sympathetic cosmology that was emergent, which produced fate in their lives. Its purpose was to either enable them to reach their full potential as individuals or to live in harmony with the world, adopting a holistic approach. Both of these versions of a theory of fate are Stoic-like. Fate as a pattern is considered in more detail later in this chapter.

In contrast, Cicero's fate, a style of hard-incompatibilism, which has been central to most of the polemics against astrologers for the last two thousand years, gained little support. Cell E6, Fig.2, is for the combined selection of fate as inevitable and its source being the result of determinism. This was selected only 12 times. However, the view of fate as determinism attracted some interest when linked to God's plan, or as a full potential or harmony option. The lowest number of responses was for the idea that fate was an illusion and only a construct of the human imagination—column H.

In summary, the vast majority of the astrologers who completed my questionnaire considered that astrology gave them a personal tool to work with fate. They tended to select more than one option when deciding between: 'to reach one's full potential' or 'to help find harmony in the world' while the source of fate in their life was the result of living in a divine cosmos and the soul's desire for evolution or, was the result of living inside a pattern. The experience of living inside a pattern can give rise to emergent events. Emergentism is a philosophical position that holds that higher-order phenomena (such as consciousness or life) emerge from more fundamental physical processes but are not reducible to them; their origins cannot be directly causally linked to the outcome.[10] Hence, an event arises, the person senses that the event is 'correct' and belongs to a larger concept, but the event appears to be a coincidence or happenstance. This phenomenon is explored later.

These questions only explored two components of a theory of fate: source and purpose. However, these results indicate a theory of fate partly based on Plato's views on the existence of the soul and its desire to 'evolve', but with the twist that the soul was embedded in the current life, the material world, and did not seek transcendence to find the divine, but instead sought the divine within the material world. This is a Stoic-like version of fate. The soul's purpose or journey was to find and support the divine in nature. This in turn, led to questions about astrologers' beliefs about the divine.

Secular or non-secular astrology

With the classical theories of fate having strong links between fate and the idea of the divine, I asked the astrologers directly if they considered the notion of a divine was a prerequisite for their view of fate.

The astrologers had already been asked whether they considered that the purpose of astrology was to help them understand a divine plan (Q.4.2.4). To this they were also asked whether fate was a part of a divine cosmos (Q.5.1.3). Both questions were aimed at confirming the non-secular nature of astrology. The astrologers selected a response from a Likert scale coded from -2 to +2. Tallying the responses from both responses produced a score which shifted from -4, 'strong disagreement' to both statements to +4, 'strong agreement'. Fig. 3 shows a level of ambiguity around the divine role in astrology. Less than 5% strongly believed that astrology and the cosmos were secular (non-divine), while 5% took the opposite position. However, 52% of all astrologers produced scores of 0 (unsure) or less than zero (not a spiritual subject) for these questions, while 48% of astrologers produced a positive score (+1 to +4), showing a level of acceptance of astrology requiring a divine presence.

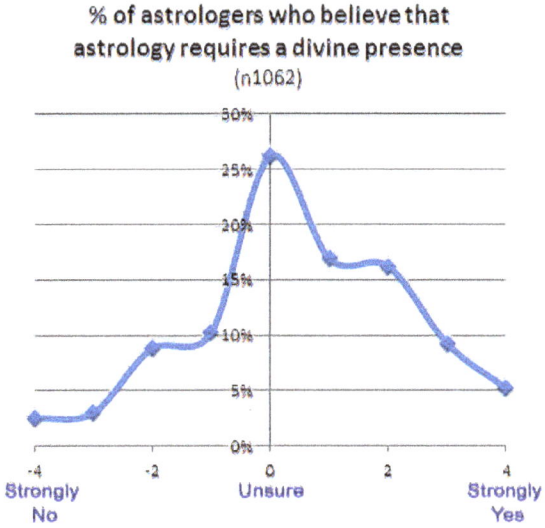

Figure 3: Belief that astrology was linked to a divine plan, and that astrology required a divine cosmos.

These results (Fig. 3) are a snapshot of astrologers' opinions in the early twenty-first century. They challenge the arguments of Steve Bruce in 1995 and Gordon Melton in 2001 that astrology was a form of new religious movement.[11] Apart from the complexities involved in defining religion, if religion requires a divine force, then these results indicated that only 48% of the 1062 astrologers surveyed accepted the need for a divine force within their practice of astrology. These results align with those shown in Fig. 2, which indicate a roughly even split between astrologers who viewed fate as the soul's need for evolution (non-secular) and those who considered it the result of living in a pattern (secular).

The results shown in Fig.2 reveal that a large number of astrologers see the role of astrology as helping them live in harmony with the planet. The fact that 52% view their astrology as secular builds a picture of a type of ecological Stoicism, which, as Aladakan pointed out, 'appears to be a philosophy that invites men [and women] to take their relationship with the world seriously'.[12]

Fate as pattern and telos

Some astrologers believed that fate comes from God's plan (see Fig.2 Row 1); however, many astrologers held other views. These astrologers answered questions about the nature of fate and how it was created.

The belief of living in a pattern, first revealed in Fig.2 column G, is an ontology promoted by Alfred Whitehead. It implies that the pattern will impose some form of limitation on the future, a style of teleology where the future (the pattern) can influence the present (to move in a way to form the future pattern). Commenting on teleology, F. J. K. Soontiëns argued that a person is a teleological being, as they direct their actions towards future ambitions. He argued that humanity, therefore, could not be the product of an a-teleological world, stating,

> If nature and evolution are a-teleological, then we are either obliged to conclude that human teleology stems from a non- (extra-, super-) natural source, or we are obliged to conclude that human teleology is only an illusion.[13]

Apart from the questions listed in Fig. 2, there were three additional questions that focused on astrologers' attitudes to this Whiteheadian argument on teleology. These questions were:

    i. Q.3.3, asked about the expected similarities in family members' horoscopes, thus suggesting that the family was holistic, an emergent pattern to which the unborn child's future horoscope would either choose to engage or was required to conform to the family pattern.

ii. Q.4.1.7 asked if the astrologer thought the source of fate resulted from naturally emerging patterns in the web of life.

iii. Q.4.2.5 asked if the astrologer thought that the purpose of astrology was to live in harmony with the patterns of the world.

For each question, the astrologer was presented with a Likert scale. By using a consistent scale for the answers to all three questions (-2 to 2), an individual's overall score for a belief in fate as teleology and/or pattern was assessed. A 'strong disagreement' on all three questions gave a score of -6 to that respondent, while 'strong agreement' produced a score of +6. Total neutrality for all three questions would result in a score of zero. Fig.4 is the graph of the results for the scores from each of the 1062 astrologers.

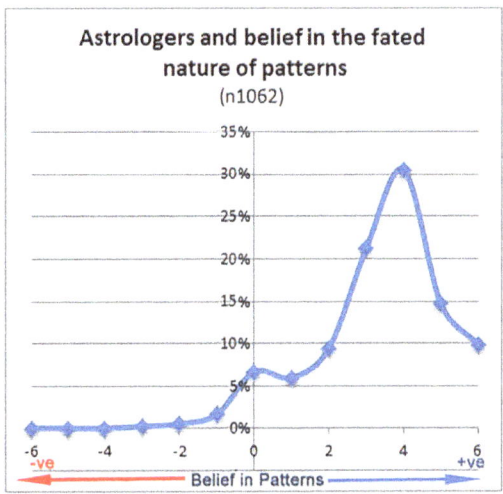

Figure 4: The individual scores for the astrologers' belief in patterns as the source of fate. A value of -6 for an astrologer represented 'strong disagreement' while a value of +6 represented 'strong agreement' to all three pattern questions.

The results displayed in Fig.4 showed that the astrologers avoided the 'disagree' side of the Likert scale. Instead, 91% of astrologers scored on the positive side (between 1 and 6) for the questions. However, over 30% of the astrologers scored a value of +4, indicating that these astrologers 'strongly agreed' with at least two of the three questions. This result suggests that these astrologers envision themselves living a life as part of a sympathetic world, — an interconnected, responsive web with which one seeks to be in rapport; a world that is, in a sense, ensouled. For them, living in harmony, in accord with the world, was their goal. Astrology helped them, in varying ways, to understand their part of this sympathetic cosmos and be supportive, or at least neutral to any ups and downs.

From a Classical perspective, this understanding of fate aligns closely with Stoic philosophy, as well as the writings of the first-century CE Stoic astrologer, Claudius Ptolemy, cited in Chapter Two. He wrote of the need to accept one's fate as part of living in a sympathetic cosmos. The underlying theme was an ethical imperative to live in harmony with the world. Today, this theory of fate also resonates with contemporary environmental thought, particularly the recognition of the deep interconnectedness of all living and non-living systems. This perspective culminates in forms of 'dark green religion', rooted in a Spinozist-Stoic worldview, wherein, as Bron Taylor observes, 'nature is sacred, has intrinsic value and is therefore due reverent care'.[14] With the questionnaire highlighting this view, it was explored in greater depth in the interviews.

Prediction and fate

Many astrologers use astrology to make predictions that logically require a belief in fate. Astrological predictions are derived from the movement of the planets and/or the celestial sphere against the background of the person's horoscope – birth chart. The astrologer first locates the timing of a potential event, a geometrical exercise based on the determinism of celestial mechanics. With this timing established, the astrologer has to decide what will happen at that time. Hence, there are three expectations an astrologer can have of their predictions:

> (1) a hard incompatible astrologer (working with Cicero's fate) would seek to predict both time and event;
>
> (2) a compatibilist astrologer (working with negotiable fate) would seek to predict just the timing but not an exact event;
>
> (3) a libertarian astrologer (no fate) would seek to predict neither time nor event.

The fourth option, a prediction of an event without timing, may fit into any exploration of divination; however, it does not align with the astrologer's expectations. A significant difference that is often overlooked when defining astrology as divination.

The questionnaire asked the astrologers about what they thought they could predict: time, event, both, or neither. Fig. 5 shows the results of these questions, which are also grouped by the number of years the person had been studying astrology. The vast majority agreed that the horoscope could provide them with a fixed timing of a future event but not the fixed nature of the event, and the acceptance of this version of fate increased over time spent studying astrology.

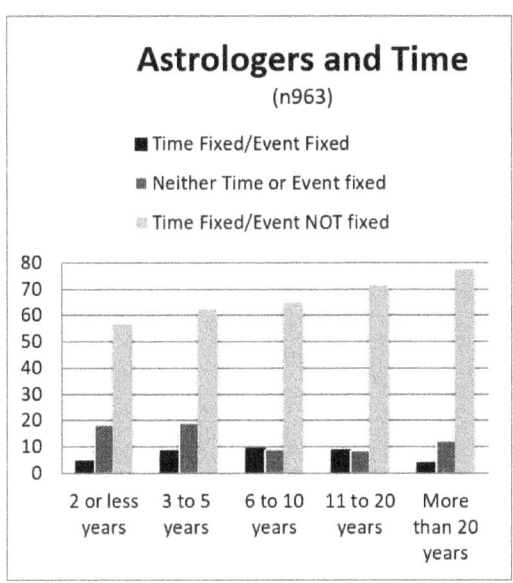

Figure 5: Percentage response of astrologers to Q. 2.6 and Q.2.7 grouped by years of involvement with astrology. The black bar represents those astrologers who hold a natural hard incompatibilist belief that both time and event are inevitable. In contrast, the grey bar represents those astrologers who accept a natural compatibilist belief that time is fated but not the nature of events. The blue bar is non-acceptance of either premise.

Nichols, in his research into determinism and philosophy students, posed two questions of the influence of culture on an individual's intuitive beliefs and whether training as a philosopher could alter one's intuitions about determinism.[15] He did not reach a conclusion. However, his questions were addressed within the astrological community. The questionnaire revealed that for those new to astrology (between 1 and 5 years), 56.8% accepted that fate indicated only the timing, but not the exact event. However, after 20 years, 77.4% of astrologers supported this view of fate and time. Hence, the longer people where involved with astrology, the more they adopted a type of compatibilism, a negotiable fate.

Many of astrology's critics claim that adopting an astrological lifestyle implies the acceptance of an inevitable future, viewing astrology as imposing this belief on its gullible followers, as Adorno claimed, submitting to a higher external authority. Dawkins, Dean, Kelly and Mather also argued that astrology moves a person into accepting giving up control of their lives.[16] If this were the case, then one would expect that the longer a person was involved in astrology, the higher their response would be towards accepting a hard incompatibilist option. My research indicates that these opinions are not valid and that, in contrast, negotiable fate is a feature of contemporary astrology.

Furthermore, such a view of a future time is time embedded with quality, and is similar to the ancient Greek notion of *kairos*, a term that refers to the right, opportune, or critical moment.[17] The actions of *kairos*, for the astrologer, placed moments in their future that are filled with a fated quality. In contrast to *kairos*, which focuses on the qualitative nature of time and the opportune moment, *chronos* is about the quantitative flow of time, the ticking of the clock that governs our daily routines and schedules. For non-astrologers, the future holds forthcoming events in one's daily life, weekly commitments, social gatherings, and anniversaries. However, the astrologer's calendar also contains additional dates, times when they are fated to 'meet' an event, to experience fated critical moments. Accepting the existence of these future moments, but not the exact event they will meet, shows a compatibilist attitude among astrologers. The timing was fixed, but the actual expression of the event was somewhat open, thereby allowing the astrologer to take some form of action to try to 'adjust' the expression of the forthcoming event—a form of hybrid fate, in which a part of fate was fixed (timing) but part was open to change (the event).

Additionally, as cited in the previous chapter, Shoshana Feher argued that attitudes to prediction were a dividing point between astrologers. She claimed that there were two types of astrologers. She defined one type as New Age astrologers who viewed astrology as a spiritual practice and, according to her, did not engage in predictive astrology. The second group she viewed as non-New Age, secular astrologers who did engaged in prediction.[18] To explore Feher's argument, I divided the respondents into the two groups she identified. Those who 'strongly agreed' that fate was an expression of God's will or the 'will of the gods' were placed into the spiritual group. The second group consisted of those who 'strongly disagreed' and were placed into a non-spiritual group. In total, this represented 429 astrologers of the total data of 1062. The responses of these 429 astrologers to their expectations of astrology to predict were then tabulated and shown in Fig. 6.

	Hard incompatibilist: Time and Event Fixed	Compatibilist: Time Fixed Event NOT Fixed	Libertarian: Neither time nor event fixed	Number of astrologers
Spiritual Astrologers	8.4%	76.2%	6.6%	227
Non-Spiritual Astrologers	8.4%	72.8%	12.4%	202

Figure 6: This table shows % of astrologers and their approach to predictive astrology divided into spiritual and non-spiritual groups.

These results do not support Feher's thinking on spiritual and non-spiritual astrologers, as 8.4% of both the non-spiritual and spiritual astrologers were hard incompatibilists, that is, they adopted a hard incompatibilism as their model of fate by seeking to make exact predictions of both timing and the event. This group justified their ability to make exact predictions by aligning themselves with the use of astrology to read God's will. In contrast, 76.2% of spiritual astrologers and 72.8% of the non-spiritual astrologers selected options that revealed that they were compatibilist astrologers working with a negotiable fate, as they sought to predict the timing of the event but agreed that the nature of the event was not fixed. Only 6.6% of the spiritual astrologers were libertarians, predicting neither time nor event, while 12.4% of the non-spiritual astrologers also selected the option that astrology could not be used to predict either the timing or the nature of the event. In this regard, astrologers who viewed their astrology as a spiritual pursuit were just as likely to engage in predictive astrology as those who did not consider that it needed a divine component for its efficacy.

Astrology, authoritarianism and moral responsibility

The questionnaire also explored the assumption, namely, that of the sceptical literature, which argued that the acceptance of fate and astrology implied that a person relinquished control over their life.[19] To consider this assumption, as well as look at how attitudes to fate related to matters of moral responsibility, the questionnaire asked questions aimed at measuring the astrologer's response to events or situations predicted by their horoscope. For each question, the astrologer could select that they: (1) calmly accepted the inevitability of the consequences with a Ptolemaic/Stoic-like attitude; (2) became angry and blamed the planets but took no other action; (3) developed fears around the forthcoming event; or (4) just braced for the worst. Selecting these options would imply

Adorno's argument that astrologers accepted a lack of control over their lives. Alternatively, the astrologers could choose from other possibilities that showed that they would seek to change the expected fate by negotiating or engaging with it in some way. The questions covered various situations, from trivial events with no real consequences, thus non-emotional, to events with high emotional consequences (see the appendix for the actual questions used).

Astrologer's Action	Q.2.4 Non-emotional	Q.3.2 Low emotions	Q3.1 High emotions
Acceptance	13.4% 142	1.55 16	0.3% 3
Blame	9.8% 104	0.8% 8	0.2% 2
Fear	0.7% 7	2.4% 25	5.1% 54
Brace	5.2% 55	12.3% 131	6.4% 68
Total – Fate as fixed	29.0% 308	16.9% 180	12.0% 127
Negotiate	21.7% 230	21.0% 223	3.1% 33
Co-create	47.7% 507	60.9% 647	84.1% 893
Total – Fate as negotiable	69.4% 737	81.9% 870	87.2% 926

Figure 7: The percentage and raw numbers of astrologers' responses to Qs 2.4, 3.1, & 3.2, (n1062) to the questions concerning attitudes to and acceptance of fate over various non-emotional and emotional situations. Each column represents the answers to one question.

Fig.7 shows that, when asked about a possible predicted minor event (Q.2.4), 29% of astrologers selected a possible authoritarian response: they allocated blame to the planets, they feared the forthcoming event, or they submitted to it and braced for it, expecting the worst. However, when the same group was asked a similar question about a predicted event which had high emotional content (Q.3.1), this number more than halved, with only 12.0% accepting a possible authoritarian response. Hence, there was only minor support for Adorno's claims of submission to an external authority.

The other set of options, however, received the most significant support. These options were to negotiate with, that is, to view the forthcoming astrological event as an opportunity to engage with fate and seek to change its expression. For the non-emotional event, 69.4% selected these options, which shifted to 87.2% with the highly emotional event. Hence, the greater the concern of the astrologer regarding a future event, the greater their belief in being able to alter the outcome. This duplicated the same compatibility levels found in theories of fate table, Fig. 2.

These results echoed the philosophical arguments discussed in Chapter Five on moral responsibility and determinism. Briefly, Wolf surmised that the philosophical debates about determinism and free will were focused on a false dichotomy. She argued that the discussions needed to be focused on moral responsibility.[20] David Cockburn expanded Wolf's argument, suggesting that moral responsibility should be privileged in this dichotomy and that determinism had to fit into the gaps left by moral responsibility.[21] Additionally, in the field of experimental philosophy, Nichols found that lay-people's beliefs around the role of determinism in their lives varied depending on the moral content of the situation.[22] Later, Nichols and Knobe surveyed what they described as lay-people, or the philosophically naïve.[23] They found that lay-people's acceptance of the truth of determinism in their own lives was inversely proportional to the moral or emotional content of the situation. Nichols had also found that 46% of his philosophy students accepted that life was governed by determinism (hard incompatibilism). However, only 28% of those same students still maintained their hard incompatibilism in the face of the crime of murder.[24] Nichols and Knobe labelled this shifting view of the efficacy of determinism as 'folk intuition'.[25]

It was apparent from my research that the astrologers who completed my questionnaire were displaying Nichols' and Knobe's 'folk intuition'. For them, this involved negotiating with fate. Wolf's argument that moral responsibility takes precedence over determinism is reflected with the astrologers; fate in their life needs to fit into the gaps within their moral responsibility. Hence, these three diverse groups all share the same belief, which holds that 'what is meant to be' can be altered if it clashes with one's emotional well-being. These three groups are first, Nichols and Knobe's group of lay-people, second, Nichols' group of philosophy students, and now my group of astrologers.

In summary, my questionnaire was completed by 1,062 astrologers from 40 different countries, who were asked in various ways and through different vignettes about their views on fate. The key findings were that there was no single version of fate. A small number of astrologers were hard incompatibilists (Cicero's fate) as they believed in an inevitable fate. This number was consistent across the results, representing between 8%-11% of the astrologers. However, around 89%-92% of astrologers adopted a version of fate that produced a compatibilist position (negotiable fate). The actual nature of this negotiable fate varied. For about half of these astrologers, fate had a divine source, while for others, it resulted from living in a pattern. However, regardless of its source, this fate was not inevitable; instead, it was a hybrid fate. Part was inevitable (timing), but part was negotiable (events). Additionally, fate's influence was reduced, or rather, the astrologer deemed they had more control over the events as the possible emotional potential increased.

Finally, once a person engages with astrology, they stay with the subject, and the longer their involvement with it, the more their views and expectations of fate are shaped into a compatibilist mould. To understand this more fully, the voices of astrologers, their stories, hopes, fears and dreams are the topics of the following two chapters.

CHAPTER EIGHT

NOTES IN A BOTTLE

This chapter presents the notes the astrologers included when they completed the questionnaire. These non-structured, freely given thoughts on fate and astrology provided insights into the life of an astrologer. They offered what Clifford Geertz referred to as a 'thick description' to the questionnaire data.[1] 'Thick' data, according to Geertz, can disclose a deeper level of what it means to live within a particular culture, data that contains subtle nuances of phrases or snippets of conversations that accumulate and slowly reveal the nature of participation within a community. Geertz referred to these pieces of 'thick' data as 'notes in a bottle', a term that captures the random and unexpected nature of these notes' arrival onto the shores of my desk.[2] Each note was an isolated and self-contained 'note in a bottle', but slowly, they piled up on each other to form a picture of life within the community of astrologers.

These notes represented a different form of interview. They were free from the structure of an arranged interview and instead were unsolicited thoughts about the social world in which the astrologers lived. As Sarah Matthews commented, data collected with no questions and free from any influences represents the best chance to collect 'information that makes it possible to see the world through informants' eyes'.[3] The notes are unstructured and informal, and in that regard, they are a form of participant observation.[4] That is to engage an collect unstructured data, with the role of the 'observer' being filled by the questionnaire itself, as it offered a blank canvas on which the astrologers could then anonymously scribble their thoughts.

These messages covered a wide range of subjects, from personal stories to criticisms of the questionnaire's focus. They included poetry, worries, different spiritual views, different non-spiritual views, likes and dislikes of various forms of astrology, fatalism, comments on astrological techniques, views that expressed undiluted libertarianism, and others that expressed opinions of the dominance of God's providence. The notes were generally written using astrological jargon and terms, incorporating astrological shorthand, which reflects the colloquial language of one astrologer to another.

The discussion on these notes uses pseudonyms which reflect the astrologers' self-identified gender. Geertz commented that, with any ethnographic research into a community, 'The trick is to figure out what the devil they think they are up to'.[5] These 'notes in a bottle' offer an insight into what astrologers' 'think they are up to'. In total, 902 astrologers contributed a note, and the notes made up over 77,000 words of information.

Echoes of ancient theories of fate

Amongst the notes were various threads of different classical theories of fate. These notes offer concrete examples that illustrate how these ancient concepts remain relevant in contemporary astrological practices. The astrologers echoed these theories by demonstrating their understanding and interpretation of fate. They often emphasised specific points with words in capitals or italics, which are retained when quoting them.

Cicero's hard incompatibilism

Although, according to the questionnaire, only a small minority of astrologers adopted Cicero's mechanical-like view of fate, some of these messages in a bottle captured fate as hard incompatibilism. From the US, 'Megan' was a sixty-four-year-old woman who had studied astrology for the last thirty years. She described astrology thus:

> It is like an equation in calculus. It does nothing, but "DESCRIBE" the past, present and future. Just as algebra works so beautifully — so does the astrology that I practice.[6]

She had faith that astrology would give her clear exoteric information about her daily life, saying that it allowed her to feel confident in believing people when they say that 'the check is REALLY in the mail'. She also used it to make judgments of her relationship to others: 'I also like the fact, I can avoid people that have really negative aspects to my own chart'. Megan did not see astrology as an expression of the divine in her life, and this was repeated in her questionnaire responses as she denied the existence of soul or divinity of any description. Indeed, what she disliked in astrology were 'the crazy religious nutters in some groups…' Additionally, she disliked the contemporary practice of medieval astrology, saying of astrological authors who use medieval astrology that, 'They have castrated a very complex linguistic system since he [she names a well-known astrologer] started learning medieval astrology'. Megan saw herself as a modern astrologer, defining the concept of modernity through the diverse array of astrological techniques she employed. However, she appeared to lack ways of accommodating fate, which implied she adopted a hard incompatibilism position. In her questionnaire responses, she showed that she dealt with the varying emotional situations of life by 'bracing' for the forthcoming events, considering herself powerless before them.

Also adopting a version of fate that seemed to be consistent with hard incompatibilism was 'Michael', a forty-five-year-old American male who had worked with astrology for ten years. He talked of his thoughts on the role of fate in his life:

> I am completely deterministic in my outlook because after watching myself and others for the last 10 years I can't find anything or anyone whose actions are not completely determined by their natal chart. ... Others may reach other conclusions, but for myself, the universe is nothing more than a series of wheels spinning out series of unchanging fated events.[7]

Michael's focus was on financial astrology. In his questionnaire responses, he indicated that the source of fate was God's plan, and he felt that the purpose of life was to embrace this, accepting it unquestioningly. Astrology produced an inevitable future for him; his drive was to use it to seek consistent and reliable predictions.

Although fate, which for him was derived from God's will, was directed solely at human endeavours, for he did not accept that it also applied to other life forms, such as his pets. Michael's attitude was one of acceptance of the inevitability of the life planned for him by God. He wrote, 'I am a curious person and astrology lets me understand things like why evil occurs. I worry less'. Given his interest in financial astrology, he sought to profit from his knowledge of these mechanical 'spinning' wheels. His preferred astrological authors were classical and medieval astrologers, such as the Roman Julius Firmicus Maternus (c. 330), the Persian astrologer and astronomer Abū Ma'shar (787–886), and the contemporary medieval astrologer Robert Zoller. These astrologers did not promote the natural hard incompatibilism of Michael's astrology, but they did seek to make predictions about the external world.

Michael did not accept the psychological developments in astrology of the second half of the twentieth century and wrote, 'I think most psychological astrologers delude themselves in thinking that clients evolve'. With his strong monotheism, selecting the questionnaire option of 'strongly agreed' to all questions about the efficacy of God's will, along with his reference to 'evil' in the world, his astrology appeared to be driven by Augustinian theology. For Michael, his horoscope showed God's will at work in his life.

Both Megan and Michael believe in the horoscope's inevitability but support very different theories of fate. Megan saw fate as the expression of the algebra of a cosmic order. She spoke as an astrologer who disliked the association of spirituality with astrology and the modern use of medieval astrology, seeing both as a blight on her idea of a non-divine, rational approach. In contrast, Michael was deeply religious. For him, fate was an expression of God's will, and he embraced the ways of medieval astrology to help him understand God's plan for his life. He considered the modern notion of psychological astrology as 'delusional'.

These two astrologers represent the 8% to 11% of astrologers who accept a version of fate as described by Cicero, equivalent to hard incompatibilism. The comments by Megan and Michael revealed a diversity of thoughts on fate. Both viewed fate as inevitable, but Megan lived in a 'beautiful algebra' run by a set of undefined natural laws, while Michael lived within God's plan, and his astrology was his way of understanding that plan.

Plato and the freedom of the soul

Another classical position represented in the 'notes in a bottle' was the dualist theory of fate implied by Plato. He taught that the more one reached for a divine spark and drew closer to the divine, the freer one became of the necessity produced by the planets.[8] This view was promoted by the astrologer Alan Leo (1860–1917). According to both Campion and Curry, Leo was the most influential astrologer of the early twentieth century.[9] Curry added that, 'Modern astrology is difficult to imagine without his intervention'.[10] His teaching had a long reach into twentieth century Western astrology, and he viewed the soul as being entangled with the fate of matter:

> …the spirit and the body (or 'matter'), man's soul is at some times bound, at others free — never wholly free, nor wholly bound, but linked to both states of existence by subtle bonds and thus ever harnessed to the Circle or 'Wheel' of Necessity.[11]

Leo mirrored Platonist concepts by writing: '…Man is a spirit, or to speak more correctly a SOUL, with a body. His "spirit" [which he also defined as character] is free, immortal, undying and permanent, but his soul is imprisoned in the "matter", or bodies, through which it manifests on the lower planes'.[12] He then placed the moral responsibility of one's life in one's own hands by teaching that one's past lives produce the quality of the current life, and that past lives were reflected in the horoscope:

> The horoscope of any man is the outcome of his thoughts, desires and motives in previous lives. These have materialised into a web or garment, as it were, in which the soul is clothed; and this constitutes his 'karma, fate or Destiny'.[13]

Thus, where Plato believed that the soul could have some choice in its future life, Leo saw the future life as a necessary expression of one's past. The horoscope became the vehicle that revealed not only the soul's spiritual journey in its desire to refine itself through the journey of many lifetimes but also the nature of the soul's fate in its current life. Adding to this, Leo taught that one needed to rise above one's fate and thus the effectiveness of the horoscope to foretell exoteric events was, he considered, the sign of a weak-willed soul. Leo saw this as the plight of many people for he wrote, '…many cases are found in which an unprogressive soul sticks in the rut of the radical [birth] horoscope…'[14], suggesting that many people failed to commit to the soul's spiritual journey which freed them in this life from the full influence of the fate of matter.

A note from 'Rachel' contained this life philosophy. She was a forty-six-year-old English woman who was involved with astrology for twenty-three years. Fate, for her, was produced by the law of karma, the actions of her immortal soul in her previous lives, and the purpose of this life was, as Plato pointed out, to improve the soul and help it in its journey back to the divine.[15] She mirrored Alan Leo's views when she commented:

> Yes, my experience is that the more spiritually evolved/conscious a person is the less likely it is their life can be predicted. In any case I don't think it's possible to predict actual events in someone's life, although you can make estimated guesses, just the quality of experience of events.[16]

Similarly, a female South African astrologer echoed Leo's Platonism when she commented that,

> I see our ultimate soul purpose as seeking a return to the wholeness (purity) of the divine circle (God); to me our natal astrology chart represents the point where our soul is on that evolutionary journey back to God.[17]

Another South African woman working with astrology for forty years summed up Alan Leo's argument by stating, 'Your horoscope is your fate ONLY if you don't use your free will to guide your own life'.[18] These astrologers were using astrology to reach for freedom from fate. This was freedom that their actions could achieve, and for them, their astrology provided the tools to help them achieve this goal. Their life philosophy could be described as 'user-actioned libertarianism'.

Stoicism and Spinozian thinking – fate and acceptance

In the first century, the astrologer Claudius Ptolemy argued for the value of knowing the future. He suggested that the purpose of astrology was to gain knowledge of the future to enable mental preparation for maintaining a more harmonious disposition through life, rather than to lead one into futilism, the belief that human efforts are ultimately pointless. He wrote of this in his defence of astrology:

> ... if, however, such events should have been foreknown, the mind will have been previously prepared for their reception, and will preserve an equable calmness, by having been accustomed to contemplate the approaching event as though it were present, so that, on its actual arrival, it will be sustained with tranquillity and constancy.[19]

Ptolemy's words were reflected in the note from 'Jane', a fifty-one-year-old US woman who has been working with astrology for ten years. She discussed her resignation as an inevitable part of her future and her struggle with what she perceived as her 'fate'. Unlike Michael, who accepted his fate as God's will, and Megan, who considered it a beautiful algebra but braced for any difficulties, Jane took a Stoic position. She followed Ptolemy's advice, finding comfort in its acceptance:

> Yes. I would like to change events that you know are coming... but you really can't. And I knew that terrible things were coming for me in the past few years, and I tried to use the energies in positive ways, but in the end, it was just as bad as I thought. The difference however was that by expecting troubles, I was able to reserve more patience and understanding and not resort to anger, and limit my frustration. Maybe that in itself was 'easier', BUT I now believe there is NO escaping your chart, just enduring and preparing and learning to take the high road.[20]

According to her questionnaire responses, Jane accepted that she lived in a sympathetic cosmos where she sought harmony. In this view of the cosmos,

Jane acknowledged the importance of patterns and recognised that all life was intricately involved in the patterns of the cosmos. She did not believe in God, or even in gods, and was neutral on matters concerning the existence of the human soul; however, she did believe in the importance of attaining harmony with the cosmos. Indeed, Jane continued to talk of her own impending death:

> It [astrology] has given me a comfort of dying and moving on, not that I want to. I was not sure about fate or total free choice/blank slate theories, but now I believe that astrology is fate based, and to me the lesson is about how you handle the difficult patches that are coming whether you like it or not, with grace and humility and patience, not becoming bitter and resentful and bringing that energy forward. My chart has been horrible for the past seven years and I only have 6-8 months or so left, so I've given this thought.

Jane's words were reminiscent of those of the Stoic philosopher Epictetus cited earlier, who wrote, 'I must die. But must I die groaning? I must be imprisoned. But must I whine as well? I must suffer exile. Can anyone then hinder me from going with a smile, and good courage, and at peace?'[21]

There was also the Spinozian philosophical theme of knowing the self through detachment. Spinoza had argued that a method of gaining a concept of oneself was to use a form of detachment, which could facilitate a deeper understanding of oneself and allow a person to accept their situation.[22] Many of the notes from astrologers described how astrology provided them with a sense of self, remarking on the way it allowed them to understand their history with detachment while at the same time giving them greater compassion towards those around them. Indeed, this was one of the major themes of the notes, with over 25% of the astrologers referring to this feature of astrology.

According to Hazel Markus and Shinobu Kitayama, the Western view of self is as an '...independent, self-contained, autonomous entity who (a) comprises a unique configuration of internal attributes... and (b) behaves primarily as a consequence of these internal attributes'.[23] For astrologers, some of their attributes of self consist of their uniquely personal combination of zodiac signs, planets, aspects, and so forth, which make up their horoscope. These celestial attributes, allocated at birth, injected a form of fate into the astrologer's view of themselves. However, the same instrument that placed fate in their life also placed uniqueness, as no two horoscopes were the same. This uniqueness was a key part of what Giddens considered essential for an individual to understand themselves in 'terms of her or his biography...[and]... across time and space...'

and that the individual needed to have a concept of themselves as well as of others.²⁴ For many astrologers, their horoscope reinforced this notion and provided them with a distinct sense of self that fosters a Spinozian detachment, highlighting their uniqueness while simultaneously connecting them to the cosmos.

Sophie, a thirty-eight-year-old American astrologer who has been working with astrology for seven years, commented on what it was like if one accepted fate, which she called determinism, through the detached vehicle of the horoscope. She wrote:

> [It] helps you and the client to accept your life for what it is – determinism can be a fairly optimistic outlook or at least one that does not blame the subject for the bad things that happen. I think free will plays a somewhat limited role in what happens to us. You work as much as you can or make the effort that you are satisfied with, and you will still fulfil a pre-destined framework to a large degree. There can be a lot of acceptance and compassion built into this outlook. You stop judging others as severely (they are dealing with limitations that won't change significantly despite awareness and efforts to change in some cases). You also stop judging yourself as severely for the same reasons. You do whatever you define as 'your best' and try to accept predestined limitations that same way.²⁵

'Emily', a fifty-nine-year-old British woman who had been working with astrology for twenty years, captured both Giddens' idea of a personal biography and the Spinozian concept of detachment, when she wrote,

> What I love about astrology is its ability to show me that life is a journey not just a destination. As a developmental tool it gives meaning to life. It gives me insights, tolerance and understanding into my own predispositions and behaviours and those of others.²⁶

Emily's astrology was secular, and she held a life philosophy that enabled her to see '...that the bad times won't last forever and the ability to make "lemonade out of lemons" and to make the most of the good times when they are here'. Similarly, another British woman who had practised astrology for over forty years commented that,

> Astrology has given me confidence to be who I am, and accept myself. It guides me through life, with the transits and gives purpose to my journey. I have more compassion and understanding of others, and am less judgemental because of astrology.[27]

From the US, a forty-year-old male astrologer wrote of astrology, 'It is a wonderful tool to assist you in gathering more information about who you are and why you may tend to behave in the manner in which you do. As such, it offers a means to make you a better, more actualised person'.[28] A forty-year-old Australian woman who has been doing astrology for eight years writes, 'It has allowed me to see other people as different from me, with different ways of thinking and being'.[29]

For these respondents, their horoscope provided them with their concept of 'self' as described by Giddens, a concept of the 'self' as a unique being in relationship to a larger whole. In this way, they used their horoscope as a Spinozian instrument of detachment to enable them to be more accepting of life events.

These themes were summed up by 'Paul', an American astrologer in his early thirties who had been studying astrology for nine years. He appeared to be deeply embedded in Stoic themes as well as Spinoza's detachment when he wrote of what astrology added to his life:

> The sense of connectedness primarily, the depth and fullness of a meaningful religious (spiritual) connection. An ability to see the challenging and invigorating parts of my life from a larger perspective and the ability to experience meaning beyond the secular experience. Also the realisation that extremely personal aspects are able to be understood by virtue of their being parts of larger historic and collective patterns experienced by others in different but related ways.[30]

Other astrologers reflected Paul's Stoic and Spinoza-like comments. The order of the cosmos which placed fate into their lives, also gave them a sense of belonging to a rational, ordered world. A fifty-eight-year-old Canadian man wrote that astrology provided the '…capacity to illuminate human behaviour within the context of a larger natural order'.[31] A forty-seven-year-old American woman, who had been working with astrology for twenty years, wrote that this order transcended any of her other beliefs:

> It gives me a deep, peaceful sense of order in a world that often seems chaotic. It anchors me. It is the one thing I always fall back on when things are tough in my life. Religious and spiritual beliefs have changed throughout my life, but never my connection with astrology. It meets all challenges and I always come out a winner.[32]

One astrologer from the US focused on this notion of detachment that the horoscope provided and stated that it enabled her to deal with her life:

> I like the idea that astrology allows me to dissociate from the events and feelings that I am experiencing - and see them from a broader - more cosmic perspective. It allows me to let go of the past, and prepare myself more fully for the future.[33]

Many astrologers repeated this theme. 'John', a thirty-one-year-old astrologer from the US who had only been studying astrology for five years, wrote that what he liked about astrology was the Stoic approach to his life that it offered him:

> The mental preparation it gives me; even when I'm on the lookout for the expression of an upcoming transit, I sometimes don't see the event as that expression until it has passed. Even so, acceptance comes so much more easily; Acceptance of my level (without judgment) of awareness with that particular part of life.[34]

These notes reveal how many astrologers sought personal definitions for themselves or their clients. In this pursuit, they naturally turned to Giddens' concept of the self, a self which is viewed as both unique and in relation to others. They utilised the Spinozian/Stoic concept of detachment as provided by the horoscope, to help them gain a personal perspective, and used the horoscope's fate to reinforce their unique membership in a sympathetic cosmos.

Stoic time and cycles

As shown from the questionnaire results, the astrologers linked fate to time. The Stoic view of time was that it was closed. The Christian philosopher Nemesius (c. 390) wrote of Stoic time as follows, '... when the stars are moving again in the same way, each thing which occurred in the previous period will come to pass... The periodic return of everything occurs not once but many times'.[35] This concept of repeating time exists within astrology, but it is based on the cycles of the planets rather than the Stoic notion of the great cycle of conflagrations.

Dane Rudhyar, born Danel Chennevière (1895–1985) in Paris, wrote of astrological fate based in emerging cycles. Rudhyar produced a considerable body of astrological work between 1936 and the early 1980s; most of it is still in print today. Campion cited him as the most influential American astrologer of the twentieth century.[36] The astrology of Rudhyar and Alan Leo helped Theosophy's Platonist esotericism move into astrological literature. Rudhyar, however, added more than Platonism to astrology. He developed the idea that fate was linked to emerging cycles.

Cycles, by definition, are repeated times, such as the 24 hours of a day. The philosophy of Stoicism developed the notion that great cycles were linked to inevitable events. This was the Stoic concept of closed time, where the great cycle of the conflagration produced inevitability.[37] Friedrich Nietzsche (1844–1900) also linked time to events, creating an inevitability that he defined as the eternal recurrence of the same events.[38] Rudhyar, however, focused on the cyclic nature of astrology and its association with planetary cycles and separated these from closed time by coining the term 'spiral time'. Rudhyar suggested that these cycles, whether astrological or not, were emergent, with each new cycle being influenced by the last.[39] In this way, Rudhyar voiced the difference between the astrological use of planetary cycles and the closed time of Stoic philosophy or Nietzsche's eternal recurrence.

Due to his popularity, Rudhyar implanted the concept of emerging cycles into twentieth-century astrology, drawing, perhaps intentionally, on Whitehead's emergent philosophy. Rudhyar combined the idea of emergence through cycles, where individuals could use their knowledge of cycles to strive for personal wholeness. This approach stressed the individual's autonomy as they were engaged in self-creation. As Deniz Ertan stated, Rudhyar used astrology to redefine the notion of 'self'.[40] Rudhyar taught that this view of 'self' was reflected in the horoscope as a unique seed.[41] Leo promoted the horoscope as representing the world of fated matter, which needed to be resisted in a Platonist-like manner. In contrast, Rudhyar presented the horoscope as a profoundly personal, sacred object—a view of the ideal self to be embraced rather than avoided.

A thirty-nine-year-old American woman captured Rudhyar's views on the ideal form of 'self' wrote,

> I love the free will that astrology provides. The chart provides you with possibilities; it's up to you to recognise and take advantage of them. Your chart is a fail-proof tool for living up to your full potential — not a map to your destiny.[42]

A forty-four-year-old Australian woman, who took up astrology in 1992, wrote of one of the most important concepts that astrology had given her: 'It taught me about cycles, hard times do pass as do happy ones. It gives us the opportunity to make the most/best of any situation'.[43] A forty-two-year-old Norwegian woman who has been doing astrology for twelve years wrote, 'When life is difficult, astrology gives it meaning and hope, even in the darkest hours. You know that soon this too will pass'.[44] Another example came from 'Nancy', a fifty-nine-year-old woman from the US who became involved with astrology in the mid-1970s. Drawing on her thirty-four years of living an astrological life, she offered this comment about one of the ways that she used astrology:

> The cyclical quality that it presents to us. If you live long enough, you see those cycles coming back. If you've learned anything at all, then when the tough ones come back, you handle them better and when the great ones come back, you appreciate them more.[45]

Her responses in her questionnaire showed she embraced fate, which, for her, had its source in God's will and her soul's relationship to that will. For her, astrology was a way of life, giving meaning to her life's ups and downs.

'Grace', a sixty-seven-year-old British woman who has been involved with astrology for thirty-four years, described a participation-emergentism theory of fate which drew together acceptance, emergent cycles, and order:

> I believe there is an order in the cosmos, unfolding in time cycles that are predetermined. But the universe is also in a state of flux, a continuous state of becoming. So the future is also open-ended. Our fate is limited by its patterning, but as we participate in the universe's creative consciousness, so we can also be inventive and transform. Thus on one level we have free will, and on a deeper level we don't, and on one level we are governed by cosmic laws, and on another the human spirit is free.[46]

Grace's theory of fate embraced both the idea of cycles and an emergent cosmos. For her, as in Stoic philosophy, God emerged in the on-going act of creation, evolving via union with all of life and matter.[47] Her notion of free will enabled her to be inventive in the expression of future patterns.

The astrologers also discussed how they create personalised, fate-filled calendars. Such calendars, Giddens argued, were a feature of creating a lifestyle which contains a life plan, and he talked of this plan as:

...the reflexively organised trajectory of the self... Life-planning is a means of preparing a course of future actions mobilised in terms of the self's biography. We may also speak here of the existence of personal calendars or life-plan calendars, in relation to which the personal time of the lifespan is handled.[48]

Many notes wrote of using the horoscope to plan the life through the timing of future events. An American astrologer summed this up as,

It [astrology] gives me the ability to see how things work together and why, as well as the opportunity to plan ahead to make the best use of whatever transits are available at any given time.[49]

A forty-two-year-old Australian astrologer wrote of what he gained from astrology by stating that it is its 'ability to see timing which few other systems can do well'.[50] Locating oneself in time and space was also the focus of 'Molly's' comments. A sixty-two-year-old American astrologer of some forty years' experience, she wrote that astrology provided a map of where she was in her life:

It's one of the mathematical systems of the universe and simply tells you where you are in time and space and what is likely to happen and how you are likely to deal with the situations in your life. I believe everything is there in the map [horoscope] and mistakes are made not because the information isn't there but because, like a doctor, we don't always understand what we are seeing.[51]

Molly used Ptolemy's argument that any errors in reading the horoscope were due to lack of knowledge by the astrologer, not the lack of efficacy of the horoscope. Ptolemy wrote of the astrologer that, 'although he may have attained to the greatest possible accuracy in the science, must still be liable to frequent error, arising out of the very nature of his undertaking, and from the weakness of his limited capacity in comparison with the magnitude of his object'.[52] Molly's note, with her paraphrasing of Ptolemy's words, was an example of the 'traditions' of astrological belief, which date back to the first century.

All of these astrologers held a compatibilist attitude to fate and free will. Neither fate nor free will excluded the other. Instead, for many of the astrologers, fate provided their own private calendar of life, their personal story that they believed gave them an overview and allowed for a more effective use of their free will.

Calcidius's theory of fate

In the fourth century, Calcidius postulated fate as a cosmic force and the consequences of one's actions. He wrote:

> Now the preceding merit [fate] which can take one of two directions is caused by a motion of our mind and a judgment and an agreement and desire or avoidance, things put within our power, because these things as well as their contraries are for us to choose. So in this ordinance of things and according to a most ancient law some things are said to result from a preceding decision and are in our power; what comes after them, however, is the result, bound by necessity.[53]

A female Australian astrologer reflected Calcidius arguments. She had been studying astrology for twelve years and wrote, 'The answer to the argument of Fate versus Freewill lies in a view that it is not one or the other, but rather it is both together. Our fate creates the opportunity to use our freewill which in turn creates our fate'.[54] A female lecturer in classics from the US, almost paraphrasing Calcidius, wrote, 'Your "fate" is what happens to you when you exercise your free will'.[55] A fifty-three-year-old British woman, an astrologer of twenty years, wrote a note that was musing over these points,

> I do believe that some things are fated and beyond my control. ...I don't know how one would reconcile it but I do believe in the chart's potential and us creating our own fate, so to speak, together with a belief that some things are fated. I have seen both these things happening in my own life.[56]

According to Calcidius, and for these astrologers, one's actions are descriptive of one's fate and, thus, a description of oneself. Arguing within philosophy about the nature of free will, J. Lucas noted that such a view of free will was also part of the contemporary notion of self-agency and central to beliefs about free will.[57] Additionally, Wolf, in her discussions on free will, wrote of being an 'autonomous agent' which enabled a unique view of the world, reinforcing moral responsibility.[58] These astrologers, reflecting Wolf's arguments, are examples of those who took responsibility for their fate, seeing it, as argued by Calcidius, as linked in some way to their actions.

Fate as an illusion

In contrast to the above were a few astrologers who were libertarians. 'James' is a thirty-seven-year-old man from Ireland who has been working with astrology for fifteen years.[59] He commented that, '…astrology is a thing unto itself that is largely a human imaginal process using the heavens as a guide to chart and map the human condition using cycles, mythology and archetypal patterns to elucidate meaning. …'

For James, astrology was about patterns and was concerned not with certainty but with relationships. He defined himself as a psychological and humanistic astrologer, indicating that he was more concerned with the world of the human mind than the exoteric world of events. James' astrology was secular; he stated that he, 'no longer believes in god as a figure…' and feels that astrology does not require a divine cosmos:

> [I do not] believe that to believe in something [divine] is required of astrologers. Astrology reflects the human experience and the rhythmic unfoldment of life, of which there is an intrinsic fate (whether chosen or random) — the fate of the initial conditions of life.

Thus, for James, fate is nothing more than being born into a material life, and the consequences of that materialism. Astrology could be used as an imaginal tool, to help understand the complexities of this life. James indicated that he had read Rudhyar and Leo, and although not following their Platonist dualist arguments requiring free will to be located in the human soul, he appeared to adopt a Cartesian view that one's free will was totally separated from the influence of fate. James seemed to be that other form of incompatibilist, the libertarian. For him astrology was simply a tool that could help with the personal mystery of life.

Similarly, 'Betty', a fifty-six-year-old Canadian woman who was a professional astrologer who saw clients and had been involved with astrology for thirty-eight years, also adopted a natural libertarianism. In her questionnaire responses she 'strongly agreed' that fate is only a human illusion. For her, astrology was:

> [An] …archetypal language …Although there are other symbolic languages, astrology is one that can be viewed from both a 'fixed' and 'relative' perspective, due to its mathematical nature and its adaptability to the reader's viewpoint and belief system.[60]

For Betty, astrology was a way of gaining a perspective on life. As such, in her questionnaire responses, she 'strongly disagreed' with any suggestion that the future was inevitable and even rejected one of the almost universal tenets of astrology: its ability to give the timing of events, if not the event itself. Betty considered astrology to be a 'neutral medium' that can facilitate an externalisation of issues, like a blank screen that the astrologer can paint upon. She saw its true value in its ability to have 'the power of suggestion', which professional astrologers should use to help their clients. Within her own spiritual beliefs, she revealed a Thomist or Cartesian philosophy as she saw the human soul as an independent entity, untouched by the fate or determinism of the material life. However, according to her replies to the questionnaire, she did not extend her spiritual views to her astrology, seeing it as a neutral secular medium.

From the entire matrix of the theories of fate discussed in the last chapter, only 37 astrologers (3.5%) held similar views to James and Betty, that fate was an illusion and the purpose of astrology was to provide comfort or to help find harmony in life. On the bell curve of beliefs about fate, these astrologers represented the other extreme to Michael and Megan cited at the beginning of this chapter.

Living as an astrologer in a sympathetic cosmos

Among the notes were also insights into the daily life of the astrologers. These comments were not concerned with their philosophy, but with what they do daily with their astrology. From the US, 'Lucy', a forty-eight-year-old who has been involved with astrology for ten years, wrote:

> Just because something is in the stars, free will can change the outcome. An example is Mercury retro[grade], during the transit I pay close attention to my car, computer, finances, relationships, not sign any contracts etc... [these are objects ruled by Mercury] I also maintain a very positive attitude during the transit, because how I perceive the transit (gloom & doom versus time to revisit and learn) has a tremendous effect on my experiences during that time. I don't boldly challenge the retrograde, I honor Mercury with respect, so my lessons are easier.[61]

Lucy's note revealed a common practice of astrologers. At times when it is believed that a planet is dominating one's daily activity, in this instance when Mercury appears to move backwards through the heavens, Lucy felt that by focusing on those areas of her life that she considered linked to that planet and paying attention to them—she called this honouring the planet—then she can influence the external events which happen around her. This idea echoes the work of C.C. Zain, born Benjamin P. Williams (1882–1951) in Iowa, US. A naturalist and a spiritualist, he became a prolific US astrological author. In 1932, he founded the Church of Light in Los Angeles, which promoted astrology as a cosmic religion, the 'Religion of the Stars', and claimed that 'True Religion and True Science are One'.[62] He promoted the idea of a *Law of Affinity*, where he believed that by maintaining harmony with the planets, one could change the external events that are 'attracted' to one's life. In 1922 he wrote:

> Man cannot more prevent these periods of planetary harmony or those of planetary discord that enter his life than he can prevent sunshine or rain. But as their effect upon him is determined by his mental response to their influence, he may determine what events and conditions they will bring into his life... For he may cultivate thoughts and emotions that will ...attract events such as would be expected from the actual corresponding planetary relations.[63]

Zain's *Law of Affinity*, although offering a version of fate that one could control with one's mental outlook, at times produced a more worrying perspective. 'Margaret', a thirty-four-year-old British astrologer who had worked with astrology for ten years, stated that she was filled with apprehension in how she lived with astrology, as she did not find any solace in its future messages. She wrote:

> I struggle with the whole fate aspect. I don't like the way that working with future planetary transits and progressions [predictive astrology techniques] you can see tough times ahead, and this makes you 'dread' them, you then start looking at difficulties and negativity — does this mean you create it as you expect it?? I have a [transiting] Pluto conj [my natal] Moon coming in a year or so — and although I have heard all the positive manifestations of this — I have also been (at lectures / classes etc) told how awful it can be. To be honest this has made me wary of astrology — which has made me question it. Having said that even when I have a break for a while from working with it and checking my ephemeris [table of planetary movements] — when I have had a rough time and I do look what's been happening I ALWAYS find its reflected in the astrology!! So am I kidding myself that there's any way of avoiding the events /energies? And should I at least go

in to them with awareness? But if so how do I avoid going into it loading my belief with negativity? I am struggling with these questions massively right now.[64]

There is much in this story of doubt and fear. Margaret was using her astrology to look ahead, much like Giddens' argument about lifestyle and the production of personal calendars, but what she saw worried her. Without any apparent surrounding philosophy to inform her knowledge of astrology, such as the dualism of Rudhyar's humanism or finding comfort through Ptolemy's Stoicism, her knowledge of the future did not give her control, facilitate harmony, or enable her to understand her personal journey, but instead produced apprehension. As C.C. Zain had written, she was concerned about the power of her own thoughts to influence the future, but did not take the mental step to understand that this implied the future was not fixed. She tried to step back from astrology, but in times of difficulty, she returned to the mechanical order of the ephemeris and, almost as a self-fulfilling prophecy, found confirmation of the validity of the subject.

Another personal story also captured this doubt and confusion. 'Olivia', like Margaret, is a thirty-four-year-old British astrologer who has been studying astrology for four years. Her story is similar to Margaret's but seems to have moved one small step closer to a personal theory of fate:

Paradoxically, I dislike the fact that astrology seems so accurate, every time I look in the paper there are often deaths or incidents happening to or around people in their first or second Saturn return years, for example. Seeing these things and the patterns at work takes away the feeling of having some control over your life, that 'ignorance is bliss' feeling. Instead, I sometimes feel that we are all interconnected and my fate is not just a matter of cause and effect — the consequences of choices that I make, but I see that it is interlinked with my children and their developmental needs — and the same with my father. He died when Saturn transited my [natal] sun (immediately after my Saturn return), and that had a huge effect of change upon me and my siblings and our relationship with each other. So, it left me thinking, 'would he have died if Saturn wasn't transiting my Sun?' I saw him out of the blue on the day he died, I was the last to speak with him on the phone — an hour before he killed himself. It raises a lot of questions for me that I wish I didn't have to consider. You can't un-know what you come to know from learning astrology.[65]

Olivia was struggling with her perception of the fate of astrology. She had accepted it, but it clashed with her culture's beliefs about the inherent free will of the individual. Like Margaret, she floundered in a sea of doubt and confusion. This doubt and confusion resulted from the synchronicity of the movement of the planet Saturn over the zodiacal location of her natal Sun, both this luminary and planet in astrology are symbolic of the father. [66] This celestial/horoscopic event occured at the time when 'out of the blue' she encountered her father only an hour before his suicide. An occurrence that produced for her an astrological epiphany. This epiphany was located outside her established belief systems. Olivia was left to either abandon the implications of this epiphany or abandon her previous worldview. Her narrative captured the moment of the making of an astrologer; if she stepped into the new landscape of a sympathetic cosmology that supported the epiphany, she would most likely never return to her old way of seeing the world.

Olivia's story may offer a clue as to why astrologers tend to stay in the subject, as revealed by the questionnaire in the previous chapter. The adoption of astrology into one's life requires a shift in one's thinking about the nature of the universe, a shift that alters one's expectations of the world, and once having made that shift, it places the astrologer in a different 'landscape', one that appeared for them to offer greater meaning or understanding of life, and thus many are reluctant to let that go.

Finally, to complete this analysis of the 'thick' data, which, in its diversity and density, exposed facets of how astrologers think and live with fate, was a note from a fifty-six-year-old Canadian astrologer who has been practising for twenty-five years. Her note embraced the vast majority of opinions:

> So here's what I think about fate, just so you're clear: I believe the course of our lives is largely, and possibly entirely, predetermined from the moment we're born. I'm not sure to what extent we have free choice in small events, but certainly in large ones I think we have none. Though I believe in reincarnation, I have no idea if the soul chooses the moment it is born, or what kind of life it will take on in a particular incarnation. I do feel the following is an appropriate metaphor for how astrology works: 'We cannot direct the wind, but we can adjust our sails.' i.e., we have no control over what events happen to us, but we have some control over HOW we respond in any given situation – I think![67]

In summary, these 'notes in a bottle' revealed a personal or intimate view from inside the astrological community. They exposed thinking that many critics of astrology could attack; yet, the candid nature of these notes paints an image of a community that is actively concerned with the problems of free will and fate in relation to their own lives. Their thoughts lack a philosophical language structure and are wrapped in personal doubts and worries. However, the very fate that was the cause of their doubts also provided their sense of self and their personal calendars, giving meaning to their lives by offering them membership in a sympathetic cosmos.

CHAPTER NINE

CONVERSATIONS ABOUT FATE

The questionnaire and the 'notes in a bottle' give an insight into the nature of fate from the grass-roots level of the astrological community. The resulting depiction of fate is both classical and varied. To further explore these perspectives, I conducted interviews with a group of astrologers involved in consulting, lecturing, writing, and teaching. Most of the astrologers interviewed held undergraduate degrees, with many also holding a Master's degree. Three held PhDs. These tertiary qualifications included classics, medieval studies, ancient languages, Romance languages, music, psychology, English literature, drama, economics, archaeology, history, philosophy, and cultural studies. All of them were published authors.

Each interview became a unique conversation, focusing on the astrologer's views on fate, how they incorporated these views into their lifestyle, and how this perspective influenced them. This material explores the lived experience of fate through the unique perspectives of individuals who have dedicated their professional lives to working with fate. Common themes emerged, many of which were those expressed by the grass-roots astrologers.

Fate as the order of the world

In the *Timaeus* Plato postulated that the cosmos was governed by the World Soul, whose essence was reason.[1] In the third century, Diogenes wrote of the Stoic cosmos as alive and rational and, in the fourth century, Calcidius argued, 'So the World-Soul is fate as a substance'.[2] The classical view of the cosmos was that it was a rationally formed and sympathetic entity. According to Plato, divine reason permeated the cosmos and produced its sympathetic nature. Aristotle considered it bound by divine love, while the Stoics thought that the need for the co-creation of the divine bound all things together in a sympathetic web through the workings of fate.[3] Regardless of the nature of the binding force of the cosmos, in the third century, Plotinus argued that the entire cosmos was enchained in a sympathetic web.[4] Astrologers have not abandoned these classical arguments. Self-evident in the 'notes in a bottle' presented earlier was the theme of living in a purposeful cosmos. This was also reflected in the views of the professional astrologers.

I interviewed the American Hellenistic astrologer Demetra George in August 2009. Hellenistic astrology is the contemporary interpretation and practice of the astrology that developed in the Mediterranean region roughly between the third century BCE and the seventh century CE. George captured the fundamental theme of a sympathetic cosmos in present-day astrology when she replied to my question on the nature of fate and astrology as follows:

> Well, one of the things that I consider is that astrology can only work in a model where there is soul, intelligence, and conscience in the cosmos. If our worldview is that we live in a random, chaotic, dead world, then there is no way that astrology can make any sense whatsoever.

George's 'dead world' was a world of passive matter that was not sympathetically linked in a chain of being. Ben Dykes, the classics scholar and self-professed Stoic-oriented astrologer, also from the US, embraced this theme of a living cosmos and spoke of fate as order, an order that was immanent within the universe. He mused on this when considering the origins of fate as follows:

> Um.. I guess.. err.. where does fate itself come from? ...My guess, it's from the way that the cosmic reason operates. ...In reality, where did we come up with the idea... um... I am sure it was people reflecting on cosmic processes.

I asked Dykes if this imposed immanent order was, for him, like the operating system on a computer in that it was something that was in the background but laid down all the rules on how the system worked. He laughed and replied:

> I never heard it said like that... but yes it is the immanent way in which the universe operates even if there are levels of reality in which there are some Platonic forms that sort of guide the being.

Liz Greene, a British Jungian psychologist and psychological astrologer, acknowledged determinism but, like the other astrologers I interviewed, saw fate itself as something more organic than a purely deterministic concept. Psychological astrology integrates concepts from psychology, particularly those related to personality, behaviour, and emotional dynamics. The work of Carl Jung and other depth psychologists has influenced the practice and goals of this astrology. In January 2010, Greene spoke of her view of fate, reflecting her psychological approach:

> What happens is you get a sort of alchemical mix, there is the individual's temperament, there are psychological inheritances, family complexes, physiological inheritance, environment, choices the parents make at any given time, choices the individual makes…

And then to this mix of determinism, she added another level of order, that of emergentism, and patterns:

> …I think there are patterns that operate on levels that are not explainable. Jung calls them archetypes, they are also the form of myths. But they are in the fabric of life, they are the stuff of life, they are alive, they are here, they are everywhere. We are not… it is not that we go and grab a handful of the pattern, we are part of the pattern. Every person is part of it. So those patterns do not have a logical cause. And they are becoming 'creativity' through some kind of process of livingness that is intelligent but which I don't think is sort of up there someone looking down. It is actually in the stuff of living of the world. It is in the stuff of everything.

Greene's view of the forces imposed on an individual encompassed both material determinism and cultural and/or psychological determinism, but she also added the Jungian concept of an archetype, which influences the actions or thoughts of an individual.[5] This was expressed in patterns, stories, and mythology, and, in her view, the individual was born into a 'part of the pattern', and the nature of the pattern at that moment was their fate.

The American esoteric astrologer Alan Oken expressed another point of view. Esoteric astrology is the branch that focuses on the spiritual and soul-centred aspects of an individual's life. It draws on Theosophy and other mystical traditions, aiming to understand the soul's purpose, spiritual growth, and the evolution of consciousness. I interviewed Oken in March 2010, and when I asked for his opinion on the source or nature of fate, he spoke of a spiritual dimension. He used the Platonic and Stoic notions of fate to talk of it as an instrument of the divine:

> …and that divinity, I believe, has a destiny whose dynamic transcends all of the individual parts, meaning your fate and my fate. So there is an overriding movement of fate which is really the life force and the life destiny of that divine entity… So I do not know of any time when fate does not exist. Fate, to me, always exists, [and we have to] accept that

> there is a dynamic of an expansion of awareness which allows freedom of choice to transcend a previous fate as you move into another fate.

For Oken, fate was the substance of the World Soul, the living divine force that reached through the entire cosmos. For Oken, this force didn't override free will; instead, it could be harnessed to navigate different levels of fate, progressively drawing closer to the divine.

Tolerance was the theme of fate for British humanistic astrologer Roy Gillett, whom I interviewed in November 2009. Humanistic astrology is an astrology that emphasises personal growth, self-awareness, and the potential for positive transformation. I asked Gillett about the source of fate and his reply, like George, involved a sympathetic cosmos:

> ...the universe is based on tolerance. The planets tolerate each other. There are cycles in the heavens and when anything happens something else happens. ...I think you do have a certain amount of control over your destiny. If you are conscious of the cycles you are free up to a point within the range of possibilities. [We are] parcels of water sucked into and pulled one way and another. And the extent to which we can work with this is like a ship sailing through the ocean....You cannot master fate, but you can work with fate. You can turn what can be a very difficult situation into a much better one.

Gillett saw fate as influenced by material determinism, like Greene. However, for Gillett, the 'great chain of being' and the sympathetic cosmos represent pressure on the individual based on the balance and counterbalance of the 'tolerance' of the planets. Gillett held a compatibilist view of fate, positing that individuals who were aware of these influences could use their free will to work with these energies for a better outcome.

Among these varying opinions on the source of fate, however, all of these astrologers upheld two common themes: a sympathetic cosmos and the ability to use freedom of choice. Dykes, from his Stoic philosophy, talked of a force that guided the being. With her Jungian perspective, Greene saw humanity enmeshed in pattern but talked of the 'choices the individual makes'. Oken, arguing from a Platonic esoteric position, considered that we had 'freedom of choice' to transcend levels of fate. At the same time, Gillett saw the theme of tolerance as the balancing force of the cosmos and used the metaphor of sailing a boat to describe fate and its relationship to free will.

Fate and the soul

With any mention of fate, the interviewees tended to shift the subject to the soul. The soul and its relationship to fate were central to the classical period's exploration of free will. Plato believed that the divine formed the soul and placed a spark of the divine soul into each individual. The soul held both the attributes of reason and what Plato termed as 'what was up to us'. With these features, the soul's responsibility was to seek a union with the World Soul.[6] Aristotle differed and pondered on the human soul's mortality and considered it the life force, the 'essence of the whole living body', and that it was the tool by which humanity reached for mortal perfection.[7] Later, in the thirteenth century, Aquinas followed Aristotle and aligned the soul with the body. He, however, acknowledged its immortal features. He considered that the soul functioned in both the temporal world of matter and the divine realm of spirit.[8]

In August 2009, I interviewed British psychological astrologer Clare Martin, president of the UK-based Faculty of Astrological Studies from 2000–2009. I asked about her views on fate, and she moved the conversation to talk about the soul and its relationship to fate:

> Well I think we are multi-levelled, yes. I do not feel that our bodies can transcend our charts as I think that the charts are maps of time and space. We are embodied in time and space. It is our bodies which are here. In our bodies we are born and die and we are subject to time. But I do not think that that is all that we are so I would subscribe to the sort of ancient view that we have a soul that comes and goes and that it is timeless and that is not subject to time.

Martin appeared to accept fate and questioned whether we had free will. Greene also addressed the issue of the soul's nature and relationship to fate and framed it in Humean empiricism, a human construct:

> …the idea of soul seems to be something that humans do construct in particular ways when they encounter these patterns which are experienced as fate. Because they are overwhelming, you can't do anything about them. It is the place where we are suddenly reduced to the recognition that we are simply part of life, that we don't have autonomous control over it. So the idea of soul as a divine spark that has come down between reincarnations and will fly up home again once the body decays could be our view of human hope.

Greene suggested that our perceptions created the soul, our sense of awe and wonder when we recognised our life as part of a pattern, and that by creating the idea of the soul, we maintained the hope of our uniqueness. Some astrologers expanded on this idea by discussing the trials of life. I interviewed Brian Clark, an Australian humanistic astrologer, in April 2010, and when I asked him about free will, he shifted the conversation to poetry and the nature of the soul:

> I came across John Keats the other day. I was reading his *Ode to Psyche* and then the notes that he wrote about soul. About the veil, Earth, the world being the veil of soul and so on. He wrote those three days before he wrote this *Ode to Psyche* and he talked a lot about it as if it was this kind of world of pain, 'the test and tasks of life that made soul', so what I …to cut a long story short …free will I think is to recognise that… I guess the soul is made. I like Keats' idea of 'soul making'. So it is as if… I see soul as what makes …infuses our lives… it infuses and gives meaning …so I see soul as the sort of meaning of life, if you will.

Clark saw the soul as something learned or shaped by life, and one's free will was to recognise and accept this struggle. For Clark, free will was the tool used to help to 'make the soul'. Greene also talked of this idea of soul-making by sharing one of the dreams she had while recovering from surgery:

> When I was coming out of hospital I had a couple of very strange experiences, one of which was a bizarre dream. I was doped up on the pain killer drugs and I dreamt about souls. I was seeing …these …it was the most bizarre combination of Platonic and Complexity, it had everything in it. There were these individual souls and they were geometric. They were like cubes or hexagons and there were the Platonic shapes and they were all connected by these very delicate kind of cords. But they were moving around so they weren't in any kind of order. And all of them were in the process of transformation and some of them had writing on them and it was either Hebrew letters or hieroglyphs or alchemical symbols. They all had this symbolic writing on them, some of them were base metal or just sort of clay and they were turning… they were transforming through all metals like an alchemical… some were silver or bronze becoming copper and they were souls. And it was clear that they were souls being formed by life, by life experience, and eventually they might become gold or silver. But they did not start like that.

Greene, coming from her Jungian perspective, then commented on her dream of souls:

> What it said to me was that the potential for a soul, that the sort of base stuff that could be a soul, is there maybe in all things, maybe even in rocks. But it does not automatically become this kind of… we are not automatically incarnating with it, such as pure gold people, a pure gold piece of god in us. We are just part of life. We work at it and we transform it and we struggle and we become more conscious and it may or may not transform.

Greene's dream and Clark's reference to John Keats's soul-making suggest that this concept of soul-making could be considered a Platonist view of the soul, where the soul is born into mortal flesh and then struggles to improve its nature. Plato wrote of the soul's responsibility to improve itself: 'So all things that contain soul change, the cause of their change lying within themselves and as they change they move according to the ordinance and law of destiny….'[9] Thus, the soul in this context was a vehicle, divine or a human construct, with which the individual engaged with the sympathetic cosmos, and the narrative of the struggle of this engagement was one's fate.

Clark viewed the work of soul-making as a journey of connecting with specific tasks assigned to one's mortal life, while Greene contemplated whether the raw material of the soul was exclusive to humanity or was part of the entire material world. She wondered if the soul was real or just a version of human hope. In this regard, Greene's version of soul was more attuned to Spinoza's view of *conatus*, defined by Steven Smith as 'the presence of an urge, however poorly understood, to live rationally or intelligently. We desire not just to live but to enjoy the fullness or plenitude of life'.[10] Hence, one could understand soul-making as a Spinozian journey of self-understanding.

Other astrologers, however, saw the soul in a Cartesian manner in that it did not require the body for its existence. Such a soul was not engaged in a union with the physical world that produced 'soul-making' but was already perfectly formed, possessing reason and free will. Alan Oken wrote of this in his book *Soul-Centered Astrology*: 'The more we are attached to the personality, the more we are materially oriented, in and of the Earth. As the Soul becomes an ever-increasing Presence in our lives, we begin to become more Light-oriented'.[11] For Oken, 'light-oriented' was the nature of existence of the soul when it was no longer tied to a body, 'It is to Light that we also return…'[12] When interviewing Oken I asked him about his view on the soul. He linked it to free will by saying:

Free will is relative to the expansion of consciousness that the individual achieves to help to transcend his or her biology …So here is where the soul comes in. As we move into that place of free will we move into the realm of the soul… [this is the place where] what I like to call 'free creative radicals' are available to us, so that we have what appears to be some greater choice but that greater choice is still within the parameters of some larger energetic unit which has movement and life being and destiny of its own, except that its destiny is larger than that of the individual who has not achieved that awareness.

Although these astrologers had diverse opinions about the nature of soul, they all considered that the soul was the holder of a unique feature of the individual beyond 'personality', which Oken saw as a minor expression of the soul in its material guise. From this, another question emerged: If the soul was unique and a holder of the will, or free will, what did these astrologers think was its relationship to the natal horoscope, the very instrument of fate in their lives?

Fate, soul and the horoscope

Philosophers of the classical, late antiquity, and medieval periods assigned the attributes of the divine soul as reason and the will, which lay beyond the domain of earthly fate. But this was not the only position available. In the third century, the philosopher Plotinus believed that the union of the immortal soul with the material realm occurred when the soul traversed the cosmic circuits of the planets. Each planet, in turn, affected the soul, clothing it with both its nature and its future fate.[13] This offered a middle ground for the soul to engage with the fate of the horoscope while maintaining its immortal character.

Astrologers, however, are divided over whether to accept or reject the idea that the soul is contained in the horoscope and, thus, whether the soul is subject to fate. In the early twentieth century, Alan Leo wrote that the horoscope was the holder of the material fate, but the soul was the holder of the will and reason and hence was not contained in the horoscope. In contrast, by the mid-twentieth century, the work of Margaret Hone, the co-founder of the UK's oldest school of astrology, the Faculty of Astrological Studies, argued in 1951 that the soul, reason, character, and material fate were all contained within the horoscope, she wrote:

Inasmuch as a man identifies himself with his physical self and the physical world about him, so he is indissolubly part of it and subject to its changing pattern as formed by the planets in their orbits.[14]

Hone used the term 'psyche', which she defined as body, mind, spirit, soul, personality, individuality and the will, and argued that:

> the entire psyche of a person cannot be dissected into such divisions, but that all combine to form the whole, all contained in the horoscope. The art of Astro-analysis is in blending the indications given by these pointers [horoscopic points].[15]

Hone's arguments were ground breaking in astrological thinking as she placed the horoscope in the centre of the astrologer's life, to be embraced rather then viewed, as argued by Leo, that it was the material burden of the soul. For her, the soul was a part of the material world; she did not view it as a captive creature seeking to return to the heavenly realms.

In 2008, Demetra George published a book titled *Astrology and the Authentic Self*. In this work, she acknowledged this split among astrologers. Offering advice to the consulting astrologer, George wrote: 'If we [the astrologer] consider the possibility that an individual can take conscious action to alter the indications of the chart… we [the astrologer] give guidance as to the strength of the human will to overcome obstacles'.[16] George argued that if the astrologer considered that the human will (soul, intellect, or reason) was free and existed outside the chart, it could be used to alter the expression of the horoscope. If, on the other hand, the astrologer considered that the 'character' was fixed within the horoscope, then, George suggested, the astrologer should advise the client to find inner harmony while accepting '…the objective conditions of our lives'.[17] This was a Stoic perspective.

George's opinion on this question was that 'A planet's condition does not predispose a person to act in good or bad ways – moral behaviour remains in the sphere of the free will; what it indicates is the presentation of fortunate or difficult life events and the likely outcome of those situations'.[18] George considered that the will was free and that this freedom was essential to ensure moral responsibility. This view echoed Susan Wolf's philosophical arguments about the balance between free will and determinism.

Greene's position was different. In her interview, she voiced Spinozian-like concepts, indicating that ignorance made one passive and thus, one was 'thrown about like a football' by determinism.[19] Coming from a monist psychological perspective, Greene talked of the horoscope (chart) and its relationship to fate by stating:

> I do not think that charts are equal in terms of,.. I mean, that is nonsense to think that people are equal in terms of their charts. Not every moment is the same as every other moment and that is all a chart is, a moment. The life form is not always the same it has extremes; there are times when it is flowing and times when it is at war with itself and times it wants to kill itself and times when it… it is different all the time and if you are born under a time, at a time when life is going through a sort of nauseous bit, you are going to have a rougher time – it is not about fairness. Fairness does not come into it. But even then, you can still tamper. The more openings you can make, the less compulsive the flow of the water. There are people that are just deeply unconscious, they have no idea and they do not want to know. So they are thrown about like a football by their complexes and by anything that happens to them. And they invariably follow the least conscious version of their pattern. And other people are in there struggling with it, and maybe having a really rough time but they are trying to work with it and they get a lot better results out of it.

Greene's astrological arguments reflect Arthur Schopenhauer's (1788–1860) concept of the world as chaotic. Schopenhauer saw the world as pessimistic and hence his idea of fate was being born into this pessimistic world—the World as Will.[20] Greene, however, was more optimistic; the individual was born into an emergent cosmos. To quote Greene, 'The life form is not always the same it has extremes; there are times when it is flowing and times when it is at war with itself… .' For Greene, the nature of this life force at the time of birth decided a person's fate.

The British financial and humanistic astrologer Christeen Skinner, whom I interviewed in November 2009, offered another view of fate and the horoscope. She described how the horoscope contained fate but that it was not inevitable. She used an analogy from music:

> ….Yamaha managed to come up with an electronic piano that played itself. It was terrible, this thing was playing a perfect A, perfect B flat but actually it is the imperfections that makes a piece of music into something that touches your soul — so, yes, one of the beauties of astrology which is like art or music or anything else is that it is very slightly flawed or that it requires a little poetry, it requires… it has an organic part to it.

For Skinner, the horoscope was not inevitable but a mixture of inorganic and organic. To live with it was like working with an instrument; the music produced (the story of one's life) was a combination of an instrument and a musician. The non-inevitable horoscope was also the style of thinking embraced by Dutch psychological astrologer Karen Hamaker-Zondag, whom I interviewed in Amsterdam in September 2008. Speaking in English, she talked of how she spoke of fate to her students:

> What I tell my students is that from the moment that I am born, my progressions and transits are fixed, so I can actually see what is happening when I am ninety years old. And I know that things will happen in accordance with the core meaning of those planets but I cannot see what exactly. So... there is a kind of pattern that wants to unfold and it has its own timing and it does unfold. So, yes, that you can consider as fate.

Hamakar-Zondag voiced the issue of fate and time that was evident in the questionnaire responses—time was fixed, but the actual event was not. This seemed to be a nearly universal belief among astrologers.

Fate, time, and the horoscope

I asked Robert Hand, a Hellenistic/Medieval astrologer, if we ever had a choice of avoiding the fated time dictated by the geometry of the horoscope. He only laughed and replied: 'You will not miss a transit. You may not notice it, but you will not miss it'. Martin also wrote of this: 'In our natural state we live under the sometimes tyrannical dominion of the planets. But what we do with our birth chart, and how we choose to live it, is up to us'.[21] Here, Martin accepted the limitations the horoscope imposed on the timing of life's events but saw the will as free. I asked Martin to expand on her understanding about fate and time and she replied:

> I mean you cannot trade that in, that is what you are given. Now in the birth chart is the period of history we are born in because of the cycles of the great planets. We are all subject to that. We are all part of a period in history and we are all born into a certain culture and that is our fate. Also it is our fate to... I mean you can look at a baby's chart and see that when that baby is going to be 75 years old you can see that Pluto is going to be crossing over the ascendant. And we know exactly how that chart is going to be triggered for the rest of that person's life. We can talk about the exact date. That is also our fate.

Thus, for the astrologer, the timing of a future event is fixed, inevitable and non-negotiable, and as Martin stated: 'This is also our fate'. I explored this notion with Skinner. She was discussing a potential time when the planet Saturn would transit into a specific position in its orbit, which was related to the geometry of her horoscope. I asked her: 'Do you believe that at this time you are going to encounter 'Saturn'?' Skinner replied:

> Yes, I am going to encounter something. I cannot say for sure what that thing will be, but I know what the music is that needs to be played at that time. I have a choice. I can decide that I do not want to play in that concert in which case I suspect that the cosmos will come and force me into the one next door which will be twenty times more painful. Or, if I am going to take part in it, do I want to prepare for it?

Skinner was implying that although the timing was fixed, based on her horoscope, she had a choice. She could be willing to engage in the potential of the forthcoming event, or use her free will to ignore it, with the caveat that ignoring it could make it 'twenty times more painful'. In contrast, she could 'prepare for it' by choosing to 'take part in it'. I asked Skinner how she would prepare for a forthcoming 'encounter with Saturn'. She continued with her musical metaphor:

> I know what time the performance is going to be [the time of the transit]. I do not know how the audience is going to be, or if anybody is going to show up, but I know when that performance is. So therefore, like for example I am getting old and Saturn is supposed to be [associated with] the bones, so that it would not be a bad idea to check that I am having enough calcium and things before this happens. So I am doing things that are essentially only like weather forecasting in that I am taking the umbrella out with me beforehand. But I am trying to take a healthy, well what I hope is a healthy approach to it.

Hand discussed similar ideas. He reflected on Rudhyar's view of cycles when he commented on his experience of the cycles of Saturn—a Saturn return occurs every 29.5 years of a person's life. He spoke of his own Saturn return as follows:

> …they are nevertheless, only a pre-figuration, they are not going to be repeated. Nothing is ever repeated. For example, both [my] Saturn returns, interestingly enough, coincided with the same style of personal problems but the second one worked out fine. More recently, I have

had Saturn squaring those same points and its manifestations have been entirely health. And there is no reason based on where Saturn is transiting why it should have made that difference?

In referring to his life events, inherent in his conversation was the concept that one Saturn cycle would not produce the same events as the first. Indeed, all the astrologers interviewed saw time embedded with quality. For them, the event's timing was inevitable, but the event itself was less formed, although it would conform to the nature of a planet being 'met' at that time. This is the hybrid fate, as discussed in Chapter Eight, and it was part of how these professional astrologers used the instrument of their horoscope to enable them to focus on or gain some understanding of their future.

Fate and reason

Plato spoke of reason as the divine gift that enabled the individual to 'subdue that turbulent, irrational mass [of their material being] by means of reason'.[22] Many astrologers, both in the 'notes in a bottle' and in the interviews, reflected that the notion of 'reason' or consciousness was the instrument with which they avoided, negotiated, or transcended fate. Oken linked consciousness directly to free will and, in his interview, said, 'Free will is relative, it is very relative. Free will is relative to the expansion of consciousness that the individual achieves to help to transcend his or her biology and the psychological dynamics enthused in that biology', indicating that for him, consciousness was the ability to resist the physical desires or worries of worldly life.

Sue Ward, a UK astrologer who practices traditional astrology, exemplified by William Lilly, took a different approach to the role of consciousness. I interviewed her in April 2010, and I asked her whether we could change the fate that was indicated within the horoscope, she replied:

> We are all to a greater or lesser degree the subjects of heavenly forces, influences, to a greater or lesser degree. We can reduce that if we believe that the stars incline, we can reduce that inclination or compulsion by sorting ourselves out. …which I think explains my attitude far more than any other. It is that if you can gain control of yourself…, if you can gain control of yourself, purify yourself as they would have said, then you can become the mistress of your own fate. You can, as [William] Lilly said, "Rise above the stars" and that is what he means when he says that.

For Ward, astrology allowed the individual to gain knowledge of themselves; through this knowledge, they gained a greater understanding of their 'inclinations or compulsion'. She suggested that this was the way a person can gain control of themselves and thus become the 'mistress of your own fate'. I asked if one could break the bonds of fate in this way and she replied:

> Yes that is the potential, in that I think it is highly unlikely that you're not going to know that it is happening, particularly if you have a horrible Saturn in your nativity, but what you can do is re-adjust. This is the principle, this is the theory, that you re-adjust so that you do not allow it, you are able to resist, so that your life is based on choice.

Ward suggested that one could be free of fate through awareness, but that one's fate, as stated in her reference to 'the horrible Saturn in your nativity', may make it more difficult, reminiscent of Greene's comments that not all people are equal in their fate. Melanie Reinhart, a tutor and lecturer at the Faculty of Astrological Studies, also emphasised the need for awareness. She told a story of two twins with very similar charts, both experiencing events in their lives at the same time, yet one being far worse than the other. I asked Reinhart the question: 'What makes the event different for each twin? Does free will come in here'? Reinhart replied:

> I think that if one is plodding along relatively unconsciously in any area of life then the experience of choice is often either not possible or in fact it is an illusion or... yes, basically one of those two. So the more conscious someone is the more choice they have,... the more the possibility of free choice does arise.

Although not her intention, Reinhart was answering Cicero's challenge regarding twins who lived different lives. She argued that the different levels of consciousness between the two twins could alter the expression of events in their lives, ultimately leading to non-similar lives. Reinhart's argument necessarily assumes that consciousness is separate to fate.

The astrologers I interviewed tended to accept the Platonic relationship between fate and reason. Some astrologers, such as Oken, considered that fate could be transcended, thus reflecting the Platonic idea of consciousness. Others, such as Greene, accepted that consciousness could increase knowledge of oneself to reduce the internal pain of one's mind, reflecting the Stoic and Spinozian arguments. However, for all these astrologers, self-knowledge was central to their approach to living with fate. All the astrologers assumed the autonomy of the self, an assumption not necessarily classical in its view but one that reflected modern notions of the self, as argued by Giddens.

Living with fate

I also asked the astrologers how they handled the fate they saw in their own lives. In October 2009, I asked Dutch business astrologer Faye Cossar (Blake) what she would do if she saw a problematic event in the future. She replied:

> I try and use it. I will try and negotiate and co-create and think what can I do with that. ....I might not necessarily then think 'shit I must do that'. But I would be aware of that. Like with the Neptune transit, I was aware I do not want it to go into addiction, so I think it might be a good time to get into a photography course.

Cossar was a compatibilist as she considered that she could give fate another outlet in her life. For her, the planet Neptune was associated with matters to do with addiction as well as issues to do with illusion and artistic endeavour, hence Cossar's reference to photography. To her eye, the future held an encounter with 'Neptune'; this was fated. However, instead of waiting for the encounter, she strove to prepare for it, hoping to shape its expression. Oken took the same compatibilist approach to his fate. Using the language of astrology, he described a fated difficult time ahead of him, which could have been violence or even death and, given this, he made a series of decisions to change his living situation:

> I knew that that aspect was on its way for yearsssssss before it happened. *[Oken stressed the years drawing it out])* I said OK let's get some place safe. Let's gets some place safe so that that can happen in a comfort zone.

Oken became aware of his meeting with a fated time, established by the future movement of planets and the geometry of his horoscope. He accepted this fated encounter and decided to relocate to allow this fate to express itself safely.

> So I move to very safe place because I know that that aspect will be brutal, at the very least life challenging, and maybe even be life threatening and, because I have nothing else to support Mars in my chart, 'Let's get some place where there is a lot of nurturing, let's get some place where I can be nurtured. Now let's get to a place where the dynamics of the way I nurture will be tested and it will be okay for me to be tested there'. So I did that. I moved to Lisbon, Portugal.

Oken accepted that he could not avoid his fate but like Cossar he sought to choose the expression of this 'meeting'. The events for Oken, as for Cossar, were not inevitable; what was inevitable were the timing and the quality. Oken knew the timing, and he believed, in his own words, that it would be brutal. He continued with his personal story:

> Now I took a very cushy apartment in Lisbon and I have a lot of very close friends in Lisbon and the thought was that 'OK, this will be a safe place for Pluto opposing Mars'. So what happens, right… I fall down, my foot is badly injured, I am starting to age very rapidly, I need all of those friends to bring food and groceries and to help me to get to my teaching classes, because I am hobbling. The elevators for the entire time I lived in this beautiful apartment on the sixth floor of a seven-story building kept breaking down. I sometimes would be isolated in that apartment for days at a time because my foot was really bad. I could not walk, my maid robbed me while I was in London on a teaching trip, I got ripped off financially, and I also came into a whole bunch of money. So I got financially regenerated as well as robbed, as well as ripped off, as well as ageing… my whole level of compassion grew for people who are ill, for people who are suffering, for people who have less than a good group of friends to take care of them.

I asked Oken if this was, in his opinion, how he had used his free will, choosing to move to Portugal, but he quickly replied, 'The free will was my attitude, not so much in moving to Portugal'.

British humanistic and homeopathic astrologer Sue Tompkins, whom I interviewed in November 2009, also spoke of what it was like to live as an astrologer:

> A few years ago, I have this group of south London friends and we tend to do things on people's birthdays. One of the group was about to have a 60th birthday and she wanted us all to go to Morocco. And this is a discussion in April for something which is happening in the following November. I looked at the transits in November and I thought, 'Oh God, I don't want to go away in November'. It was massive Saturn, you know, which is not horrendous but — … but on the other hand I could not because it was —… anyway, so masses of Saturn transits and we went to Morocco and I had a great holiday! But basically, the whole place was full of Saturn because it was a city which

was a walled city. Everywhere there are donkeys, beasts of burden. We went up the Atlas mountains, there was impoverishment, it was uncharacteristically cold, so we were all wearing all! You know, it was just Saturn all the way through. But hey! We had a great holiday. So one still meets the symbolism, we have all done this, one meets the symbolism of whatever the given planet is. BUT I could not have predicted that.

Tompkins commented that, for her, she still encountered the planet Saturn, but instead of the depression or difficulties she had expected, the planet's symbolism revealed itself as a walled city, beasts of burden, impoverishment, and the cold, all textbook expressions of Saturn.[23] Here, Tompkins did not try to reshape the encounter as Oken did, but instead took her chances with the holiday at what she considered a difficult time, only to find, from her perspective, that the symbolism was fulfilled benignly.

Clark gave another approach. When I asked him about how he dealt with forthcoming predicted difficult events which he saw in his horoscope, he first used astrological terms to describe what was happening for him—his planetary fate and then talked of his experience:

> The last time I had a major Pluto transit, I found my neighbour — (I have moved since then), I rushed over to her house and found her— ... she had been on the floor of her bathroom all night. I knew that something was wrong, I just knew it.

> I helped her up and blah blah blah... *[Brian waves his hands in the air]* and she eventually died. But to cut a long story short, this [his current] neighbour I am having the problem with — his birthday is the same day as mine and he just turned 30 and I have just turned 60 so we are like —... and I laugh because I can see ... The astrological images allow a kind of ... I don't know it is like 'Hah hah haaaa', you know? It got me!

(Clark was referring to the fact that, with a shared birthday, the neighbour's natal sun was in the same zodiacal position as his thus he knew that the neighbour was also 'meeting' the planet Pluto via his natal sun.)

> But what it does is that, well, he is a very nasty person but what it does is lessen my —...if, if ... if I sit with it I feel very rage-full and I am going to go over and smash this person, but really when I reflect on it,

because of what I know about it, it lessens that —... There is... there is something bigger going on, and I have to find the answer to that so when I see these things and I use the astrological images, whatever they are, I am trying, as much as possible, be alert to them, to the potentialities and possibilities of them and to be more reflective and be understanding, to try to not, in any way, circumvent life but to live it, and to live it with the knowledge of what is going on around me.

Clark's story is of a person who lives in a sympathetic cosmos. He defined this as participating in life, giving him a different perspective on life's situations. He found himself in a situation where he was enraged by his neighbour. However, using the information in his astrology, he could detach from that rage and resist his desire to 'smash this person'. Instead, another deeper story was at stake, fated and a little mysterious for him. From his perspective, Clark believed that there was another level of meaning to the situation with his neighbour, which he did not understand, but was certain that something bigger was at stake. So, he waited and contemplated what it might be in light of his past history. Clark's story of his struggle with his emotions and his resistance to the normal flow of events resonated with Spinoza's philosophy. Clark accepted his fate and used an instrument of detachment— his horoscope, which provided an inner and unbiased self-image—to reduce the heat of his anger. He engaged his reason by pondering the deeper significance of the events. For Clark, this was participating in his life, rather than just blindly living it.

Clark's example, which was not unique, showed him reaching for the Spinozian concept of an instrument of *sub specie aeternitatis,* where his reason could function without reference to time.[24] He pondered the death of an elderly neighbour many years before, while also talking of present difficulties, both for him linked in a timeless moment. Clark was aware that, by stepping into this detached place of reason, he was able to reduce his rage and respond differently, rather than being a pawn in the flow of events. For Clark, the expression of his free will was in a compatibilist manner, as he did not deny the workings of fate in his life but considered that he could attempt to control his reactions.

Fate-Casting

In the fourth century, Calcidius promoted the use of astrology to choose the best times for initiating a chain of fate. This philosophical approach to fate is a form of libertarianism, as the individual becomes a fate-caster and can choose the time for casting a new chain of fate. This philosophy was central to William Lilly's practice of horary astrology, cited in Chapter Four.

Today, an active community of astrologers follow Lilly's work. I spoke to one of them concerning this idea of fate-casting. Barbara Dunn is a published author in the field of Horary astrology, the astrology of casting a horoscope for the time of asking a question. I interviewed her in April 2010, and she discussed how she would use her knowledge of horary astrology in her daily life. She commented that she often sought to cast the fate for a developing situation by astrologically waiting for a good time before asking a question. She spoke about waiting to hear about a forthcoming job opportunity:

> I can remember years ago when I was working for... I was trying to get a job on *Cosmopolitan* and I remember thinking that I would do a horary today, and I thought, 'No I won't, bad day'. And this went on for about three or four weeks until I got a good day. So I asked the question, I mean you can never be sure because of the minute, but you can have a rough idea. I asked the question, 'Will I get the job?' – Yes, it looks good. I get the job. And I wonder. I still have the chart and I still look at it and I sort of wonder how that works? I am not quite sure about that either.

With her mental knowledge of the daily position of the planets, Dunn posed the question in her mind, asking if this was a good time to ask this question. She would not ask the question if she mentally calculated it was not a good moment. However, after some weeks, she considered that the planets were now in auspicious places for asking the question. However, retrospectively, she wondered about the ontological mechanism underpinning her being the fate creator. Dunn's next example reflected this dilemma again.

> And another awful instance with a friend of mine about ten years ago. She had a lump in her breast and she said to me, we were in the car. 'I've got this lump, but it won't be anything', and I thought to myself, 'No it won't be anything but I will do a horary', I thought in my head. And the horary was dreadful, but I had thought that it would be good. I had made a mistake; I thought it was going to be a good horary, a good chart for her. I did not tell her —... I did the chart and it was awful and she did have cancer. I mean she survived it, but I was not sure what was going on then either. I was trying to help because I thought that if I get a good horary and if I am casting fate I am going to help her.

Dunn worried about the moral responsibility of being a fate-caster. Calcidius warned of this problem, but his solution was to visit an astrologer for help.[25] Dunn, as the astrologer, did not have this option. Her concerns were that horary astrology assigned self-agency to the individual, and it was up to the individual to avoid the consequences of the fate cast by a difficult horoscope. The implications of this power mean that the fate-caster is morally responsible for the fate they cast. Dunn's comments suggest that horary astrologers adopt a libertarian stance; however, when they were the originators of the question (when they are the fate casters) concerning the well-being of another person, they held responsibility for the outcome.

In conclusion, the interviews provided valuable insights into the astrologers' perspectives on fate and its integral role in shaping a personal ontology. Their twenty-first-century understanding of fate was deeply rooted in classical cosmological frameworks. All the astrologers adhered to the concept of a sympathetic cosmos, wherein all entities, whether tangible or conceptual, interact in a non-causal manner. Their horoscopes served as a medium to explore their relationship with this cosmos. Fate, distinct from determinism, was perceived as the organising principle governing the order of their world, whether through divine agency or as part of the natural laws of the cosmos.

Some astrologers referenced fate in the context of the soul, which they identified as the seat of will and reason. The soul, conceptualised as a form of consciousness akin to awareness, was regarded as an essential tool for navigating the challenges posed by fate. Some of the astrologers adopted a Platonic dualistic perspective, believing that by cultivating awareness, they could transcend their material fate, aligning with either Leo's or Rudhyar's astrological interpretations. Conversely, others endorsed a Stoic viewpoint, asserting that awareness facilitated a deeper understanding of their material fate. These astrologers described this process as 'soul-making' and adhered to a naturalistic philosophy that resonated with Hume's pragmatic approach. They viewed astrology as a means of elucidating the ongoing internal dynamics between the conscious mind and the unconscious or mental complexes.

The astrologers all rejected Cicero's assertion that the horoscope predetermines an individual's life with inevitability. Instead, they embraced a compatibilist perspective that integrates time and event into a cohesive framework. They accepted the inevitability of timing, acknowledging that regardless of their actions, they would inevitably 'encounter' a specific planetary symbol at a predetermined point in their future. However, while the timing was fixed, the event itself was not predetermined, this is a hybrid fate. The nature of the event was seen as only partially shaped by fate, understood as an interaction with a symbolic representation. This symbol was conceptualised as a broad palette, yet monochromatic, offering various shades of a single colour. For these astrologers, the exercise of free will lay in their capacity to choose a particular tone or tint from this palette, thereby shaping the specific manifestation of the event.

The interviews also explored the astrologers' experiences of living with fate. Some astrologers approached their horoscopes as tools for objectively interpreting fate's signals, while others adopted a Spinozian-inspired philosophy, using their horoscopes as a means of detachment. This detachment facilitated their acceptance of being an integral part of nature, allowing them to step back and reflect. Such reflection enabled them to examine the nature of the symbols they encountered and to respond with greater insight. Ultimately, it became evident that, regardless of whether the astrologer subscribed to esoteric and Platonist-influenced theories of fate, such as those espoused by Alan Oken, followed a pragmatic humanistic approach like Sue Tompkins, drew inspiration from mythological and emergent astrology like Brian Clark, or embraced a Jungian-Spinozian perspective like Liz Greene, they all shared a common approach to living with fate. These astrologers perceived themselves as residing within a sympathetic cosmos, where they believed it was possible to engage with and to negotiate with fate. This shared outlook formed the foundational theme of their personal theory of fate.

James Davidson gave a light-hearted critique of astrology in 2004 and wrote: 'Getting into astrology is like being drawn through the door of your own private cathedral or seduced by a fugue constructed out of the letters of your name'.[26] Davidson's comments suggested that astrology was a self-indulgent subject. In his criticism, however, he echoed a truth, for a cathedral, or even a fugue, is a place where one comes closer to something larger and more mysterious than the self. Astrology is a discipline centred on the self, emphasising the uniqueness inherent in each individual, as reflected in the distinctiveness of every horoscope. However, the very tool that underscores this individuality also integrates the astrologer into a sympathetic and mysterious cosmos. This connection paradoxically challenges the boundaries of the unique self, exposing the individual to the influences of this interconnected world, an experience they perceive as fate. In response, astrologers endeavour to reclaim their autonomy by acquiring knowledge of this fate, enabling them to navigate their lives with greater awareness and intention.

CHAPTER TEN

A TOPOGRAPHY OF FATE

This work aimed to address the assumption that fate and determinism were equivalent concepts. By tracing the nature of fate through the writings of philosophers, theologians, and astrologers across history, and extending this exploration into the contemporary era through the perspectives of modern astrologers, a picture of fate emerged.

The initial assumption that fate and the thesis of determinism are the same implies that fate is inevitable. Cicero articulated this in the first century BCE, and to avoid any challenge to free will, he argued that fate did not apply to humanity. Cicero's assumptions have persisted, leading to a commonly accepted view that fate is inevitable. Since that time, any arguments that fate plays a role in human life are, by and large, treated with disdain, and any consideration that it is a topic worthy of serious inquiry is dismissed.[1] Despite this assumption and dismissal, an acceptance of fate has persisted as a part of the lived experience of people for over two thousand years.

To understand fate's persistence, the earlier assumptions need to be set aside to allow for a fresh consideration of the question. My approach to researching fate was to try and think through fate, in the manner of Amiria Henare, Martin Holbraad and Sari Wastell:

> With purpose naïveté, the aim of this method is to take 'things' encountered in the field as they present themselves, rather than immediately assuming that they signify, represent, or stand for something else.[2]

Hence, I allowed fate to present itself through its nature in classical and medieval societies, both in the philosophical discourse and astrological writings. This historical research provided a context for investigating beliefs in fate in today's society. In the latter part of the project, I turned to the modern astrological community—a tradition that has engaged continuously with the concept of fate for millennia—to examine how fate is understood and lived today. This research showed that, contrary to the common assumption that fate implies inevitability and the necessary surrender of free will, my findings revealed a far more nuanced picture that differed in many ways from the thesis of determinism.

Fate, however, was elusive and, in both historical and contemporary contexts, it resisted being reduced to a single definition. Nonetheless, within this complexity, a discernible topography of fate was found.

Fate, a different ontology

A principal and universal feature of fate is that it requires a sympathetic cosmology. This is a worldview in which the cosmos is perceived as an interconnected, living whole, where all parts of the universe—human, natural, celestial, and divine—are bound together through relationships of sympathy and correspondence. This was the ontology developed by classical philosophers who employed either inspiration or observation in their pursuit to understand the world, observing the interconnectedness of life. They saw that all things were in a perpetual state of change, interconnected through recurring cycles.

Heraclitus (540–480 BCE) famously encapsulated this notion with his metaphor of a river, which remains a river but is continuously in flux: 'the river where you set your foot just now is gone—those waters having given way to this, now this'.[3] It was the Stoics, however, who addressed this constant change by conceptualising the world as a living, rational entity, interconnected like a single organism.[4] They termed this concept *sumpatheia*, the belief that all elements of life and non-life exist within an interwoven cosmos where everything influences everything else.[5] For the Stoics, a divine breath, known as *pneuma*, permeated all existence and mediated the universe's interconnectedness. Plato and Aristotle proposed other forms of sympathetic cosmology. Plato envisioned the world as being created and sustained by the World Soul, while Aristotle described the cosmos as composed of four fundamental qualities which were mixed by the movements of the heavens, each interacting and seeking to return to its proper place. Regardless of the specific binding agent, a sympathetic cosmology suggests that some events emerge in a manner independent of a cause-and-effect framework. They appear to work by what is known as cause-at-a-distance (sympathy or correspondence), where one object or event can influence, or echo, another without any apparent physical connection or immediate contact between them.

For a person to accept any such interconnectedness in their life, they need to have some form of Classical sympathetic cosmology in their ontology. An ontology informs a person of what is and is not possible and defines their view of the rational.[6] An ontology, a theory of being, that places synchronicities, serendipities, superstitions, divination, lucky and unlucky events, jinxes, omens, curses, prayer and blessings into a rational framework, also supports the existence of fate. Such an ontology belongs in what Lucien Lévy-Bruhl (1857–

1939) defined as a mystical mind. This mind sees reality in both the regularity of an ordered world and the interruptions that occur to that regularity.[7] Lévy-Bruhl argued that such a mind was indifferent to questions of how.[8] The matter of a physical causal link is non-relevant since the mental focus for the individual is on the 'what'—what is the meaning of the event, rather than 'how' does this event happen?

As Lévy-Bruhl wrote,

> As soon as it is a matter of mystical experience or action, the consideration of the laws of nature fade into the background; they are not denied, but in so far as they could constitute an obstacle, they are put aside, and there is seen to us the very framework of the ambient world, the characteristic fluidity of the mythical world which is unaware of it.[9]

Importantly, the idea is that the rational, logical world dominated by the laws of science is not, for an individual, challenged by alternative ontologies. Henare, Holbraad, and Wastell noted that the practical and the mystical should not present a situation of binary oppositions for the researcher.[10] A person with a belief in fate should not, therefore, be viewed as holding a primitive mind, ignorant, or delusional about the rational world defined by the sciences. A belief in one does not threaten a belief in the other. A science-informed ontology enables individuals to operate within a causal, logical, material world. Simultaneously, they may draw upon another ontology—one rooted in the organic world—characterised by complex networks of thoughts, emotions, social systems, relationships, and other living uncertainties. This additional ontology helps them navigate the density of the lived experience. The two ontologies can and usually do coexist in the same person, and the person, as Lévy-Bruhl claimed, moves seamlessly between them.

This ontology, as defined by Lévy-Bruhl's mystical mind, does not need to stand outside of mainstream thought. Although determinism's universality is central to the laws of nature and thus it claims the dominant worldview, it is challenged by self-organising systems. Christian Fuchs *et al.* argued that self-organising systems appear to be governed by '...less than strict determinism... [as] a touch of indeterminism enters causal relationships that involve self-organising systems, for the systems themselves select one of the several possible ways to react'.[11] Klaus Brunner commented that, within a system undergoing self-organisation, 'Different inputs may lead to the same output, and the same input may lead to different outputs. So causes and effects are not coupled unambiguously'.[12] These 'less than strict' deterministic situations contain the potential for an effect to emerge as a pattern whose final form is not inevitable. Brian Goodwin commented on this type of pattern-forming behaviour:

> Such unexpected, orderly patterns from disorderly elements are known as emergent properties. In general, they cannot be predicted from a knowledge of how individuals behave and how they interact.[13]

Emergent behaviour is a widespread phenomenon observed across organic systems, including social, political, cultural, and even individual lives, contributing to the inherent unpredictability of these systems.[14] Goodwin posited that emergent self-organising systems exhibit cyclical patterns, where new order arises in a manner that is similar, yet not identical, to previous cycles. This is a concept known as self-similarity.[15] Michael Bütz pointed out that self-similarity is a property of an object or system in which its parts resemble the whole, either exactly or approximately, across different scales or levels of structure.[16] The fronds on a fern, where each small leaflet is shaped like the whole frond, showing repeating patterns at multiple levels of magnification, the branches of a tree, where the limbs branch into twigs, and so on, each resembling the whole in structure, are examples of self-similarity. Additonally, Bütz argued that self-similarity applied to behavioural patterns, stating that, 'This process can be applied to an individual, a family, a community, and so on — in a self-similar manner.[17]

This organic emergent behaviour can be studied in the mathematics of fractals. Fractals reveal how layered repetitions and feedback loops produce variations in patterns, which are not produced uniformly.[18] Named by Benoit Mandelbrot (1924–2010), a fractal is an image generated by certain equations undergoing iterations, a process in which the outcome of one application of the equation becomes the input for the next (feedback).[19] A fractal image forms through these repetitions (each repetition adding a dot to the pattern). With each repetition of the cycle influencing the next, it progresses through time in an emergent process, which demonstrates self-similarity.[20] Fractals reveal, in a simple way, how time and cycles bring transformation to organic systems. This transformation is not a smooth progression, but is instead a nested rhythm of emergent structures that encode memory (of the previous pattern), adaptation, and change. Notably, the behaviour of such systems cannot be fully explained or predicted through deterministic principles.

Human life exists within an emergent system; the lives of individuals, families, communities, and social systems all function as emergent systems.[21]

These systems are in a constant state of emergent transition due to the activities of life. The repeating activities of life are the rhythms of the calendar, the working week, and the repetitions of daily events—ranging from rising to sleeping, eating, working, and socialising—all of which include feedback, and hence, by emergence, a shape or pattern of one's life is created. This pattern of life can be seen as a living fractal—revealed through encounters or events, or through synchronicities that connect distant moments and experiences across different scales in a self-similar way. Therefore, it is not an enormous leap of faith for an individual to quietly accept the role of Stoic *sumpatheia* in their lives, not as a conscious choice, but rather as an internal acceptance that provides them with meaning for the patterns they experience. This adoption of a sympathetic ontology is without concern for its conflict with the laws of nature, for as Lévy-Bruhl argued, the laws of nature are 'put aside' when the mystical sympathetic ontology offers greater meaning to the situation.[22]

Fate as story

The phenomenon of living inside an emergent system is akin to finding oneself in a story, but only glimpsing part of the plot line at times of serendipity or personal reflection. Like emergentism, stories are teleological and driven by a purpose defined by their ending. They involve collecting facts and people together and organising them into a pattern which provides them with meaning.[23] As a story progresses, if we can see enough of the pattern, we can guess the ending.

Fate is like a story. When fate is experienced, it has a sense of already being written. As Broadie stated, when fate is sensed, it seems to have 'an agency concerning which... all we know, is that it has a certain purpose'.[24] Just as a story will have a purpose and remain loyal to its theme, this also appears to be the perception of fate. Fate is sensed when one seeks to understand a string of apparently disconnected events across time that 'conspire' to a specific purpose. Edward Morgan Forster, In his 1908 novel, *A Room with a View,* had one of his characters, George, when told that it was a coincidence that he had arrived where he was, proclaim, 'It is Fate. Everything is Fate. We are flung together by Fate, drawn apart by Fate—flung together, drawn apart'.[25] Forster implies that George views these unexpected meetings as being orchestrated by something larger, a hidden pattern at work.

If fate is the perception of an emergent system, then the patterns and cycles of self-similarity explain the characteristics of fate as being teleological and purposeful. Teleology, which is procession with purpose, is not merely motion, but motion shaped by an end. It gives the view that life is not a series of accidents but instead a purposeful journey, and that particular moments feels like they participate in a larger, meaningful trajectory. These are the features of a story as well as the experience of fate. This type of fate, teleological and repetitive, is central to David Mitchell's work, *Cloud Atlas: A Novel*, when his character Sonmi-451 stated, 'Our lives are not our own. We are bound to others, past and present, and by each crime and every kindness, we birth our future'.[26] The novel features six interconnected stories spanning centuries, where each story centres on characters who are seemingly unrelated but subtly linked through reincarnation, echoes of past decisions, and inherited consequences. In this framework, coincidence is never random, but part of a larger pattern.

These are the features of fate in popular culture: the believer requires an ontology that at least acknowledges holism and then perceives fate as a teleological force that operates with purpose and meaning. It is within astrology that fate takes on some additional features.

Fate and astrology

When the thesis of determinism was developed in the seventeenth century by Baruch de Spinoza, he pointed out that mind, reason, and spirit were not free. Consequently, as discussed in Chapter Five, philosophical debates have sought to reconcile free will with universal determinism. However, astrologers stayed with fate. For astrologers, their tool for stepping into their sympathetic ontology is to plot the emerging pattern by turning to the cycles of the heavens. They believe that the celestial cycles echo (across scale and by self-similarity) their own lives. These cycles are deterministic, governed by Kepler's Laws of planetary motion; however, this is the source of fate that astrologers have historically accepted. It is part rigid, being constructed by the celestial cycles, but also it is part story, being blended with the emergent nature of life.

A hybrid fate

One of the key features of fate for astrologers is that it imbues future time with specific qualities. For them, fate dwells in calendars, consisting of two components: time and event. At a particular moment, one meets a fateful event. No action the astrologer can take will alter the timing of their fated 'encounters,' as the celestial movements determine the timing. The date is fixed. However, the other part of fate is an emergent story, and thus what they meet at that fated time is less clear and, in varying ways, subject to alteration. The encounter is viewed as one with an ambiguous symbol. Astrologers will recognise the significant features of the symbol and, once noted, endeavour to take action to influence it, hopefully producing a favourable manifestation, or accept it and view it as part of their journey of self-understanding. In practice, the astrologers acknowledged that fate dwells on the road of life, and they seek to identify the times of these encounters and, at the very least, prepare for them or, at best, change them.

Fate for many people is perceived as being in 'the right place at the right time' or, conversely, in 'the wrong place at the wrong time', depending on the nature of the event. However, astrologers believe that they can remove the element of surprise from the timing of the encounter, and with this knowledge, they seek to negotiate, manipulate, or influence the outcome of the meeting.

Fate and participation

The vast majority of contemporary astrologers sought to participate in their fate and thus be active agents in their life story. Lévy-Bruhl wrote of this type of participation, arguing that 'It is immanent in the individual, a condition of existence. To exist is to participate in mystical forces, essences and reality'.[27] Maurice Leenhardt in the preface to Lévy-Bruhl's *Notebooks* wrote,

> Participation is not accounted for, it cannot be explained, it ought not to be, it has no need of legitimation, yet one sees its necessary place in the human mind – and as a consequence its role in religion, metaphysics, art, and even in the conception of the entirety of nature.[28]

Lévy-Bruhl argued that participation was experienced both individually and collectively, thereby providing the individual with membership in a larger whole.[29] This membership was, according to Lévy-Bruhl, experienced as 'a matter of consubstantiality, of communion, of an identity even (dual-unity) between things and objects'.[30]

The astrologers in my research used the concept of participation with the celestial bodies in order to influence their future. They participated by 'honouring the planet', which was achieved through rituals, meditation, or practical activities associated with the symbolism of the respective planets. The process also gave them membership to a larger whole, the cosmos, and provided them with a sense of control or at least an understanding of life events. It was through participation that the astrologers revealed one of the key features of fate: fate is negotiable.

Fate, self-identity and the horoscope

The practice of participation requires the astrologer to believe they have personal agency, a self in relationship, in some way, to the cosmos. In discussing self-identity, Anthony Giddens argued that the uniqueness of self was a feature of contemporary culture, and he commented that the post-traditional view of self was one where the individual had the ability and freedom to be concerned with questions such as 'What to do? How to act? Who to be?' He saw these as the focal questions for everyone living in circumstances of late modernity.[31] He added to this argument by claiming that self-identity also required a personal ongoing biography:

> A person's identity is not to be found in behaviour nor — important though this is — in the reactions of others, but in the capacity *to keep a particular narrative going*. ...It must continually integrate events which occur in the external world and sort them into the ongoing 'story' about self.[32] [Giddens' italics]

For astrologers, this 'particular narrative' encompasses both the past and future, based on planetary cycles, and yields a life chronicle. This is part of their unique view of self and their relationship to the cosmos, which formed what Giddens called the ongoing story about the self. Giddens added:

> A person with a reasonably stable sense of self-identity has a feeling of biographical continuity which she is able to grasp reflexively and, to a greater or lesser degree, communicate to other people. ...self-identity is bound up with the fragile nature of the biography which the individual 'supplies' about herself.[33]

The uniqueness of the individual horoscope linked with the life narrative based on planetary cycles, therefore, provides a stable self-identity. For the self-identity of the astrologer is bound to their horoscope. Allocated at birth, it places fate into the astrologer's life, but at the same time, it offers them uniqueness, as no two horoscopes are the same. Additionally, the planetary cycles provided the astrologer with 'biographical continuity', the story of their life. This uniqueness was a key part of what Giddens considered essential for an individual to understand themselves in 'terms of her or his biography...[and]... across time and space...' and that the individual needed to have a concept of themselves as well as of others.[34]

The horoscope, however, offered more than a stable self-identity with its continual biography. During challenging periods, the astrologers employed their horoscopes to obtain an objective perspective on the planetary configurations affecting them. It offered them an instrument of Spinozian detachment, a means of viewing things *sub specie aeternitatis*, that is, as Scruton defined, 'in a timelessness mode'[35]. The horoscope, fixed from birth, holds an image of the self-detached from the current problems and provides the astrologer with an objective, non-emotional explanation, embedded in their history of similar events that have occurred in their life.

It is this feature of fate and the horoscope—that of unique self-identity—that can explain the robustness of astrology in Western culture. Once a person adopts their astrological identity, that is, their horoscope, with its past and future narratives, it can become foundational to the individual's view of the self.

In discussing the lived experience, Christopher Tilley argued that a distinction exists between Being and Being-in-the-World, and that a gap separates these two states. He considered that this gap between the notion of self and the outer world created a space that humans bridged in various ways.[36] Tim Ingold also acknowledged this gap, and he claimed that how a person filled this gap revealed their ontological foundation, how they constructed their world.[37] For astrologers, fate read through their horoscope, fills the gap between self-concept and the external world, between being and being-in-the-world. In this regard, for today's astrologers, fate is a genuine phenomenon, felt and experienced tangibly through the voices of the heavens, planets, and stars. In this way the fate contained in astrology provides the individual with a unique self, a self in relationship with a holistic cosmos. The practice of astrology is a cultural carrier of classical fate in today's world.

To conclude, the thesis of determinism is required to maintain the integrity of natural laws, and it must be universal, consistent, and immune to personal influence or desire.[38] Determinism is linear and causal, describing a universe filled with passive matter and governed by fixed sequences of cause and effect. By contrast, the sense of fate is inherently personal and non-universal, functions by emergentism in a sympathetic cosmology and is thus adaptable. Where determinism is objective, fate is subjective; where determinism is sequential, fate is patterned. The thesis of determinism underpins the function of the laws of nature, while a theory of fate appears to provide meaning or context to the human lived experience.

Astrology is a home for fate. People who sense that there are meaningful patterns that appear to shape their lives find acceptance of their worldview within astrology. The astrologers in my research did not discover fate, or have it forced upon them, through astrology. Instead, astrology provided them with a home for their natural sense of fate. Furthermore, once they adopted astrology, it then shaped their view of fate. The longer they practised astrology, the more their views on fate shifted to a compatible model; in short, their work in astrology taught them that they could negotiate with fate.

Ultimately, one must ask: Is fate merely a construct of human imagination—a projection of a mystical mindset—or does it reflect a genuine, though elusive, phenomenon? Fate gains ontological weight when understood as the perception of existence within an emergent system or a sympathetic cosmos. Within this framework, synchronicities and coincidences become perceptible expressions of deeper, emerging patterns. These moments may hint at underlying meaning, even if their full significance remains inaccessible to the individual. Thus, from the perspective of emergentism, fate constitutes a legitimate phenomenon—an aspect of reality situated at the margins of human perception. Whether one chooses to map, measure, ignore, or engage with it, the existence of fate as a part of the lived experience should not be dismissed just because it requires a non-linear ontology.

Shakespeare's character Hamlet told his friend Horatio how, by chance, things had gone well for him, he mused on the happenstance of events by saying, 'There is a divinity that shapes our ends, rough-hew them how we will'.[39] Rough-hew them may be all we can do to try and shape our fate, but since its earliest representations in the Egyptian scenes of the Weighing of the Heart, humanity has acted in the hope that fate was open to change.

APPENDIX

THE QUESTIONNAIRE

The Questionnaire

This document is a request for your thoughts on fate and determinism within your astrology. It is an academic survey conducted by Bernadette Brady in regard to her doctoral studies at Bath Spa University, UK. While you are at UAC please take 15 minutes to complete this questionnaire. As a thank you for your time I can, once I am back in the UK, also email you a special report on the results of *your* answers *(example shown below)*.

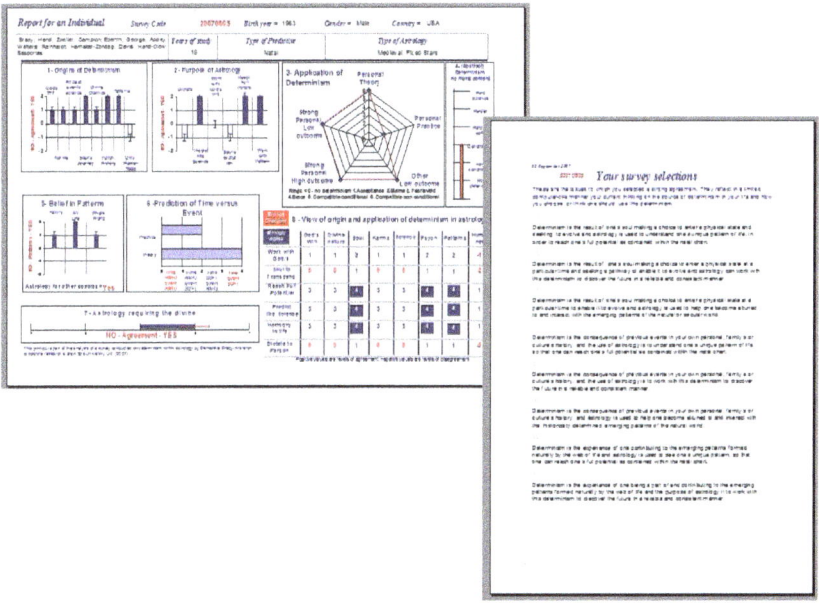

Additionally, apart from learning some things about yourself you will contribute to this global research project. The questionnaire **will take you about 15 - 20 minutes.**

Please read this first.

A central tenet of astrology is that something is written at the moment of a birth or a moment in time and place and some component of this moment has a bearing on the future. In this questionnaire, this component, which astrology explores via horoscopes, is labelled the "fate" of a person's life or the "fate" contained in a moment in time.

It is often assumed by non-astrologers that astrologers believe that one's entire life and life decisions are dictated by the "stars", yet no one has actually asked astrologers about their ideas on fate, destiny and free will. Thus your answers are important as they will go towards building a concept of fate (or determinism) as used in 21st-century Western astrology.

If you wish me to email you back your personal determinism/fate report then please *clearly* print your email address.

email address: _____

Section 1 – About You

    a) What year were you born? _____

    b) Male/Female _____

    c) In what country do you live? _____

    d) How long, in years, have you been studying astrology? _____

    e) As there are different types of astrology, could you please circle the type that you *now* prefer to use.

Horary   Medical   Financial   Esoteric   Psychological   Humanistic   Medieval

If your type is not listed then please enter your preferred astrology

    _____

    f) Who do you consider to be some of the major authors who have influenced your study of astrology?

_____

Section 2 – Predictive Astrology

2.1 Please choose the statements that best fit your understanding of the nature of predictive astrology. Predictive astrology is:

    a) The *application of particular mathematical techniques* (like transits, progressions and returns) to a horoscope in an attempt to gain information concerning the future.

    b) The use of a horoscope *intuitively* to divine the future.

c) The *application of a set of rules* to a horoscope for the moment of an event in order to foretell the likely outcome of *that* event – horary astrology.
d) Working with a person's natal horoscope to seek insights into their future behaviour by *understanding their personality and/or psychological makeup* – reading a natal chart.

If you do not use any form of predictive or natal astrology, please now move to **Section 3**

2.2 Please choose one statement that best fits how you think predictive astrology helps you in your life:
   a) I use it to understand why life can be so difficult at times.
   b) It allows me to relax and let my chart inform me of the path to take in my life.
   c) It gives me an understanding retrospectively of why things have happened in my life but I never use it to look at the future.
   d) It explains the past and also tells me what will happen in my life, and when, so I am mentally prepared for the problems.
   e) It allows me to know the time for doing spiritual practices to help me balance the planetary energies.
   f) It gives me a framework for understanding, not only what has happened, but also how to make the most of the potential contained in future patterns.

2.3 Please choose one statement that best fits how you would use predictive astrology when something unpleasant happens in your life:
   a) I look at my chart to simply see what it was astrologically.
   b) I use it to find out why it happened and understand what the "planets" had in store for me.
   c) I look at the astrology and worry about the next time the same astrological indicators will be present.
   d) I look at the astrology to be prepared for a similar problem in the future.
   e) I meditate on the planetary energies and seek to work with them more effectively in my life.
   f) I look at the astrology and use this information to help shape my path of action in the future.

2.4 In the history of a person's life, every time they have had transiting Mars conjunct their Ascendant they "accidentally" break a plate. Would you expect them to break another plate when Mars next conjuncts their ascendant? *Please select one statement:*
   a) No.
   b) Maybe.
   c) Depends on their level of awareness.
   d) Probably.
   e) Almost certainly.
   f) Yes.

2.5 If the person does break another plate on their next Mars transit, in your opinion: *Please select one statement*
   a) It was only an accident and has nothing to do with their Mars transit.
   b) They could not have avoided breaking a plate.
   c) It was their fault as they should have been extra careful around plates on that day.
   d) They were "waiting" to break the plate.
   e) It was a good thing as it was a simple way to use the Mars energy on that day.
   f) They are "out of tune" with Mars and need to undertake some Mars meditation or ritual to help them work with it in the future.
   g) They may want to find a more productive outlet for the expression of Mars.

2.6 Astrological predictions can contain both timing (when something may happen) and event (what that something may be). For example, a Saturn transit will happen at a certain time and will have a particular quality of expression. Does the *length of time* being examined (e.g. one year into the future or ten years into the future) have an influence on the capacity to predict the when and what? *Please select one statement.*
   a) No, I am able to predict both the timing of the event and the actual event regardless of how far it is in the future.
   b) Yes, I have a reduced ability to define the event as the timing moves further into the future.
   c) Yes, I have a reduced ability to define the timing as the expected event moves further into the future.
   d) Yes, I have a reduced ability to define both the timing and the event as it moves deeper into the future.

2.7 In two years' time your natal chart is going to have a series of "once in a life time" transits. Do you: *Please select one statement*
- a) Be concerned about the events you know will happen in two years' time but feel that there is nothing that you can do about it.
- b) Start to take action now that will optimise a positive outcome, whatever the events are in two years' time.
- c) Take the events into consideration but take no action as you are unsure of the timing.
- d) Not think about it as it is too far away to reliably predict either events or timing.

Section 3 – Natal Charts - If you do not use natal charts, then could you please move to Section 4.

3.1 If your primary relationship was having difficulties and you found out that your partner's time of birth was not what you thought, and this introduced different aspects between you and your partner, would you: *Please select one statement.*
- a) Try to change the relationship to reflect the new astrological picture.
- b) Break up the relationship, knowing now why it was having difficulties.
- c) Not look at the chart combinations as you would rather deal with the issues without knowing the astrology.
- d) Look carefully at your partner's new chart to see if the relationship is worth the emotional work of repairing it.
- e) Meditate on the planetary combinations to try to adjust their expression in your lives.
- f) Look at the new aspects and use them to help you and your partner work through any possible relationship issues.

3.2 You meet someone and you discover that their chart contains particular aspects, and you have in the past clashed with people who have such aspects. What do you do? *Please select one statement:*
- a) Break away from the possible friendship, feeling that no matter how much you try it will only cause you emotional upset.
- b) Worry, as there is reason to assume that there will be problems this time around.
- c) Cannot say as you do not want to know about the charts of your friends.
- d) Not end the new friendship but be ready to discontinue it if the suspected problems you see in their chart emerge.

    e) Look at your own problems with the aspects and meditate on the planetary energies to help you deal with them in a new manner.
    f) Learning from previous experience, take a different approach to the friendship in the hope that it will avoid the problems of the past.

3.3 Do you expect to find that members of your own family have similar astrological features or themes in their individual horoscopes, for example, a Sun-Saturn or Capricorn theme? *Please select one statement:*
    a) You have not looked and do not intend to look.
    b) You have looked but have not noticed any themes or patterns in your family's horoscopes.
    c) Yes, but you think of them as just a coincidence.
    d) Yes, your family has one or more horoscopic themes, which you think has meaning for your family.
    e) Yes, and you not only consider that they have meaning but you expect these themes to be reflected in some way in other generations of your family.

3.4 If you knew the birth data of a pet, would you do its chart? Yes/No *please circle*

3.4.1 If you know your pet's chart do you expect to see similar astrological features in their chart as you would in one of your family members?
    Yes/No *please circle*

3.5 If you are trying to select the timing of a birth which is going to be a caesarean or inducted but unexpected events occur which alter this timing do you consider that the infant has chosen their own time of birth?
    Yes/No / Never considered it *please circle*

Section 4 – Your views on fate, destiny or necessity

There are different philosophical positions on the nature of determinism (fate), and also on why, if at all, it is present in our life. This section of the questionnaire is asking your opinion on some of these positions. *With each statement, please select one option of the five choices offered. If you do not believe in fate then please move to Section 5.*

4.1 To what extent do you feel that the experience of fate in your life comes from:
    1) the will of a single divine entity (God) in your life.
strongly disagree / disagree / neither agree or disagree / agree / strongly agree

2) a divine cosmos/nature (as gods, goddesses, spirits or energies expressing itself in your life.
strongly disagree / disagree / neither agree or disagree / agree / strongly agree

3) your soul making a choice to enter a physical state at a particular time to enable it to evolve.
strongly disagree / disagree / neither agree or disagree / agree / strongly agree

4) your actions in a previous life.
strongly disagree / disagree / neither agree or disagree / agree / strongly agree

5) the combination of <u>all</u> that has happened in the past with the physical laws of nature which fixes a unique and possible future.
strongly disagree / disagree / neither agree or disagree / agree / strongly agree

6) previous events in your own personal history, and/or your family's history and/or your culture's history.
strongly disagree / disagree / neither agree or disagree / agree / strongly agree

7) your life being part of and contributing to the emerging patterns formed naturally by the web of life.
strongly disagree / disagree / neither agree or disagree / agree / strongly agree

8) the human desire for a pattern which strings together what is only a series of coincidences into something which appears to be meaningful.
strongly disagree / disagree / neither agree or disagree / agree / strongly agree

4.2 Below are some statements on the purpose of astrology, for your clients as well as for yourself. To what extent do you believe that the purpose of astrology is:

1) to be used like a news report about what has happened, what can happen and what cannot happen.
strongly disagree / disagree / neither agree or disagree / agree / strongly agree

2) to show the place from which the journey of spiritual evolution begins, with the expectation that the chart will eventually becoming obsolete.
strongly disagree / disagree / neither agree or disagree / agree / strongly agree

3) to be used as a guide to learn your unique pattern of life, mortal and spiritual, so that you can reach the potential as *reflected in your natal chart*.
strongly disagree / disagree / neither agree or disagree / agree / strongly agree

4) to be used to help you become aware of, and attuned to, the unfolding will of a divine entity in the cosmos.

strongly disagree / disagree / neither agree or disagree / agree/ strongly agree

5) to be used to help you become attuned to and interact with the emerging patterns around you – the natural or secular world.

strongly disagree / disagree / neither agree or disagree / agree/ strongly agree

Section 5 – Your feelings about Astrology

5.1 How do you feel about the following statements? With each statement please select one option of the five choices offered.

1) The future is <u>fully</u> formed and astrology provides a tool to help read that future.

strongly disagree / disagree / neither agree or disagree / agree / strongly agree

2) Small events in your life can act as indicators of forthcoming, apparently non-related, larger events.

strongly disagree / disagree / neither agree or disagree / agree / strongly agree

3) The practice of astrology requires a divine presence in the universe – God, gods or spirits.

strongly disagree / disagree / neither agree or disagree / agree / strongly agree

These last two questions are only if you have the time to write a few lines.

What do you like about astrology?

_____

What do you dislike, if anything, about astrology?

_____

Do you wish to add anything further:

_____

Thank you for your time

NOTES

Introduction
The Modern Enigma of Fate

1 Sarah Broadie, 'From Necessity to Fate: A Fallacy?', The Journal of Ethics 5, no. 1 (2001): pp.21–37 (p.28).
2 Robert Solomon, 'On Fate and Fatalism', Philosophy East and West 53, no. 4 (2003): pp.435–54 (p.440).
3 Anthony Giddens, Modernity and Self-Identity. Self and Society in the Late Modern Age (Cambridge Polity Press, 1991), p.113.
4 Dalya Cohen-Mor, A Matter of Fate: The Concept of Fate in the Arab World as Reflected in Modern Arabic Literature (Oxford: Oxford University Press, 2001), p.xvi.
5 Cohen-Mor, A Matter of Fate: The Concept of Fate in the Arab World as Reflected in Modern Arabic Literature, p.xvii.
6 Carl Hoefer, 'Causal Determinism', The Stanford Encyclopedia of Philosophy (2010). http://plato.stanford.edu/archives/spr2010/entries/determinism-causal/. [Accessed 25 Aug 2016].
7 Evander Bradley McGilvary, 'Freedom and Necessity in Human Affairs', International Journal of Ethics 45, no. 4 (1935): pp.379–98 (p.382).
8 Pascal Massie, Contingency, Time and Possibility, an Essay on Aristotle and Duns Scotus (Maryland: Lexington Books, 2011), p.52.
9 Solomon, 'On Fate and Fatalism', p.443.
10 Richard Bargdill, 'Fate and Destiny: Some Historical Distinctions between the Concepts', Journal of Theoretical and Philosophical Psychology 26 (2 January 2006): pp.205–20 (pp.205–06).
11 Solomon, 'On Fate and Fatalism', p.435.
12 Nicola Gess, Primitive Thinking, Figuring Alterity in German Modernity, trans. Erik Butler and Susan L. Solomon (Berlin: Walter de Gruyter, 2013 [2022]), p.270.
13 Gess, Primitive Thinking, p.2.
14 Stuart A. Vyse, Superstition : A Very Short Introduction, First edn (Oxford: Oxford University Press, 2019), p.87.
15 Gillian Bennett, '"If I Knew You Were Coming I'd Have Baked You a Cake", The Folklore of Foreknowledge in a Neighborhood Group', in Barbara Walker, ed., Out of the Ordinary: Folklore and the Supernatural (Logan, UT: Utah University Press, 1995): pp.122–42 (p.135).
16 Eugene Subbotsky, Magic and the Mind: Mechanisms, Functions, and Development of Magical Thinking and Behavior (Oxford University Press, 2010), p.52.
17 Grant Bailey, 'Terrified of Friday 13th? These Are Brits' Top 30 Superstitions', The Mirror, 17 October 2017.
18 Orr Levental, Udi Carmi, and Assaf Lev, 'Jinx, Control, and the Necessity of Adjustment: Superstitions among Football Fans', Frontiers in Psychology 12 (2021): pp.1–10 (p.2).
19 Levental, Carmi, and Lev, 'Jinx, Control, and the Necessity of Adjustment: Superstitions among Football Fans', pp.1–10 (p.5).
20 Michaela Schippers and Paul A.M Van Lange, 'The Psychological Benefits of Superstitious Rituals in Top Sport: A Study among Top Sportspersons', Journal of Applied Social Psychology 36, no. 10 (2006): pp.2532–53 (p.2532).

21 Jeremy Burrus and Neal J. Roese, 'Long Ago It Was Meant to Be: The Interplay between Time, Construal, and Fate Beliefs', Personality Social Psychological Bulletin 32, no. 8 (2006): pp.1050–58 (p.1050).

22 Burrus and Roese, 'Long Ago It Was Meant to Be: The Interplay between Time, Construal, and Fate Beliefs', p.1050.

23 Eugen Bleuler, Textbook of Psychiatry, trans. A.A . Brill (New York: Macmillan, 1924;
[Lehrbuch der Psychiatrie. Berlin: Springer, 1923]). p.94.

24 Nicholas Campion, Astrology and Popular Religion in the Modern West (Surrey: Ashgate, 2012), p.1.

Chapter One
Fate: its Western roots

1 Jan Assmann. Death and Salvation in Ancient Egypt. Translated by David Lorton (Ithaca, NY, and London: Cornell University Press, 2005), p.55.

2 Miriam Lichtheim. Ancient Egyptian Literature [1973] 2019 edn (Berkeley, CA: University of California Press, 2006). p.107.

3 May Ahmed Hosny, 'Fate in Ancient Egypt', Journal of Association of Arab Universities for Tourism and Hospitality 19, no. 3 (2020): pp.61–68 (p.61).

4 Dorian Gieseler Greenbaum. The Diamon in Hellenistic Astrology, Origins and Influence (Leiden: Brill, 2016), p.96.

5 Ann Macy Roth and Catharine H. Roehrig, 'Magical Bricks and the Bricks of Birth', The Journal of Egyptian Archaeology 88 (2002): pp.121–39 (p.136).

6 Translation from the British Museum notes on this papyrus. https://www.britishmuseum.org/collection/object/Y_EA10470-3 [Accessed 5 June 2025].

7 Greenbaum, The Diamon in Hellenistic Astrology, Origins and Influence, p.96.

8 Assmann, Death and Salvation in Ancient Egypt, p.80.

9 Lichtheim, Ancient Egyptian Literature, p.535.

10 Edward, L. Karshner, 'Thought, Utterance, Power: Toward a Rhetoric of Magic', Philosophy & Rhetoric 44 (2011): pp.52–71 (p.51).

11 L.M. Zucconi, 'Medicine and Religion in Ancient Egypt', Religion Compass 1, no. 1 (2007): pp.26–37 (p.31).

12 Angus M. Bowie, 'Fate and Authority in Mesopotamian Literature and the Iliad', In Adrian Kelly and Christopher Metcalf, eds, Gods and Mortals in Early Greek and near Eastern Mythology, pp.243–61 (Cambridge: Cambridge University Press, 2021), p.244.

13 Francesca Rochberg, The Heavenly Writing, Divination, Horoscopy, and Astronomy in Mesopotamian Culture (Cambridge: Cambridge University Press, 2004), p.196.

14 James B. Pritchard, ed., Ancient near Eastern Texts (Princeton, NJ: Princeton University Press, 1969). p.179.

15 Bowie, 'Fate and Authority in Mesopotamian Literature and the Iliad', p.243.

16 James B Pritchard, ed. Ancient near Eastern Texts. (Princeton: Princeton University Press, 1969), p.65.

17) Pritchard, Ancient near Eastern Texts. The Lament for Sumer and Urim, lines (1–3p.64.

18 Bowie, 'Fate and Authority in Mesopotamian Literature and the Iliad', p.246.

19 Rochberg, The Heavenly Writing, Divination, Horoscopy, and Astronomy in Mesopotamian Culture. p.2.

20   Francesca Rochberg, 'Fate and Divination in Mesopotamia', Archiv für Orientforschung, Beihefte 19 (1982): pp.363–71 (p.363).
21   Simo Parpola, Letters from Assyrian Scholars to the Kings Esarhaddon and Assurbanipal Part 1 (Germany: Butzon and Kevelaer, 1970), Letter 292.
22   Nicholas Campion, The Dawn of Astrology. A Cultural History of Western Astrology, the Ancient and Classical Worlds (London: Continuum Books, 2008), p.64.
23   Hesiod, Works and Days, Theogony and the Shield of Hercules, trans. Hugh G. Evelyn-White (New York: Dover Publications Inc., 2006), p.95, L.215–219.
24   Homer, Iliad, trans. Samuel Butler (1898; Digireds.com Publishing, 2009), p.24, L.210–16.
25   Homer, Iliad, trans. E.V. Rieu (London: The Penguin Classics, 1964), p.22, L.230–40.
26   Simone Weil, 'The Iliad, or the Poem of Force', Chicago Review 18, no. 2 (1965): pp.5–30 (p.6).
27   Weil, 'The Iliad, or the Poem of Force', pp.5–30 (p.15).
28   Walter R. Agard, 'Fate and Freedom in Greek Tragedy', The Classical Journal 29, no. 2 (1933): pp.117–26 (p.119).
29   Sophocles. Oedipus the King, trans. F. Storr (Cambridge, MA: Harvard University Press, 1912), L.792–97.
30   Sophocles, Oedipus the King, L.824–30.
31   E. R. Dodds, 'On Misunderstanding the "Oedipus Rex"', Greece & Rome 13, no. 1 (1966): pp.37–49 (p.43).

Chapter Two
Fate in Classical Philosophy

1   Timaeus, trans. Donald J. Zeyl, in John M. Cooper, ed., Plato Complete Works (Cambridge: Hackett Publishing Company, 1997), 34b.
2   Plato, Laws, trans. Trevor J. Saunders, in John M. Cooper, ed., Plato Complete Works (Cambridge: Hackett Publishing Company, 1997), 903b.
3   Plato, Laws, 894e-95b.
4   Plato, Timaeus, 41e-42a.
5   Plato, Timaeus, 42b-c.
6   Plato, Timaeus, 42d.
7   Francis M Cornford, Plato's Cosmology (1935; Cambridge: Hackett Publishing Company, 1997), p.35.
8   Plato, Phaedo, trans. G.M.A Grube, in John M. Cooper, ed., Plato Complete Works (Cambridge: Hackett Publishing Company, 1997), 66b; Gunther S. Stent, 'Epistemic Dualism of Mind and Body', Proceedings of the American Philosophical Society 142, no. 4 (1998): pp.578–88 (p.578).
9   Plato, Timaeus, 27d.; Cornford, Plato's Cosmology, p.24.
10   Plato, Phaedo, 66a-b.
11   Plato, Republic, trans. G.M.A and rev Grube, and C.D.C. Reeve, in John M. Cooper, ed., Plato Complete Works (Cambridge: Hackett Publishing Company, 1997), 617d.
12   Plato, Republic, 618c.
13   Plato, Republic, 620e.
14   Plato, Republic, 617e.

15 Richard Broxton Onians, The Origins of European Thought About the Body, the Mind, the Soul, the World, Time and Fate (1951; London: Cambridge University Press, 1954), p.349.
16 Plato. Republic, 617c.
17 J.O. Urmson, The Greek Philosophical Vocabulary (London: Duckworth, 1990), p.20.
18 Dorian Gieseler Greenbaum, The Diamon in Hellenistic Astrology, Origins and Influence (Leiden: Brill, 2016), pp.240–244.
19 Plato, Timaeus, 42c.
20 Plato, Laws, 903c.
21 Plato, Phaedrus, 249a.
22 lham Dilman, Free Will: An Historical and Philosophical Introduction (London: Routledge, 1999), p.35.
23 Aristotle, Metaphysics, trans. Hugh Tredennick, Loeb Classical Library (London and Massachusetts: Harvard University Press, 1933.), Bekker 1074a 10-13, pp 97–101.
24 Aristotle, Metaphysics, Bekker 1072a25-1072b4, pp.92–95.
25 Aristotle, On the Heavens, trans. W.K.C. Guthrie, Loeb Classical Library (London: Harvard University Press, 1939), Bekker 284a 25. pp.134–35.
26 Aristotle, Meteorologica, Book I, Chapter 2, in Meteorologica, trans. H. D. P. Lee, Loeb Classical Library (Cambridge, MA: Harvard University Press, 1952), Bekker 339a10–339b25. pp.20–25.
27 Aristotle, Categories, Book I, Chap. 5, in Aristotle, Categories, trans. J. Cook and H. P. Tredennick, Loeb Classical Library (Cambridge, MA: Harvard University Press, 1963), Bekker 1b25–2a10. pp.35–37.
28 Aristotle, Physics, Book II, Chapter 3, in Physics, Vol. I, trans. R. P. and R. K. Gaye, Loeb Classical Library (Cambridge, MA: Harvard University Press, 1930), Bekker 194b23–195a10. pp.106–111.
29 Andrea Falcon, 'Aristotle on Causality', The Stanford Encyclopedia of Philosophy Spring 2011 (2011), http://plato.stanford.edu/archives/spr2011/entries/aristotle-causality/ [Accessed 12 March 2019].
30 Aristotle, On the Soul, Book II, Chapter 5, in On the Soul, trans. J. A. Smith, Loeb Classical Library (Cambridge, MA: Harvard University Press, 1931), Bekker 414a25–30. pp.207.
31 Aristotle, On the Soul, III. 4-6. Bekker 429a10–430a25. pp.96–107.
32 Aristotle, On the Heavens, I.8, Bekker 277a17–278a6. pp.78–85.
33 Aristotle, On the Heavens, II.6, Bekker 288a–289a. pp..162–-169.
34 Aristotle, Physics, Book IV, Chapter 8, in Physics, trans. R. P. Hardie and R. K. Gaye, Loeb Classical Library (Cambridge, MA: Harvard University Press, 1930,) Bekker 215a20–215b30. pp.366–371.
35 Aristotle, Physics, Bekker 255b1-5, p.89.
36 Aristotle, On Interpretation, Chapter 9, in Categories. On Interpretation. Prior Analytics, trans. H. P. Cooke, Loeb Classical Library (Cambridge, MA: Harvard University Press, 1938), Bekker 18b18–19b4, pp.122–27.
37 Aristotle, On Interpretation, Bekker 18b18–19b4. pp.122–27.
38 Susanne Bobzien, Determinism and Freedom in Stoic Philosophy (Oxford: Clarendon Press, [1998] 2005), p.1.
39 Diogenes Laertius, Lives of Eminent Philosophers, trans. R.D. Hicks, Vol. II, Loeb Classical Library (1925; Cambridge, MA Harvard University Press, 2005), Book II - 139.
40 Brad Inwood, Oxford Studies in Ancient Philosophy (Oxford: Oxford University Press, USA, 2008), p.277.

41   Bobzien, Determinism and Freedom in Stoic Philosophy, p.169.
42   Requoted from: Diogenes Laërtius, 'Physics', in Brad Inwood and Lloyd P. Gerson, eds, The Stoics Reader (Cambridge, MA: Hackett Publishing Company, Inc, 2008), pp.51–112 (p.62), Cicero text 2.19.
43   A.A. Long, and D.N. Sedley, The Hellenistic Philosophers. Vol. 1 (1987: Cambridge: Cambridge University Press, 2007), p.287.
44   A.A. Long and D.N. Sedley, The Hellenistic Philosophers. p.289.
45   Mark Balaguer, Free Will as an Open Scientific Problem (Cambridge, MA: MIT Press, 2010), p.70.
46   Plato, Timaeus, 30b-c, 31b.
47   A.A. Long, and D.N. Sedley, The Hellenistic Philosophers. pp.270–79.
48   A.A. Long, and D.N. Sedley, The Hellenistic Philosophers. pp.319, 392, 394.
49   Sophie Botros, 'Freedom, Causality, Fatalism and Early Stoic Philosophy', Phronesis 30, no. 3 (1985): pp.274–304 (p.276).
50   Botros, 'Freedom, Causality, Fatalism and Early Stoic Philosophy', pp.279–80.
51   Epictetus, Discourses Books 1 and 2, trans. P.E. Matheson (New York: Dover Publications Inc, trans. 2004), p.4.
52   Bobzien, Determinism and Freedom in Stoic Philosophy, p.338.
53   Epictetus, Discourses Books 1 and 2, Book I, Ch. 1 on p.5.
54   Michael Frede, A Free Will - Origins of the Notion in Ancient Thought (Berkeley, CA: University of California Press, 2011), p.45; See Epictetus, Discourses Books 1 and 2, Book I.1.
55   Frede, A Free Will - Origins of the Notion in Ancient Thought, p.45.
56   Bobzien, Determinism and Freedom in Stoic Philosophy, p.330.
57   Frede, A Free Will - Origins of the Notion in Ancient Thought, p.102.
58   A.A. Long, 'Soul and Body in Stoicism', Phronesis 27, no. 1 (1982): pp.34–57 (p.36).
59   R. Sklenář, 'Seneca, Oedipus 980-94: How Stoic a Chorus?', The Classical Journal 103, no. 2 (2007): pp.183–94 (p.186); A.A. Long and D.N. Sedley, The Hellenistic Philosophers, Vol. 1 (Cambridge: Cambridge University Press, 1987, 2007), p.311.
60   Long and Sedley, The Hellenistic Philosophers, 1, p.312.
61   Requoted from: Aulus Gellius 7.2.1-15, in Brad Inwood and Lloyd P. Gerson, eds, The Stoics Reader, p.110.
62   Bobzien, Determinism and Freedom in Stoic Philosophy, p.1.
63   Marcus Tullius Cicero, De Divinatione, trans. W.A. Falconer, Loeb Classical Library (1923; Cambridge, MA, and London: Harvard University Press, 2001), I lv.125.
64   Cicero, De Divinatione, I lvi, p.127.
65   Cicero, De Fato, trans. H. Rackham, Loeb Classical Library (Cambridge, MA, and London England: Harvard University Press, 1942), 9, p.203.
66   Cicero, De Fato, 5, p.197.
67   Cicero, De Fato, 45, p.243.
68   Cicero, De Divinatione, II 15 p387.
69   Dorothea Frede, 'Accidental Causes in Aristotle', Synthese 92, no. 1 (1992): pp.39–62 (p.39).
70   Cicero, De Natura Deorum, trans. H. Rackham, Loeb Classical Library (1933; Cambridge,, MA: London England: Harvard University Press, 1951), II. 43, p.165.
71   Greenbaum, The Daimon in Hellenistic Astrology, Origins and Influence, p.88.
72   Cicero, De Fato, 45, p.243.
73   Cicero, De Fato, 13, p.15.
74   Cicero, De Divinatione, II XLIII 90, p.473.
75   Cicero, De Divinatione, ll vii 18, p.389.

76 David Potter, Prophets and Emperors: Human and Divine Authority from Augustus to Theodosius (Cambridge, MA: Harvard University Press, 1994), p.17.
77 Sarah Iles Johnston and Peter T Struck, eds, Mantikê: Studies in Ancient Divination (Leiden: Brill 2005), p.7.
78 David Pingree, 'Astrology', in Philip P. Weiner, ed., Dictionary of the History of Ideas (New York: Charles Scribner's Sons, 1969), p.118.
79 Daryn Lehoux, 'Tomorrow's News Today: Astrology, Fate, and the Way Out', Representations Summer (2006): pp.105–22 (p.108).
80 Claudius Ptolemy, The Tetrabiblos, trans. J.M. Ashmand (Mokelumne Hill, USA: Health Research, 1969), Book I.I.
81 Nicholas Campion, The Dawn of Astrology. A Cultural History of Western Astrology, the Ancient and Classical Worlds (London: Continuum Books, 2008), p.208.
82 Robert Hand's introduction to: Claudius Ptolemy, Tetrabiblos Book I, trans. Robert Schmidt (Berkeley Springs, WV: The Golden Hind Press, 1994).
83 Ptolemy, The Tetrabiblos, Book I Chapter II, p.2.
84 Ptolemy, The Tetrabiblos, Book I, Chapter II, p.4.
85 Ptolemy, The Tetrabiblos, Book 1 Chapter II, p.4.
86 Ptolemy, The Tetrabiblos, Book I, Chapter II, p.9.
87 Ptolemy, The Tetrabiblos, Book I, Chapter II, p.8.
88 Ptolemy, The Tetrabiblos, Book I, Chapter II, p.10.
89 Ptolemy, The Tetrabiblos, Book I, Chapter II, p.9.
90 Ptolemy, The Tetrabiblos, Book III, Chapter II, p.107.
91 Gary Gabor, 'When Should a Philosopher Consult Divination? Epictetus and Simplicius on Fate and What Is up to Us', in Pieter d'Hoine and Gerd Van Riel, eds, Fate, Providence and Moral Responsibility in Ancient, Medieval and Early Modern Thought, Studies in Honour of Carlos Steel, pp.325–40 (Leuven University Press, 2014), p.325.
92 Ptolemy, The Tetrabiblos, Book I, Chapter II, p.9.
93 Vettius Valens, The Anthology Book V & Vi, trans. Robert Schmidt (Berkeley Springs, WV: The Golden Hind Press, 1997), p.88.
94 Vettius Valens, The Anthology Book IV, trans. Robert Schmidt (Berkeley Springs, WV: The Golden Hind Press, 2010), p.77.
95 Valens, 'The Anthology', Book IV, p.77. "The Anthology " Book IV p.77.
96 Bobzien, Determinism and Freedom in Stoic Philosophy, p.5.
97 Plato, Timaeus, 29-30d.
98 Long and Sedley, The Hellenistic Philosophers, 1, p.277.
99 Requoted from: Laërtius, 'Physics', 51-112. p.62. Cicero text 2.19.Inc</publisher><label>library 22</label><urls></urls></record></Cite></EndNote>
100 Aristotle, Metaphysics. Bekker 1074a 10-13, pp 97—101; Aristotle, Metaphysics, Bekker 1072a25-1072b4, pp.92–95.
101 Aristotle, Categories, Bekker 1b25–2a10, pp.35–37.
102 Frede, A Free Will - Origins of the Notion in Ancient Thought, pp.176–77.
103 Aristotle, On Interpretation, Bekker 18b18–19b4, pp.122–27.

Chapter Three
The Threads of Fate in the Medieval Period

1 James W. Ermatinger, The Decline and Fall of the Roman Empire (London: Greenwood Press 2004), p.xxii.
2 Ermatinger, The Decline and Fall of the Roman Empire, p.80.

3 Amelia Robertson Brown, Neil Bronwen, and Maria Mavroudi, Byzantine Culture in Translation [in English] Translations from Greek into Latin and Arabic during the Middle Ages: Searching for the Classical Tradition (Brill, 2017), p.126.
4 Gyula Klima, Fritz Allhoff, and Anand Vaidya, Medieval Philosophy : Essential Readings with Commentary (Oxford: Blackwell, 2007), p.4.
5 Tim Hegedus, Early Christianity and Ancient Astrology (New York: Peter Lang, 2007), p.69, footnote 42.
6 Hegedus, Early Christianity and Ancient Astrology, pp.46–47.
7 Saint Augustine, City of God, trans. Henry Bettenson (1972; London: Penguin Classics, 2003), V.9.
8 Saint Augustine, City of God, V.8.
9 Saint Augustine, City of God, V.11.
10 Saint Augustine, City of God, V.10.
11 Gerald Bonner, Freedom and Necessity - St Augustine's Teaching on Divine Power and Human Freedom (Washington, DC: The Catholic University of America Press, 2007), pp.17–18.
12 Bonner, Freedom and Necessity - St Augustine's Teaching on Divine Power and Human Freedom, p.23.
13 See Alan G. Hill, 'Three 'Visions' of Judgement: Southey, Byron, and Newman', The Review of English Studies 41, no. 163 (1990): pp.334–50.
14 Mark Graubard, 'Astrology's Demise and Its Bearing on the Decline and Death of Beliefs', Osiris 13 (1958): pp.210–61 (p.255).
15 Campion, The Dawn of Astrology. A Cultural History of Western Astrology, the Ancient and Classical Worlds, p.283.
16 Campion, The Dawn of Astrology. A Cultural History of Western Astrology, the Ancient and Classical Worlds, p.283.
17 J. den Boeft, Calcidius on Fate (Leiden: E.J. Brill, 1970), p.134.
18 Edward Grant, Science and Religion, 400 B.C. To A.D. 1550 (Baltimore, MD: John Hopkins University Press, 2004), p.93–94.
19 A. A. Long, 'Review: Calcidius', The Classical Review 25, no. 1 (1975): pp.52–54 (p.53).
20 den Boeft, Calcidius on Fate, paragraph 154.
21 den Boeft, Calcidius on Fate, paragraph 155.
22 Massie, Contingency, Time and Possibility, an Essay on Aristotle and Duns Scotus, pp.26–27.
23 Massie, Contingency, Time and Possibility, an Essay on Aristotle and Duns Scotus, pp.2–6.
24 Aristotle, Physics, 1013b 1–15.
25 Aristotle, Nicomachean Ethics, Book III.
26 Frede, 'Accidental Causes in Aristotle', pp.39–62 (p.39).
27 den Boeft, Calcidius on Fate, paragraph 162.
28 den Boeft, Calcidius on Fate, paragraph 162.
29 den Boeft, Calcidius on Fate, paragraph 151.
30 Robert Kane, A Contemporary Introduction to Free Will (New York and Oxford: Oxford University Press, 2005), p.47.
31 Roderick M Chisholm, 'Human Freedom and the Self', in Gary Watson, ed., Free Will (Oxford: Oxford University Press, 1982), p.31.
32 den Boeft, Calcidius on Fate, paragraph 157.
33 Susanne Bobzien, 'The Inadvertent Conception and Late Birth of the Free-Will Problem', Phronesis 43, no. 2 (1998): pp.133–75 (p.161).

34 Bobzien, 'The Inadvertent Conception and Late Birth of the Free-Will Problem', p.162.

35 Bobzien, 'The Inadvertent Conception and Late Birth of the Free-Will Problem', pp.163, 174.

36 Avicenna, The Metaphysics of the Healing, trans. Michael E. Marmura (Utah: Brigham Young University Press, 2005), Book VIII, Chapter 6, Paragraph 14.

37 See Michael E. Marmura, 'Some Aspects of Avicenna's Theory of God's Knowledge of Particulars', Journal of the American Oriental Society 82, no. 3 (1962): pp.299–312.

38 Tommaso Alpina, 'Is the Heaven an Animal? Avicenna's Celestial Psychology between Cosmology and Biology', in Ricardo Salles, ed., Cosmology and Biology in Ancient Philosophy, from Thales to Avicenna (Cambridge University Press, 2021): pp.261–63 (pp.261–62).

39 Ilai Alon, 'Al-Ghazālī on Causality', Journal of the American Oriental Society 100, no. 4 (1980): pp.397–405 (p.399).

40 Marmura, 'Some Aspects of Avicenna's Theory of God's Knowledge of Particulars', pp.299–312 (p.312).

41 Al-Ghazālī, The Incoherence of the Philosophers : A Parallel English-Arabic Text, trans. Michael E. Marmura (Provo, Utah: Brigham Young University Press, 1997), Discussion 1, 10–25.

42 Sukjae Lee, 'Occasionalism', in Edward N. Zalta, ed., *The Stanford Encyclopedia of Philosophy* (Fall 2020 Edition), https://plato.stanford.edu/archives/fall2020/entries/occasionalism/. [Accessed 13 June 2025].

43 Cohen-Mor, A Matter of Fate : The Concept of Fate in the Arab World as Reflected in Modern Arabic Literature, p.8.

44 Abū Ma'shar, The Great Introduction to Astrology vol.1, trans. Keiji Yamamoto and Charles Burnett (Leiden: Brill. 2019), 3-3b-e, p.83.

45 Omar of Tiberias, Three Books on Nativities, trans. Robert Hand (Berkeley Springs, WV: Golden Hind Press, 1997), p.13.

46 Requoted from Charles Burnett, 'The Certitude of Astrology: The Scientific Methodology of Al-Qabīsī and Abū Ma'shar', Early Science and Medicine 7, no. 3 (2002): pp.198–213 (p.207).

47 Burnett, 'The Certitude of Astrology: The Scientific Methodology of Al-Qabīsī and Abū Ma'shar', pp 98–213 (p.207).

48 Burnett, 'The Certitude of Astrology: The Scientific Methodology of Al-Qabīsī and Abū Ma'shar', pp.198–13 (p.208).

49 Roger French, 'Foretelling the Future: Arabic Astrology and the English Medicine in the Late Twelfth Century', Isis 87, no. 3 (1996): pp.453–80 (pp.458–59).

50 Tiberias, Three Books on Nativities, p.6.

51 Shlomo Sela, ed., Abraham Ibn Ezra's Introduction to Astrology (Leiden and Boston, MA: Brill, 2017), p.1.

52 Abraham ben Mei r Ibn Ezra et al., Abraham Ibn Ezra Latinus on Nativities: A Parallel Latin-English Critical Edition of 'Liber Nativitatum' and 'Liber Abraham Iudei De Nativitatibus' (Leiden and Boston, MA: Koninklijke Brill NV, 2019), p.172.

53 Rabbi Avraham Ibn Ezra, The Book of Nativities and Revolutions, trans. Meira B. Epstein (ARHAT Publications, 2008), p.3.

54 Shlomo Sela, ed., Abraham Ibn Ezra's Introduction to Astrology (Leiden and Boston, MA: Brill, 2017). p.2.

55 Abraham Ibn Ezra's Introduction to Astrology, p.13.

56 See Charles Burnett, 'The Twelfth-Century Renaissance', in C. Burnett, D.C. Lindberg, and M.H. Shank The Cambridge History of Science. The Cambridge History of Science (Cambridge University Press; 2013), pp.365–84.

57 Gerald Bonner, Freedom and Necessity - St Augustine's Teaching on Divine Power and Human Freedom (Washington, DC: The Catholic University of America Press, 2007), p.5.

58 Aristotle, Categories, ed. Jonathan Barnes, trans. J.L Ackrill, in The Complete Works of Aristotle (Princeton, NJ: Princeton University Press, 1984), 4a 17–20.

59 Burnett, 'The Certitude of Astrology: The Scientific Methodology of Al-Qabīsī and Abū Ma'shar', pp.198–213 (p.212); Lynn Thorndike, The History of Magic and Experimental Science, Vol. II (New York: MacMillan, 1923), p.77.

60 Nicholas Campion, 'The Concept of Destiny in Islamic Astrology and Its Impact on Medieval European Thought', ARAM 1, no. 2 (1989): pp.281–89 (p.288).

61 Roger French, 'Foretelling the Future: Arabic Astrology and the English Medicine in the Late Twelfth Century', pp.453–80 (pp.458,75,79).

62 F. Earle Fox, 'Biblical Theology and Pelagianism', The Journal of Religion 41, no. 3 (1961):pp.169–81 (p.172).

63 Patrick Curry, Prophecy and Power: Astrology in Early Modern England (New Jersey: Princeton University Press, 1989), pp.10–11.

64 Saint Thomas Aquinas, Summa Contra Gentiles. Book 3: Providence, Part Ii, trans. Vernon J. Bourke (Notre Dame, IN: University of Notre Dame Press, 1995), 3.91.2.

65 Aquinas, Summa Contra Gentiles. Book 3: Providence, Part Ii, 3.85.9.

66 Patrick Quinn, St. Thomas Aquinas's Concept of the Human Soul and the Influence of Platonism (New York: Brill, 2009), p.182.

67 Aquinas, Summa Contra Gentiles. Book 3: Providence, Part Ii, 3.86.11.

68 Massie, Contingency, Time and Possibility, an Essay on Aristotle and Duns Scotus, p.1.

69 Saint Thomas Aquinas and Timothy McDermott, Summa Theologiae (Methuen: 1991), Part I, Question 116.

70 French, 'Foretelling the Future: Arabic Astrology and the English Medicine in the Late Twelfth Century', pp.453–80 (p.457).

71 Petr Dvořák, 'The Concurrentism of Thomas Aquinas: Divine Causation and Human Freedom', Philosophia (Ramat Gan), 41.3 (2013): pp.617–34 (p.618).

72 Robert Hand, The Use of Military Astrology in Late Medieval Italy: The Textual Evidence (The Catholic University of America, 2014), p.i.

73 Alighieri Dante and Ciaran translator writer of introduction Carson, The Inferno (London: Apollo, 2020), Canto XX.

74 Guido Bonatti, Book of Astronomy, trans. Benjamin N. Dykes (Golden Valley, MN: The Cazimi Press, 2007), Vol.1, p.20.

75 Bonatti, Book of Astronomy, Vol 1, p.3.

76 Bonatti, Book of Astronomy, Vol.1, p.14.

77 Bonatti, Book of Astronomy, Vol I, p.17.

Chapter Four
The Early Modern and Free Will

1 John Cottingham, 'Descartes', in Ray Monk and Frederic Raphael, eds, The Great Philosophers, from Socrates to Turing, pp.93–134 (London: Phoenix Paperback, 2000), p.95.

2   David Cunning, 'Descartes on the Immutability of the Divine Will', Religious Studies 39, no. 1 (2003): pp.79–92 (p.80).

3   René Descartes, 'Conversation with Burman', in Charles Adam and Paul Tannery, eds, Oeuvres De Descartes, 12 Vols (Paris: Vrin, 1996), 5.166; Requoted from: Cunning, 'Descartes on the Immutability of the Divine Will', pp.79–99 (p.80).

4   René Descartes, 'Treatise on Man', in Mark A. Bedau and Carol E. Cleland, eds, The Nature of Life: Classical and Contemporary Perspective from Philosophy and Science (Cambridge: Cambridge University Press, 2010), p.20.

5   René Descartes, Principles of Philosophy, trans. Valentine Rodger Miller and Reese P. Miller (1644; New York: Springer, 1984), Pt. II, art. 64.

6   Descartes, Principles of Philosophy, Pt. IV, art. 187.

7   Stent, 'Epistemic Dualism of Mind and Body', pp.578–88 (p.579).

8   Plato, Phaedo, see 78b - 84c. Quote - 80a.

9   Broadie, 'Soul and Body in Plato and Descartes', pp.295–308 (p.295).

10   Broadie, 'Soul and Body in Plato and Descartes', pp.295–308 (p.305).

11   Broadie, 'Soul and Body in Plato and Descartes', pp.295–308 (p.299).

12   Broadie, 'Soul and Body in Plato and Descartes', pp.295–308 (p.299).

13   Jarrett, Spinoza: A Guide for the Perplexed, p.62.

14   René Descartes: Meditations on First Philosophy, trans. John Cottingham (Cambridge University Press 1996), Meditation II paragraph 2.

15   Albert G. A. Balz, 'Cartesian Refutations of Spinoza', The Philosophical Review 46, no. 5 (1937): pp.461–84 (p.479).

16   Weimin Mo and Wang Wei, 'Cogito: From Descartes to Sartre', Frontiers of Philosophy in China 2, no. 2 (2007): pp.247–64 (p.256).

17   Robert Rethy, 'The Teaching of Nature and the Nature of Man in Descartes' "Passions De L'ame"', The Review of Metaphysics 53, no. 3 (2000): pp.657–83 (pp.682–83).

18   Daniel C. Dennett, Elbow Room: The Varieties of Free Will Worth Wanting (Cambridge, MA: MIT Press, 1984), p.18.

19   Manuel Vargas, 'Revisionism', in Four Views on Free Will (Oxford: Blackwell Publishing, 2007), pp.126–65 (p.139).

20   Baruch de Spinoza et al., [Renati Des Cartes Principia: Philosophiae. English] The Principles of Cartesian Philosophy (Hackett Pub., 1998). See Steven Barbone's Introduction to this work, pp.xxvii–xxix.

21   Dilman, Free Will: An Historical and Philosophical Introduction, p.132.

22   Baruch de Spinoza, The Ethics, trans. R.H.M. Elwes (Forgotten Books, [1883] 2008), A.3.

23   Michael McKenna and Derk Pereboom, Free Will : A Contemporary Introduction (London: Routledge, 2016), p.16.

24   Spinoza, The Ethics, Part 2. Prop. 35. Note.

25   Dilman, Free Will: An Historical and Philosophical Introduction, p.128.

26   Dilman, Free Will: An Historical and Philosophical Introduction, p.132.

27   Baruch de Spinoza, On the Improvement of the Understanding, trans. R.H.M. Elwes (MobileReference.com, 2008), Paragraph 60. Points 1-8.

28   Firmin DeBrabander, Spinoza and the Stoics, Power Politics and the Passions (London: Continuum International Publishing Group, 2007), p.36.

29   Roger Scruton, 'Spinoza', in Ray Monk and Frederic Raphael, eds, The Great Philosophers, from Socrates to Turing, pp.135–74 (London: Phoenix Paperback, 2000), p.156.

30   Hasana Sharp, 'The Force of Ideas in Spinoza', Political Theory 35, no. 6 (2007): pp.732–55 (p.740).

31   Joel I. Friedman, 'An Overview of Spinoza's "Ethics"', Synthese 37, no. 1 (1978): pp.67–106 (pp.96–97).
32   Spinoza, The Ethics, See Part 5. Prop 10. Note.
33   DeBrabander, Spinoza and the Stoics, Power Politics and the Passions, p.7.
34   Spinoza, The Ethics, Part 4. Prop. 62 also expanded in Part 2.Prop.44. Corollary 2.
35   Martin Lin, 'Teleology and Human Action in Spinoza', The Philosophical Review 115, no. 3 (2006): pp.317–54 (pp.340–41).
36   Scruton, 'Spinoza', pp.135–74 (p.164).
37   Scruton, 'Spinoza', pp.135–74 (p.164).
38   Jarrett, Spinoza: A Guide for the Perplexed, p.146.
39   Spinoza, The Ethics, Part 2, Prop. 44, corollary 2 and Part 5, Prop 2 and 4.
40   Dilman, Free Will: An Historical and Philosophical Introduction, p.134.
41   Scruton, Spinoza', pp.135–74 (p.168).
42   Spinoza, The Ethics, Part 2. Prop 21. Note.
43   Scruton, 'Spinoza', pp.135–74 (pp.147–50); Drawing on, for example, Spinoza, The Ethics, Part 3. Prop.2 and Part 4. Prop 32, Note.
44   Derk Pereboom, 'Hard Incompatibilism', in John Martin Fischer, ed., Four Views on Free Will, p.85–125 (Oxford: Blackwell Publishing, 2007), p.85.
45   Antonio Favaro, 'Galileo, Astrologer', in Nicholas Campion and Nick Kollerstrom, eds, Galileo's Astrology, pp.9–19 (Bristol: Cinnabar Books, trans. 2003), (p.17–18); Dava Sobel, Galileo's Daughter (London: Fourth Estate, 1999), p.52.
46   Favaro, 'Galileo, Astrologer', pp.13–14.
47   Favaro, 'Galileo, Astrologer', p.11.
48   See Grazia Mirti, ;Galileo's Correspondence;, in Nicholas Campion and Nick Kollerstrom, eds, Galileo's Astrology, pp.73–96 (Bristol: Cinnabar Books, 2003).
49   Biblioteca Nazionale Centrale, Florence, MS. Gal.81. This research has been conducted using photocopies and images of this material.
50   Requoted from Antonino Poppi, 'On Trial for Astral Fatalism: Galileo Faces the Inquisition', in Nicholas Campion and Nick Kollerstrom, eds, Galileo's Astrology, pp.49–58 (Bristol: Cinnabar Books, 2003), p.54.
51   See Poppi, 'On Trial for Astral Fatalism: Galileo Faces the Inquisition', pp.49–58.
52   See Bernadette Brady, 'Galileo's Astrological Philosophy', in Charles Burnett and Dorian Gieseler Greenbaum, eds, From Masha' Allah to Kepler: Theory and Practice in Medieval and Renaissance Astrology, pp.77–100 (University of Wales, Lampeter: Sophia Centre Press, 2015.
53   See Bernadette Brady, 'Four Galilean Horoscopes: A Technical Analysis', Culture and Cosmos 7, no. 1 (2003): pp.113–43.
54   Jean-Baptiste Morin, The Morinus System of Horoscope Interpretation, trans. Richard S Baldwin, Astrologica Gallica Book Twenty One (1661; Washington, DC: AFA Inc., 1974), pp.41–42.
55   Morin, The Morinus System of Horoscope Interpretation, p.43.
56   Curry, Prophecy and Power: Astrology in Early Modern England, p.29.
57   Curry, Prophecy and Power: Astrology in Early Modern England, p.28.
58   Barbara H. Watters, Horary Astrology and the Judgment of Events (Washington: Valhalla, 2012), p.3.
59   See for example William Lilly, Christian Astrology, 3rd edn (1647; London: Regulus Publishing, 1985), p.124.
60   den Boeft, Calcidius on Fate, paragraph 157.
61   Curry, Prophecy and Power: Astrology in Early Modern England, p.30.
62   Edward Grant, 'When did modern science begin?', The American Scholar 66

(1997): pp.105–13 (p.105).
    63   Gary Deason, 'Reformation theology and the mechanistic conception of nature', in D. Lindberg and R. Numbers, eds, God and Nature: Historical Essays on the Encounter between Christianity and Science, pp.167–79 (Berkeley, CA: University of California Press, 1986), p.168.
    64   Isaac Newton, Newton's Principia, the Mathematical Principles of Natural Philosophy, trans. Andrew Motte (New York: Daniel Adees, 1846). p.74.

Chapter Five
The Dilemma of Determinism

    1   Isaac Newton, Newton's Principia, the Mathematical Principles of Natural Philosophy, trans. Andrew Motte (New York: Daniel Adees, 1846), p.74.
    2   Stephen Hawking, A Brief History of Time. (London, New York, Toronto, Sydney, Auckland: Bantam Press, 1988), p.46.
    3   Fritjof Capra, The Web of Life: A New Scientific Understanding of Living Systems (New York: Doubleday, 1996), p.119.
    4   Voltaire, 'The Ignorant Philosopher', in In the Best Known Works of Voltaire (London: Blue Ribbon Books, 1932,. p.439.
    5   Pierre-Simon Laplace, A Philosophical Essay on Probabilities (New York: Cosmio, 1812, 2007), p.4.
    6   Immanuel Kant, Kritik Der Urteilskraft, ed. G Lehmann (Stuttgart: Reclam, 1971), p.340.
    7   Edward J Larson, Evolution: The Remarkable History of a Scientific Theory (New York: Modern Library, 2004), pp.79–111.
    8   Robert Bishop, 'Chaos, Indeterminism, and Free Will', in Robert Kane, ed., The Oxford Handbook of Free Will (Oxford: Oxford University Press, 2002), pp.111–24 (p.111).
    9   John Earman, A Primer on Determinism (Dordrecht and Lancaster: Reidel, 1986, p.1.
    10   William James, The Will to Believe. Essays in Popular Philosophy (London and New York: Longmans, Green and Co., 1912), p.150.
    11   Carl Hoefer, 'Causal Determinism', The Stanford Encyclopedia of Philosophy (2010), http://plato.stanford.edu/archives/spr2010/entries/determinism-causal/ [Accessed 5 May 2011].
    12   Derk Pereboom, 'Living without Fee Will: The Case for Hard Incompatibilism', in The Oxford Handbook of Free Will (Oxford: Oxford University Press, 2002), pp.477–88 (p.477).
    13   Pereboom, 'Living without Fee Will: The Case for Hard Incompatibilism', p.483.
    14   David Hume, A Treatise of Human Nature (New York: Dover Philosophical Classics, 2003), pp.407–8.
    15   Gary Watson, 'Free Action and Free Will', Mind 96, no. 382 (1987): pp.145–72 (p.145).
    16   David Hume, An Enquiry Concerning Human Understanding, ed. Eric Steinberg (Cambridge: Hackett Publishing Company, 1977; repr., 2nd), p.66; Watson, 'Free Action and Free Will', pp.145–72 (p.150); Helen Beebee and Alfred Mele, 'Humean Compatibilism', Mind 111, no. 442 (2002): pp.201–24 (p.201).
    17   Robert Kane, A Contemporary Introduction to Free Will (New York and

Oxford: Oxford University Press, 2005), pp.2–3.

18 Norman Kemp Smith, 'The Naturalism of Hume (I)', Mind (1905): pp.149–73 (p.151).

19 Don Garrett, 'Reasons to Act and Believe: Naturalism and Rational Justification in Hume's Philosophical Project', Philosophical Studies: An International Journal for Philosophy in the Analytic Tradition 132, no. 1 (2007): pp.1–16 (p.3).

20 Hume, A Treatise of Human Nature, IV.p.131.

21 Donald C. Ainslie, 'Hume's Reflections on the Identity and Simplicity of Mind', Philosophy and Phenomenological Research 62, no. 3 (2001): pp.557–78 (pp.560–61).

22 Shaun Gallagher, 'The Theatre of Personal Identity: From Hume to Derrida', The Personalist Forum 8, no. 1 (1992): pp.21–30 (p.22).

23 Hume, An Enquiry Concerning Human Understanding, p.66.

24 McKenna and Pereboom, Free Will : A Contemporary Introduction, p.232.

25 Lucretius, De Rerum Natura, trans. W. H. D. Rouse, Loeb Classical Library (Harvard University Press, 1975), II, pp.251–63.

26 McKenna and Pereboom, Free Will : A Contemporary Introduction, p.233.

27 Gary Watson, 'Soft Libertarianism and Hard Compatibilism', The Journal of Ethics 3, no. 4 (1999): pp.351–65 (p.353).

28 Harry G. Frankfurt. 'Freedom of the Will and the Concept of a Person', The Journal of Philosophy 68, no. 1 (1971): pp.5–20 (pp.6–7).

29 Frankfurt, 'Freedom of the Will and the Concept of a Person', p.7.

30 Gary Watson, 'Free Agency.' The Journal of Philosophy 72, no. 8 (1975): pp.205–20 (p.220).

31 Immanuel Kant, Critique of Pure Reason, trans. Paul Guyer and Allen W. Wood (Cambridge: Cambridge University Press, 1998), A534/B62, p.33.

32 Dennett, Elbow Room: The Varieties of Free Will Worth Wanting, p.2.

33 Isaac Newton, Principia, trans. Motte-Cajori (Berkeley, CA: University of California Press, 1966), Prop.66 Bk1.

34 See Henri Jules Poincaré, Science and Method (London: T- Nelson, 1914).

35 Nancy Cartwright, The Dappled World: A Study of the Boundaries of Science (Cambridge: Cambridge University Press, 1999), p.25.

36 Cartwright, The Dappled World: A Study of the Boundaries of Science, p.31.

37 Nancy Cartwright, How the Laws of Physics Lie (Oxford: Oxford University Press, 1984), Introduction.

38 Hoefer, 'Causal Determinism'.

39 Hoefer 'Causal Determinism'.

40 John Norton, 'The Dome: An Unexpectedly Simple Failure of Determinism', Philosophy of Science (2008): 786-98: p.788.

41 David Hodgson, 'Quantum Physics, Consciousness, and Free Will', in The Oxford Handbook of Free Will (Oxford: Oxford University Press, 2002): pp.85–110 (p.106).

42 Susan Wolf, Freedom within Reason (New York and Oxford: Oxford University Press, 1990), pp.44–45.

43 Susan Wolf, 'Asymmetrical Freedom', The Journal of Philosophy 77, no. 3 (1980): pp.151–66 (p.166).

44 David Cockburn, 'Responsibility and Necessity', Philosophy 70, no. 273 (1995): pp.409–27 (p.427).

45 Shaun Nichols, 'Folk Intuitions on Free Will', http://www.ucl.ac.uk/~uctytho/dfwNichols.html [Accessed 5 April 2010].

46 Jennifer Mason, 'Linking Qualitative and Quantitative Data Analysis', in Alan

Bryman and Robert G. Burgess, eds, Analyzing Qualitative Data, pp.89–109 (London: Routledge, 1994), p.90.

47 Cicero, De Divinatione, I lvi, p.127.

Chapter Six
Astrology from Without and Within

1 Nicholas Campion, The Dawn of Astrology. A Cultural History of Western Astrology, the Ancient and Classical Worlds (London: Continuum Books, 2008), pp.ix–x.

2 Nicholas Campion, Astrology and Popular Religion in the Modern West: Prophecy, Cosmology, and the New Age Movement (Farnham and Burlington, VT: Ashgate, 2012), p.1.

3 Philippa Waring, The Dictionary of Omens and Superstitions (London Treasure Press, 1978), p.20.

4 John Woodroff, Neil Bone, and Storm Dunlop, Philip's Astronomy Dictionary (London: George Philip Ltd, 1995), p.20.

5 Martin Ince, Dictionary of Astronomy (Teddington: Peter Collins Publishing, 1997), p.12.

6 Geoffrey Dean, Ivan Kelly, and Arthur Mather, 'Astrology', in Gordon Stein, ed., The Encyclopaedia of the Paranormal (Amherst, NY: Prometheus Books, 1996), p.35.

7 Geoffrey, Kelly, and Mather, 'Astrology', in The Encyclopaedia of the Paranormal, pp.35–36.

8 Morris Jastrow, 'Astrology', in The Encyclopaedia Britannica (Cambridge: Cambridge University Press, 1910), p.795.

9 Lawrence E. Jerome, 'Astrology and Modern Science: A Critical Analysis', Leonardo 6, no. 2 (1973): pp.121–30 (p.121).

10 George P. Hansen, 'Rationalization, Secularization, and the Paranormal: On the 'Elimination' of Magic from the World', in Academy of Spirituality and Paranormal Studies, Inc. Annual Conference (Kutstown University, PA. June 3-6 2010), pp.117–19.

11 Lilly, Christian Astrology, From 'To the Student of Astrology', p.B.

12 Robert Hand, 'The Proper Relationship of Astrology and Science', Astrological Journal 31, no. 6 (1989): pp.307–16 (p.316).

13 Michael Mayer, The Mystery of Personal Identity (San Diego, CA: ACS Publications, 1984), p.44.

14 Patrick Curry, 'Astrology', in Kelly Boyd, ed., The Encyclopaedia of Historians and Historical Writing 2 Vols (London: Fitzroy Dearborn, 1999), Vol 1, p.55.

15 Derk Pereboom, 'Living without Fee Will: The Case for Hard Incompatibilism', p.477.

16 Cicero, De Divinatione, II xlv 95.

17 St Augustine, St. Augustine Confessions, trans. R.S. Pine-Coffin (London: Penguin, 1961), p.140.

18 Hegedus, Early Christianity and Ancient Astrology, p.43.

19 Theodore Otto Wedel, The Mediaeval Attitude toward Astrology, Particularly in England (Oxford University Press, 1920), p.6; Lynn Thorndike, History of Magic and Experimental Science Part 1 (New York and London: Columbia University Press, 1923), p.514.

20 Hegedus, Early Christianity and Ancient Astrology, pp. 85–87.

21 See: Hippolytus, 'The Refutation of All Heresies', http://www.valentino-salvato.

com/Astrology/pdf/The_Refutation_of_All_Heresies.pdf; C. Moreschini, ed., St Gregory of Nazianzus, Poemata Arcana (Oxford: Oxford University Press, 1997), pp.22–23.

22   Nick Goggin, 'Astrology, Is It Harmless Fun or a Gateway into the Occult?', Watchmen Bible Study Group, http://www.biblestudysite.com/astrol.htm#3 [Accessed 9 January 2009].

23   John Chamber, A Treatise against Judicial Astrologie (London: John Harison, Rowe, 1601), pp.34,37.

24   John Levi Martin, '"The Authoritarian Personality", 50 Years Later: What Lessons Are There for Political Psychology?', Political Psychology 22, no. 1 (2001): pp.1–26 (pp.2–3).

25   See: Theodor W. Adorno et al., The Authoritarian Personality (New York: Harper & Brothers, 1950).

26   Theodor W. Adorno, 'The Stars Down to Earth: The Los Angeles Times Astrology Column', in Stephen Crook, ed., The Stars Down to Earth and Other Essays on the Irrational in Culture, pp.34–127 (London: Routledge, 1994), p.38.

27   Stephen Crook in the introduction of 'The Stars Down to Earth: The Los Angeles Times Astrology Column', pp.16–17.

28   Adorno 'The Stars Down to Earth: The Los Angeles Times Astrology Column', p.54.

29   Adorno 'The Stars Down to Earth: The Los Angeles Times Astrology Column', p.64.

30   Adorno 'The Stars Down to Earth: The Los Angeles Times Astrology Column', pp.16–17.

31   Adorno 'The Stars Down to Earth: The Los Angeles Times Astrology Column', p.64.

32   John J. Ray, 'Why the F Scale Predicts Racism: A Critical Review', Political Psychology 9, no. 4 (1988): pp.671–79 (pp.676–77).

33   Robert Wuthnow, 'Astrology and Marginality', Journal for the Scientific Study of Religion 15, no. 2 (1976): pp.157–68 (p.167).

34   Wuthnow, 'Astrology and Marginality', p.157.

35   G.A. Tyson, 'People Who Consult Astrologers: A Profile', Personality and Individual Differences Vol. 3 (1982): pp.119–26 (pp.119–20).

36   Tyson, 'People Who Consult Astrologers: A Profile', p.123.

37   Cary J. Nederman and James Wray Goulding, 'Popular Occultism and Critical Social Theory: Exploring Some Themes in Adorno's Critique of Astrology and the Occult', Sociological Analysis 42, no. 4 (1981): pp.325–32 (p.327).

38   Richard Dawkins, 'The Real Romance in the Stars', The Independent on Sunday, 31 December 1995.

39   John Bauer and Martin Durant, 'British Public Perceptions of Astrology: An Approach from the Sociology of Knowledge', Culture and Cosmos 1, no. 1 (1997): pp.55–72 (p.66).

40   Michael Dambrun, 'Belief in Paranormal Determinism as a Source of Prejudice Towards Disadvantaged Groups: "The Dark Side of Stars"', Social Behavior and Personality 32, no. 7 (2004): pp.627–36 (p.634).

41   T. L. Brink, 'Inconsistency of Belief among Roman Catholic Girls: Concerning Religion, Astrology, Reincarnation', Review of Religious Research 20, no. 1 (1978): pp.82–85 (p.82).

42   Brink, 'Inconsistency of Belief among Roman Catholic Girls: Concerning Religion, Astrology, Reincarnation', p.84.\

43   Brink, 'Inconsistency of Belief among Roman Catholic Girls: Concerning

Religion, Astrology, Reincarnation', p.85.

44   Shoshanah Feher, 'Who Holds the Cards? Women and New Age Astrology', in James R. Lewis and J. Gordon Melton, eds, Perspectives on the New Age, pp.179–88 (Albany, NY: State University of New York Press, 1992), p.180.

45   Feher, 'Who Holds the Cards? Women and New Age Astrology', p.188.

46   Focus Project, 'First Light - Preliminary Findings from the Astrologer's Survey Questionnaire in the United States', in U.A.C. '95 (Monterey, CA, 1995).

47   Nicholas Campion, 'Prophecy, Cosmology and the New Age Movement. The Extent and Nature of Contemporary Belief in Astrology' (Bath Spa University College, 2004), pp.243,248.

48   Alison Bird, 'Astrology in Education: An Ethnography' (University of Sussex, 2006), p.94.

49   Bridget McKenney Costello, 'Astrology in Action: Culture and Status in Unsettled Lives' (University of Pennsylvania, 2006), p.ii.

50   Nicholas Campion and Liz Greene, eds, Astrologies, Plurality and Diversity (Ceredigion: Sophia Press, University of Wales Trinity Saint David, 2011), p.1.

51   Duane W Hamacher, and Ray P. Norris, 'Bridging the Gap' through Australian Cultural Astronomy' [In English]. International Astronomical Union. Proceedings of the International Astronomical Union, suppl. 'Oxford IX' International Symposium on Archaeoastronomy 7, no. S278 (Jan 2011 2023-11-25 2011), pp.282–90 (pp.282–83); Also see Duane W Hamacher. The First Astronomers (Crows Nest, NSW: Allen & Unwin, 2022).

52   Campion, Astrology and Popular Religion in the Modern West: Prophecy, Cosmology, and the New Age Movement, pp.85–88.

Chapter Seven
Asking about Fate

1   Bobzien, Determinism and Freedom in Stoic Philosophy, p.5.

2   Michelle Pfeffer, 'Reassessing the Marginalization of Astrology in the Early Modern World', The Historical Journal 66, no. 5 (2023): pp.1152–76 (p.1153).

3   Zheljana Peric, 'The Decline of Astrology: A Symbol of Man's Disconnection with Nature, Self and the Cosmos' (paper presented at the Proceedings of the 53rd Annual Meeting of the International Society for the Systems Sciences, University of Queensland, Brisbane, Australia July 12-17 2009), p.1.

4   Bobzien, Determinism and Freedom in Stoic Philosophy, p.5.

5   See Appendix, Questions Q.4.1.1 to Q.4.1.8.

6   Statistical Service Centre, 'Approaches to the Analysis of Survey Data' (The University of Reading, 2001).

7   See Appendix, Questions Q.4.2.1 – Q.4.2.5 and Q.5.1.1.

8   John T Kulas, Alicia A Stachowski, and Brad A Haynes, 'Middle Response Functioning in Likert-Responses to Personality Items,' Journal of Business and Psychology 22, no. 3 (2008): pp.251–59 (p.251).

9   Deniz Ertan, Dane Rudhyar: His Music, Thought, and Art (University of Rochester Press, 2009), p.89.

10   See T. **O'Connor and H.Y. Wong**, *Emergent Properties*, in E.N. Zalta, ed., **The Stanford Encyclopedia of Philosophy** (Fall 2015 Edition). https://plato.stanford.edu/entries/properties-emergent/ [Accessed 20 August 2022].

11   Steve Bruce, Religion in Modern Britian (Oxford: Oxford University Press,

1995), p.105; Gordon J Melton, 'The Emergence of New Religions in Eastern Europe since 1989', in Eileen Baker and Margot Warburg, eds, New Religions and New Religiosity, pp.45–66 (Aarhus: Aarhus University Press, 2001), p.53.
    12   K. Alladakan, 'Stoicism, a Philosophical Basis for Ecology?', Open Access Library Journal 8 (2021). doi: 10.4236/oalib.1107237.
    13   F. J. K. Soontiëns, 'Evolution: Teleology or Chance?', Journal for General Philosophy of Science / Zeitschrift für allgemeine Wissenschaftstheorie 22, no. 1 (1991): pp.133–41 (p.140).
    14   Bron Taylor, Introducing Religion and Dark Green Religion (Oakland, CA: University of California Press, 2010), p.10.
    15   Nichols, 'Folk Intuitions on Free Will'.
    16   See Dean, Kelly, and Mather, 'Astrology', pp. 47–99.
    17   Elliott Jacques, The Form of Time (London: Heinemann, 1982), pp.14–15.
    18   Feher, 'Who Holds the Cards? Women and New Age Astrology', pp.179–88 (p.180).
    19   Adorno, 'The Stars Down to Earth: The Los Angeles Times Astrology Column', pp.34–127 (p.121); Dean, Kelly, and Mather, ' Astrology ', pp.47–99.
    20   Wolf, 'Asymmetrical Freedom', pp.151–66 (p.166).
    21   Cockburn, 'Responsibility and Necessity', pp.409–27 (p.427).
    22   Nichols, 'Folk Intuitions on Free Will'.
    23   'Folk Intuitions on Free Will', p.6; Shaun Nichols and Joshua Knobe, 'Moral Responsibility and Determinism: The Cognitive Science of Folk Intuitions', Nous 41 (2007): pp.663–85.
    24   Nichols and Knobe 'Moral Responsibility and Determinism: The Cognitive Science of Folk Intuitions', pp.663–85 (p.665).
    25   Nichols and Knobe 'Moral Responsibility and Determinism: The Cognitive Science of Folk Intuitions', pp.663–85 (p.671).

Chapter Eight
Notes in a Bottle

    1   Clifford Geertz, The Interpretation of Cultures (New York: Basic Books, 1973), p.6.
    2   The Interpretation of Cultures, p.9.
    3   Sarah H. Matthews, 'Crafting Qualitative Research Articles on Marriages and Families', Journal of Marriage and Family 67, no. 4 (2005): pp.799–808 (p.800).
    4   P. Atkinson and M. Hammersley, 'Ethnography and Participant Observation', in N. Denzin and Y. Lincoln, eds, Handbook of Qualitative Research (Thousand Oaks, CA: Sage, 1994), pp.248–61 (p.248).
    5   Clifford Geertz, Local Knowledge (London: Fontana Press, 1993), p.58.
    6   Survey code 20081213.
    7   Survey code 20081044
    8   Plotinus, The Enneads, trans. Stephen MacKenna (New York: Larson Publications, 1992), II.3.9.
    9   Nicholas Campion, A History of Western Astrology Volume Ii (London, UK: Continuum Books, 2009), p.231; Patrick Curry, A Confusion of Prophets: Victorian and Edwardian Astrology (London: Collins & Brown, 1992), p.126.
    10   Curry, A Confusion of Prophets: Victorian and Edwardian Astrology, p.123.
    11   Alan Leo, Astrology for All, 4th edn (Fowler, 1969 (1974)), The Introduction

(CD version of this book).

12 Alan Leo, The Progressed Horoscope (1905; London: L.N. Fowler, 1929), p.11; For one example of this in Plato see Plato, Alcibiades I, 130c-33c.
13 Leo, The Progressed Horoscope, p.xiv.
14 Leo, The Progressed Horoscope, p.350.
15 Plato, Laws, 903c.
16 Survey code 20080656
17 Survey code 20081170
18 Survey code 20080969
19 Ptolemy, The Tetrabiblos, Book I, Ch.III on p.13.
20 Survey code 20080680
21 Epictetus, Discourses Books 1 and 2, Book I, Ch. 1 on p.5.
22 Scruton, 'Spinoza', pp.135–74 (p.156).
23 Hazel Rose Markus and Shinobu Kitayama, 'Culture and the Self. Implications for Cognition, Emotion, and Motivation', Psychological Review 98, no. 2 (1991): pp.224–53 (p.224); See also Clifford Geertz, 'On the Nature of Anthropological Understanding', American Scientist 63 (1975): pp.47–53 (pp.47–53).
24 Giddens, Modernity and Self-Identity. Self and Society in the Late Modern Age, p.53.
25 Survey code 20080750
26 Survey code 20081667
27 Survey code 20081396
28 Survey code 20081079
29 Survey code 20080702
30 Survey code 20081074
31 Survey code 20080686
32 Survey code 20080909
33 Survey code 20081027
34 Survey code 20081028
35 Cited in Long and Sedley, The Hellenistic Philosophers, 1, p.309.
36 Campion, A History of Western Astrology Volume Ii, p.241.
37 Long and Sedley, The Hellenistic Philosophers, 1, p.312.
38 Eva Cybulska, 'Nietzsche:Love, Guilt and Redemption', Philosophy Now 86 (2011):pp. 6–9 (p.9); Elliot Wolfson, 'Structure, Innovation, and Diremptive Temporality:The Use of Models to Study Continuity and Discontinuity in Kabbalistic Tradition', Journal for the Study of Religions and Ideologies 6, no. 18 (2007): pp.143–67 (p.159).
39 Dane Rudhyar, Astrological Signs the Pulse of Life (Boulder, CO, and London: Shambhala, 1978), p.12; Sheila Rayner, Clare Rayner, and Rob Newell, Dane Rudhyar, an Interview, Oral History of the Arts Archive (Long Beach, CA: University of California Press, 1977), pp.94–95.
40 Deniz Ertan, Dane Rudhyar: His Music, Thought, and Art (University of Rochester Press, 2009), p.89.
41 Bernadette Brady, 'The Horoscope as an "Imago Mundi": Rethinking the Nature of the Astrologer's Map', in Nicholas Campion and Liz Greene, eds, Astrologies, Plurality and Diversity, pp.47–62 (University of Wales Trinity Saint David, Lampeter: Sophia Centre Press, 2011), p.59.
42 Survey code 20081287
43 Survey code 20080614
44 Survey code 20080633
45 Survey code 20081245

46 Survey code 20080627
47 Long and Sedley, The Hellenistic Philosophers, 1, p.227.
48 Giddens, Modernity and Self-Identity. Self and Society in the Late Modern Age, p.85.
49 Survey code 20081203
50 Survey code 20080979
51 Survey code 20081168
52 Ptolemy, The Tetrabiblos, Book I, Chapter II p.8.
53 den Boeft, Calcidius on Fate, paragraph 151.
54 Survey code 20080936
55 Survey code 20080919
56 Survey code 20081167
57 J.R Lucas, The Freedom of the Will (Oxford: Clarendon, 1970), p.63.
58 Wolf, Freedom within Reason, pp.44-45.
59 Survey code 20081307
60 Survey code 20081357
61 Survey code 20081153
62 Church of Light, http://www.light.org/zain1.php3.
63 C.C. Zain, Delineating the Horoscope (1922; Whitefish, MT: Kessinger Publishing, 2004), pp.6–7.
64 Survey code 20080609
65 Survey code 20080676
66 Ptolemy, The Tetrabiblos, Book III, Ch.V on p.114; Liz Greene, The Horoscope in Manifestation, Psychology and Prediction (London: Centre for Psychological Astrology Press, 1997), p.12; Sue Tompkins, The Contemporary Astrologer's Handbook (London: Flare Publications, 2006), p.73 and p.157.
67 Survey code 20081123

Chapter Nine
Conversations about Fate

1 Plato, Timaeus, 30a-c.
2 Diogenes Laertius, Lives of Eminent Philosophers, II, Book II - 139; den Boeft, Calcidius on Fate, Paragraph 152.
3 Plato, Timaeus, 48a ; Aristotle, Metaphysics, 1072b 3-4; Long and Sedley, The Hellenistic Philosophers, 1, p.277; Diogenes Laertius, Lives of Eminent Philosophers, trans. R.D. Hicks, Vol. I, Loeb Classical Library (1925; Cambridge, MA: Harvard University Press, 2005), II.140.
4 Plotinus, The Enneads, II.3.7.
5 C.G Jung, Symbols of Transformation, trans. R.F.C. Hull, 1st edn, Vol. 5 (1956; Princeton, NJ: Princeton University, 1990), p.313.
6 Plato, Timaeus, 30b-c , 41e-42a and 48a.
7 Aristotle, On the Soul, II.415b 9-12 and III 432a 1-2
8 Quinn, St. Thomas Aquinas's Concept of the Human Soul and the Influence of Platonism, p.182.
9 Plato, Laws, 904 b-e.
10 Steven B. Smith, 'What Kind of Democrat Was Spinoza?', Political Theory 33, no. 1 (2005): pp.6–27 (p.15).

11 Alan Oken, Soul-Centered Astrology (New York and London: Bantam, 1990),

p.20.
12   Oken, Soul-Centered Astrology, p.19.
13   Plotinus, The Enneads, II.3.10.
14   Hone, Margaret E. The Modern Text-Book of Astrology 5th edn. (London: L N Fowler & Co. Ltd, [1951] 1973), p.17.
15   Hone, The Modern Text-Book of Astrology, p.151.
16   Demetra George, Astrology and the Authentic Self (Lake Worth, FL: Ibis Press, 2008), p.286.
17   George, Astrology and the Authentic Self, p.287.
18   George, Astrology and the Authentic Self, pp.35–36.
19   See Spinoza, The Ethics, Part 2. Prop. 35. Note; Spinoza, On the Improvement of the Understanding, Paragraph 60, Points 1-8; Dilman, Free Will: An Historical and Philosophical Introduction, p.128.
20   Schopenhauer, The World as Will and Idea, p.23.
21   Clare Martin, Mapping the Psyche, an Introduction to Psychological Astrology. Volume 1, the Planets and the Zodiac Signs (London: Centre for Psychological Astrology Press, 2005), p.2.
22   Plato, Timaeus, 42d.
23   Hone, The Modern Text-Book of Astrology,, pp.30–31.
24   Spinoza, The Ethics, Part 4. Prop. 62 also expanded in Part 2. Prop.44. Corollary 2.
25   den Boeft, Calcidius on Fate, paragraph 157.
26   James Davidson, 'I Told You So', The London Review (2004): pp.12–18 (pp.13–14).

Chapter Ten
A Topography of Fate

1   Solomon, 'On Fate and Fatalism', p.435.
2   Amiria J. M. Henare, Martin Holbraad, and Sari Wastell, Thinking through Things : Theorising Artefacts Ethnographically (London: Routledge, 2007), p.2.
3   Heraclitus, Heraclitus Fragments, trans. Brooks Haxton (New York: Penguin Classics, 2003), fg.41.
4   Diogenes Laertius, Lives of Eminent Philosophers, II, Book II - 139.
5   Laertius, Lives of Eminent Philosophers, II, Book II - 139.
6   Michael J Loux, Metaphysics a Contemporary Introduction (London, New York: Routledge, 2006), pp.13–14.
7   Lucien Lévy-Bruhl, The Notebooks on Primitive Mentality, trans. Peter Riviére (San Francisco, CA: Harper & Row Publishers, 1975), pp.37–38.
8   Lévy-Bruhl, The Notebooks on Primitive Mentality, p.50.
9   Lévy-Bruhl, The Notebooks on Primitive Mentality, p.134.
10   Henare, Holbraad, and Wastell, Thinking through Things : Theorising Artefacts Ethnographically, p.4.
11   Christian Fuchs, Wolfgang Hofkirchner, and Bert Klauninger, 'The Dialectic of Bottom-up and Top-Down Emergence in Social Systems', (paper presented at the Problems of Individual Emergence, Amsterdam, 2001).
12   Klaus A Bruner, 'What's Emergent in Emergent Computing?', (2002), http://www.self-organization.org/results/papers/pdf/hsicpaper1.pdf [Accessed 2 March 2009].
13   Brian Goodwin, Nature's Due, Healing Our Fragmented Culture (London:

Floris Books, 2007), p.35.

14   Margaret Ward, 'Butterflies and Bifurcations: Can Chaos Theory Contribute to Our Understanding of Family Systems?', Journal of Marriage and the Family 57, no. 3 (1995): pp.629–38 (pp.630–31); van Eenwyk, Archetypes and Strange Attractors, the Chaotic World of Symbols, pp.129–37.

15   Goodwin, Nature's Due, Healing Our Fragmented Culture, pp.38–39.

16   Michael Bütz, Chaos and Complexity – Implications for Psychological Theory and Practice. (Washington, DC: Taylor and Francis, 1997), p.17.

17   Bütz, Chaos and complexity – implications for psychological theory and practice, p.18.

18   Goodwin, Nature's Due, Healing Our Fragmented Culture, pp.38–39.

19   John van Eenwyk, Archetypes and Strange Attractors, the Chaotic World of Symbols (Toronto, Canada: Inner City Books, 1997), p.52.

20   van Eenwyk, Archetypes and Strange Attractors, the Chaotic World of Symbols, p.52.

21   Patricia Shaw, Changing Conversations in Organizations: A Complexity Approach to Change. (London and New York: Routledge, 2002), pp.152–53.

22   Lévy-Bruhl, The Notebooks on Primitive Mentality, p.134.

23   Soontiëns, 'Evolution: Teleology or Chance?', p.140.

24   Sarah Broadie, 'From Necessity to Fate: A Fallacy?', The Journal of Ethics 5, no. 1 (2001): pp.21–37 (p.28).

25   Edward Morgan Forster, A Room with a View (London: Edward Arnold, 1908), p.120.

26   David Mitchell, Cloud Atlas: A Novel (London: Random House, 2004), p.320.

27   Maurice Leenhardt, The Preface of, the Notebooks on Primitive Mentality by Lucien Lévy-Bruhl, trans. Peter Riviére (San Francisco, CA: Harper & Row Publishers, 1975), p.xx.

28   Leenhardt, The Preface of, the Notebooks on Primitive Mentality by Lucien Lévy-Bruhl, p.xx.

29   Lévy-Bruhl, The Notebooks on Primitive Mentality, p.84.

30   Lévy-Bruhl, The Notebooks on Primitive Mentality, p.106.

31   Giddens, Modernity and Self-Identity. Self and Society in the Late Modern Age, p.70.

32   Giddens, Modernity and Self-Identity. Self and Society in the Late Modern Age, p.54.

33   Giddens, Modernity and Self-Identity. Self and Society in the Late Modern Age, p.54.

34   Giddens, Modernity and Self-Identity. Self and Society in the Late Modern Age, p.53.

35   Scruton, 'Spinoza', pp.135–74 (p.164).

36   Tilly A Phenomenology of Landscape, p.12.

37   Tim Ingold, 'The Temporality of the Landscape', World Archaeology 25, no. 2 (1993): pp.152–74 (p.154).

38   Cartwright, The Dappled World: A Study of the Boundaries of Science, p.3 and pp.43–46.

39   William Shakespeare, Hamlet, Act V, Scene II.

REFERENCES

Adorno, Theodor, W., 'The Stars Down to Earth: The Los Angeles Times Astrology Column', in *The Stars Down to Earth and Other Essays on the Irrational in Culture*, ed. by Stephen Crook, pp.34 –127 (London: Routledge, 1994).

Adorno, Theodor, W., Else Frenkel-Brunswik, Daniel J. Levinson, and R. Nevitt Sanford, *The Authoritarian Personality* (New York: Harper & Brothers, 1950).

Agard, Walter, R. ,'Fate and Freedom in Greek Tragedy', *The Classical Journal* 29, no. 2 (1933), pp.117–26.

Ainslie, Donald C. ,'Hume's Reflections on the Identity and Simplicity of Mind', *Philosophy and Phenomenological Research* 62, no. 3 (2001), pp.557–78.

Al-Ghazālī, *The Incoherence of the Philosophers: A Parallel English-Arabic Text*, trans. by Michael E. Marmura (Provo, UT: Brigham Young University Press, 1997).

Alladakan, K. ,'Stoicism, a Philosophical Basis for Ecology?', *Open Access Library Journal* 8(2021), pp.1–14, doi: 10.4236/oalib.1107237.

Alon, Ilai, 'Al-Ghazālī on Causality', *Journal of the American Oriental Society* 100, no. 4 (1980), pp.397–405.

Alpina, Tommaso, 'Is the Heaven an Animal? Avicenna's Celestial Pschology between Cosmology and Biology', in *Cosmology and Biology in Ancient Philosophy, from Thales to Avicenna*, ed. by Ricardo Salles (Cambridge University Press, 2021), pp.261–63.

Aquinas, Saint Thomas, *Summa Contra Gentiles. Book 3: Providence, Part Ii*, trans. by Vernon J. Bourke (Notre Dame, IN: University of Notre Dame Press, 1995).

Aristotle, *Categories*, Book I, Chap. 5, in *Aristotle, Categories*, trans. J. Cook and H. P. Tredennick, Loeb Classical Library (Cambridge, MA: Harvard University Press, 1963).

———, *On Interpretation*, Chapter 9, in *Categories. On Interpretation. Prior Analytics*, trans. H. P. Cooke, Loeb Classical Library (Cambridge, MA: Harvard University Press, 1938).

———, *Metaphysics*, trans. by Hugh Tredennick, Loeb Classical Library (London and Cambridge, MA: Harvard University Press, 1933).

———, *Meteorologica*, Book I, Chapter 2, in *Meteorologica*, trans. H.D.P. Lee, Loeb Classical Library (Cambridge, MA: Harvard University Press, 1952).

———, *Nicomachean Ethics*, trans. by W.D. Ross. The Complete Works of Aristotle, ed. by Jonathan Barnes (Princeton, NJ: Princeton University Press, 1984).

———, *On the Heavens*, trans. by W.K.C. Guthrie, Loeb Classical Library (London: Harvard University Press, 1939).

———, *On the Soul*, Book II, Chapter 5, in *On the Soul*, trans. J. A. Smith, Loeb Classical Library (Cambridge, MA: Harvard University Press, 1931).

———, *Physics*, Book IV, Chapter 8, in *Physics*, trans. R. P. Hardie and R. K. Gaye, Loeb Classical Library (Cambridge, MA: Harvard University Press, 1930).

Assmann, Jan, *Death and Salvation in Ancient Egypt,* trans. by David Lorton (Ithaca, NY, and London: Cornell University Press, 2005).

Atkinson, P., and M. Hammersley, 'Ethnography and Participant Observation', in *Handbook of Qualitative Research*, ed. by N. Denzin and Y. Lincoln (Thousand Oaks, CA: Sage, 1994, pp.248–61

Augustine, Saint, *City of God*, trans. by Henry Bettenson (1972; London: Penguin Classics, 2003).

———, *St. Augustine Confessions*, trans. by R.S. Pine-Coffin (London: Penguin, 1961).

Avicenna, *The Metaphysics of the Healing*, trans. by Michael E Marmura (Utah: Brigham Young University Press, 2005).

Bailey, Grant, 'Terrified of Friday 13th? These Are Brits' Top 30 Superstitions', *The Mirror*, 17 October 2017.

Balaguer, Mark, *Free Will as an Open Scientific Problem* (Cambridge, MA: MIT Press, 2010).

Balz, Albert G. A., 'Cartesian Refutations of Spinoza', *The Philosophical Review* 46, no. 5 (1937), pp.461–84.

Bargdill, Richard, 'Fate and Destiny: Some Historical Distinctions between the Concepts', *Journal of Theoretical and Philosophical Psychology* 26 (01 January 2006), pp.205–20.

Bauer, John, and Martin Durant, ' British Public Perceptions of Astrology: An Approach from the Sociology of Knowledge', *Culture and Cosmos* 1, no. 1 (1997), pp.55–72.

Beebee, Helen, and Alfred Mele, 'Humean Compatibilism', *Mind* 111, no. 442 (1 April 2002), pp.201–24.

Bennett, Gillian, '"If I Knew You Were Coming I'd Have Baked You a Cake". The Folklore of Foreknowledge in a Neighborhood Group', In *Out of the Ordinary: Folklore and the Supernatural*, ed. by Barbara Walker (Logan, UT: Utah University Press, 1995), pp. 122–42.

Berry, Thomas, *The Great Work, Our Way into the Future* (New York: Three Rivers Press, 1999).

Bird, Alison, 'Astrology in Education: An Ethnography', University of Sussex, 2006.

Bishop, Robert, 'Chaos, Indeterminism, and Free Will', In *The Oxford Handbook of Free Will*, ed. by Robert Kane (Oxford: Oxford University Press, 2002), pp.111–24.

Bleuler, Eugen, *Textbook of Psychiatry*, trans. by A.A. Brill (New York: Macmillan, 1924;

[*Lehrbuch der Psychiatrie*. Berlin: Springer, 1923.]).

Bobzien, Susanne, *Determinism and Freedom in Stoic Philosophy* (1998; Oxford: Clarendon Press, 2005).

Bonatti, Guido, *Book of Astronomy*, trans. by Benjamin N. Dykes (Golden Valley, MN: The Cazimi Press, 2007).

Bonner, Gerald, *Freedom and Necessity - St Augustine's Teaching on Divine Power and Human Freedom* (Washington, DC: The Catholic University of America Press, 2007).

Botros, Sophie, 'Freedom, Causality, Fatalism and Early Stoic Philosophy', *Phronesis* 30, no. 3 (1985), pp.274–304.

Bowie, Angus M., 'Fate and Authority in Mesopotamian Literature and the Iliad', In *Gods and Mortals in Early Greek and near Eastern Mythology*, ed. by Adrian Kelly and Christopher Metcalf (Cambridge: Cambridge University Press, 2021), pp. 243–61.

Brady, Bernadette. *Cosmos, Chaosmos and Astrology* (London: Sophia Centre Press, 2014).

———. 'Four Galilean Horoscopes: A Technical Analysis', *Culture and Cosmos* 7, no. 1 (2003), pp.113–43.

———. 'Galileo's Astrological Philosophy', In *From Masha' Allah to Kepler: Theory and Practice in Medieval and Renaissance Astrology*, ed. by Charles Burnett and Dorian Gieseler Greenbaum (University of Wales, Lampeter: Sophia Centre Press, 2015), pp.77–100.

———. 'The Horoscope as an 'Imago Mundi': Rethinking the Nature of the Astrologer's Map', In *Astrologies, Plurality and Diversity*, ed. by Nicholas Campion and Liz Greene (University of Wales Trinity Saint David, Lampeter: Sophia Centre Press, 2011), pp.47–62.

Brink, T. L., 'Inconsistency of Belief among Roman Catholic Girls: Concerning Religion, Astrology, Reincarnation', *Review of Religious Research* 20, no. 1 (1978), pp.2–85.

Broadie, Sarah, 'From Necessity to Fate: A Fallacy?', *The Journal of Ethics* 5, no. 1 (2001), pp.21–37.

———. 'Soul and Body in Plato and Descartes', *Proceedings of the Aristotelian Society* 101 (2001), pp.295–308.

Brown, Amelia Robertson, Bronwen Neil, and Maria Mavroudi. *Byzantine Culture in Translation* [in English] Series translations from Greek into Latin and Arabic during the Middle Ages: Searching for the Classical Tradition (Brill, 2017).

Bruce, Steve, *Religion in Modern Britain* (Oxford: Oxford University Press, 1995).

Bruner, Klaus A., 'What's Emergent in Emergent Computing?' (2002). http://www.self-organization.org/results/papers/pdf/hsicpaper1.pdf.

Burnett, Charles, 'The Certitude of Astrology: The Scientific Methodology of Al-Qabīsī and Abū Ma'shar', *Early Science and Medicine* 7, no. 3 (2002), pp.198–213.

———, 'The Twelfth-Century Renaissance', in C. Burnett, D.C. Lindberg, and M.H. Shank, *The Cambridge History of Science*. The Cambridge History of Science (Cambridge University Press, 2013), pp.365–84.

Burrus, Jeremy, and Neal J. Roese, 'Long Ago It Was Meant to Be: The Interplay between Time, Construal, and Fate Beliefs', *Personality Social Psychological Bulletin* 32, no. 8 (2006), pp.1050–58.

Bütz, Michael, *Chaos and Complexity – Implications for Psychological Theory and Practice* (Washington, DC: Taylor and Francis, 1997).

Caldwell, Roger, 'Schopenhauer', *Philosophy Now*, no. 86 (Sept/Oct 2011), pp.13–15.

Campion, Nicholas, *Astrology and Popular Religion in the Modern West* (Surrey: Ashgate, 2012).

———, 'The Concept of Destiny in Islamic Astrology and Its Impact on Medieval European Thought', *ARAM* 1, no. 2 (1989), pp.281–89.

———, *The Dawn of Astrology. A Cultural History of Western Astrology, the Ancient and Classical Worlds* (London: Continuum Books, 2008).

———, *A History of Western Astrology Volume II* (London: Continuum Books, 2009).

———, 'Prophecy, Cosmology and the New Age Movement. The Extent and Nature of Contemporary Belief in Astrology' (Bath Spa University College, 2004).

———, *Astrology and Popular Religion in the Modern West: Prophecy, Cosmology, and the New Age Movement* (Farnham and Burlington, VT: Ashgate, 2012).

Campion, Nicholas, and Liz Greene, eds, *Astrologies, Plurality and Diversity* (Ceredigion: Sophia Press, University of Wales Trinity Saint David, 2011).

Capra, Fritjof, *The Web of Life: A New Scientific Understanding of Living Systems* (New York: Doubleday, 1996).

Cartwright, Nancy, *The Dappled World: A Study of the Boundaries of Science* (Cambridge: Cambridge University Press, 1999).

———, *How the Laws of Physics Lie* (Oxford: Oxford University Press, 1984).

Centre, Statistical Service, 'Approaches to the Analysis of Survey Data' (The University of Reading, 2001).

Chamber, John, *A Treatise against Judicial Astrologie*. London: John Harison, Rowe, 1601. Chamber, John. A Treatise against Iudicial Astrologie Dedicated to the Right Honorable Sir Thomas Egerton Knight, Lord Keeper of the Great Seale, and One of Her Maiesties Most Honorable Priuie Councell. Vvritten by Iohn Chamber, One of the Prebendaries of Her Maiesties Free Chappell of Vvindsor, and Fellow of Eaton College [in English]. (London: John Harison, 1601).

Cicero, Marcus Tullius, *De Divinatione,* trans. by W.A. Falconer, Loeb Classical Library (1923; Cambridge, MA, and London: Harvard University Press, repr. 2001).

———, *De Fato*, trans. H. Rackham, Loeb Classical Library (Cambridge, MA, and London: Harvard University Press, 1942).

———, *De Natura Deorum*, trans. H. Rackham, Loeb Classical Library (1933; Cambridge, MA, and London: Harvard University Press, 1951).

Cockburn, David, 'Responsibility and Necessity', *Philosophy* 70, no. 273 (1995), pp.409–27.

Cohen-Mor, Dalya, *A Matter of Fate: The Concept of Fate in the Arab World as Reflected in Modern Arabic Literature* (Oxford: Oxford University Press, 2001).

Cornford, Francis M., *Plato's Cosmology* (1935; Cambridge: Hackett Publishing Company, 1997).

Costello, Bridget McKenney, 'Astrology in Action: Culture and Status in Unsettled Lives' (University of Pennsylvania, 2006).

Cottingham, John, 'Descartes', In *The Great Philosophers, from Socrates to Turing*, ed. by Ray Monk and Frederic Raphael (London: Phoenix Paperback, 2000), pp.93–134.

Cunning, David, 'Descartes on the Immutability of the Divine Will', *Religious Studies* 39, no. 1 (2003), pp.79–92.

Curry, Patrick. 'Astrology', in *The Encyclopaedia of Historians and Historical Writing 2 Vols*, ed. by Kelly Boyd, pp.55–7 (London: Fitzroy Dearborn, 1999).

———, *A Confusion of Prophets: Victorian and Edwardian Astrology* (London: Collins & Brown, 1992).

———, *Prophecy and Power: Astrology in Early Modern England* (Princeton, NJ: Princeton University Press, 1989).

Cybulska, Eva, 'Nietzsche:Love, Guilt and Redemption', *Philosophy Now*, no. 86 (Sept/Oct 2011), pp.6–9.

Dambrun, Michael, 'Belief in Paranormal Determinism as a Source of Prejudice Towards Disadvantaged Groups: "The Dark Side of Stars"', *Social Behavior and Personality* 32, no. 7 (2004): pp.627–36.

Dante, Alighieri, *The Inferno*, introduction and trans. by Ciaran Carson (London: Apollo, 2020).

Davidson, James, 'I Told You So', *The London Review*, (2004), pp.12–18.

Dawkins, Richard, 'The Real Romance in the Stars', *The Independent on Sunday*, 31 December 1995.

Dean, Geoffrey, Ivan Kelly, and Arthur Mather, 'Astrology', in *The Encyclopaedia of the Paranormal*, ed. by Gordon Stein (Amherst, NY: Prometheus Books, 1996), pp.47–99.

Deason, Gary, 'Reformation theology and the mechanistic conception of nature', in *God and Nature: Historical Essays on the Encounter between Christianity and Science*, ed. by D. Lindberg and R. Numbers (Berkeley, CA: University of California Press, 1986), pp.167–79.

DeBrabander, Firmin, *Spinoza and the Stoics, Power Politics and the Passions* (London: Continuum International Publishing Group, 2007).

den Boeft, J. *Calcidius on Fate* (Leiden: Brill, 1970).

Dennett, Daniel C. ,*Elbow Room: The Varieties of Free Will Worth Wanting* (Cambridge, MA: MIT Press, 1984).

Descartes, René, *Principles of Philosophy*. trans. by Valentine Rodger Miller and Reese P. Miller (1644; New York: Springer, 1984).

———, René, *Meditations on First Philosophy*, trans. by John Cottingham (Cambridge University Press, 1996).

———, 'Treatise on Man', In *The Nature of Life:Classical and Contemporary Perspective from Philosophy and Science*, ed. by Mark A. Bedau and Carol E. Cleland (Cambridge: Cambridge University Press, 2010).

Dilman, Ilham, *Free Will: An Historical and Philosophical Introduction* (London: Routledge, 1999).

Diogenes Laertius, *Lives of Eminent Philosophers*, trans. by R.D. Hicks, Loeb Classical Library, Vol. II, (1925; Cambridge, MA: Harvard University Press, 2005).

———, *Lives of Eminent Philosophers*, trans. by R.D. Hicks, Loeb Classical Library, Vol. I (1925; Cambridge, MA: Harvard University Press, 2005).

Dodds, E. R., 'On Misunderstanding the "Oedipus Rex"', *Greece & Rome* 13, no. 1 (1966), pp.37–49.

Dvořák, Petr, 'The Concurrentism of Thomas Aquinas: Divine Causation and Human Freedom', *Philosophia (Ramat Gan)* 41.3 (2013), pp.617–34.

Earman, John, *A Primer on Determinism* (Dordrecht and Lancaster: Reidel, 1986).

Eenwyk, John van, *Archetypes and Strange Attractors, the Chaotic World of Symbols* (Toronto, Canada: Inner City Books, 1997).

Eliade, M., *Traité D'histoire Des Religions* (Paris: 1949).

Epictetus, *Discourses Books 1 and 2*, trans. by P.E. Matheson (New York: Dover Publications Inc, 2004).

Ermatinger, James W., *The Decline and Fall of the Roman Empire* (London: Greenwood Press, 2004).

Ertan, Deniz, *Dane Rudhyar: His Music, Thought, and Art* (University of Rochester Press, 2009).

Falcon, Andrea, 'Aristotle on Causality', *The Stanford Encyclopedia of Philosophy* (Spring 2011). http://plato.stanford.edu/archives/spr2011/entries/aristotle-causality/.

Favaro, Antonio, 'Galileo, Astrologer', in *Galileo's Astrology*, ed. by Nicholas Campion and Nick Kollerstrom (Bristol: Cinnabar Books, trans. 2003), pp.9–19.

Feher, Shoshanah, 'Who Holds the Cards? Women and New Age Astrology', in *Perspectives on the New Age*, ed. by James R Lewis and Gordon Melton (Albany, NY: State University of New York Press, 1992), pp.179–88.

Fischer, John Martin, 'Compatibilism', In *Four Views on Free Will*, ed. by John Martin Fischer (Oxford: Blackwell Publishing, 2007), pp.44–84.

Forster, Edward Morgan, *A Room with a View* (London: Edward Arnold, 1908).

Fox, F. Earle, 'Biblical Theology and Pelagianism', *The Journal of Religion* 41, no. 3 (1961), pp.169–81.

Frankfurt, Harry G., 'Freedom of the Will and the Concept of a Person', *The Journal of Philosophy* 68, no. 1 (1971), pp.5–20.

Frede, Dorothea, 'Accidental Causes in Aristotle', *Synthese* 92, no. 1 (1992), pp.39–62.

Frede, Michael, *A Free Will - Origins of the Notion in Ancient Thought* (Berkeley, CA: University of California Press, 2011).

French, Roger, 'Foretelling the Future: Arabic Astrology and the English Medicine in the Late Twelfth Century', *Isis* 87, no. 3 (September 1996), pp.453–80.

Friedman, Joel I., 'An Overview of Spinoza's "Ethics"', *Synthese* 37, no. 1 (1978), pp.67–106.

Fuchs, Christian, Wolfgang Hofkirchner, and Bert Klauninger, 'The Dialectic of Bottom-up and Top-Down Emergence in Social Systems', Paper presented at the Problems of Individual Emergence, Amsterdam (2001).

Gabor, Gary, 'When Should a Philosopher Consult Divination? Epictetus and Simplicius on Fate and What Is up to Us', In *Fate, Providence and Moral Responsibility in Ancient, Medieval and Early Modern Thought*, ed. by Pieter d'Hoine and Gerd Van Riel, Studies in Honour of Carlos Steel (Leuven University Press, 2014), pp.325–40.

Gallagher, Shaun, 'The Theatre of Personal Identity: From Hume to Derrida', *The Personalist Forum* 8, no. 1 (1992), pp.21–30.

Garrett, Don, 'Reasons to Act and Believe: Naturalism and Rational Justification in Hume's Philosophical Project', *Philosophical Studies: An International Journal for Philosophy in the Analytic Tradition* 132, no. 1 (2007), pp.1–16.

Geertz, Clifford, *The Interpretation of Cultures* (New York: Basic Books, 1973).

———, *Local Knowledge* (London: Fontana Press, 1993).

———, 'On the Nature of Anthropological Understanding', *American Scientist* 63 (1975), pp.47–53.

George, Demetra, *Astrology and the Authentic Self* (Lake Worth, FL: Ibis Press, 2008).

Gess, Nicola, *Primitive Thinking, Figuring Alterity in German Modernity*, trans. by Erik Butler and Susan L. Solomon (2013; Berlin: Walter de Gruyter, 2022).

Giddens, Anthony, *Modernity and Self-Identity. Self and Society in the Late Modern Age* (Cambridge: Polity Press, 1991).

Goggin, Nick, 'Astrology, Is It Harmless Fun or a Gateway into the Occult?', Watchmen Bible Study Group, http://www.biblestudysite.com/astrol.htm#3 [Accessed 1 December 2008].

Goodwin, Brian, *Nature's Due, Healing Our Fragmented Culture* (London: Floris Books, 2007).

Grant, Edward, 'When did modern science begin?', *The American Scholar* 66 (1997), pp.105–13.

———. *Science and Religion, 400 B.C. To A.D. 1550* (Baltimore, MD: John Hopkins University Press, 2004).

Graubard, Mark, 'Astrology's Demise and Its Bearing on the Decline and Death of Beliefs', *Osiris* 13 (1958), pp.210–61.

Greenbaum, Dorian Gieseler, *The Diamon in Hellenistic Astrology, Origins and Influence* (Leiden: Brill, 2016).

Greene, Liz, *The Horoscope in Manifestation, Psychology and Prediction* (London: Centre for Psychological Astrology Press, 1997).

Gupta, R. K., 'Freud and Schopenhauer', *Journal of the History of Ideas* 36, no. 4 (1975), pp.721–28.

Hamacher, Duane W., *The First Astronomers* (Crows Nest, NSW: Allen & Unwin, 2022).

Hamacher, Duane W., and Ray P. Norris, '"Bridging the Gap" through Australian Cultural Astronomy' [In English], *International Astronomical Union. Proceedings of the International Astronomical Union, suppl. 'Oxford IX' International Symposium on Archaeoastronomy* 7, no. S278 (January 2011), pp.282–90.

Hand, Robert, 'The Proper Relationship of Astrology and Science', *Astrological Journal* 31, no. 6 (November/December 1989), pp.307–16.

———. 'The Use of Military Astrology in Late Medieval Italy: The Textual Evidence', The Catholic University of America (2014).

Hansen, George P., 'Rationalization, Secularization, and the Paranormal: On the "Elimination" of Magic from the World', In *Academy of Spirituality and Paranormal Studies, Inc. Annual Conference*, Kutstown University, Pennsylvania (3–6 June 2010).

Hawking, Stephen, *A Brief History of Time* (London, New York, Toronto, Sydney, Auckland: Bantam Press, 1988).

Hegedus, Tim, *Early Christianity and Ancient Astrology* (New York: Peter Lang, 2007).

Henare, Amiria J. M., Martin Holbraad, and Sari Wastell, *Thinking through Things: Theorising Artefacts Ethnographically* (London: Routledge, 2007).

Heraclitus, *Heraclitus Fragments*, trans. by Brooks Haxton (New York: Penguin Classics, 2003).

Hesiod, *Works and Days, Theogony and the Shield of Hercules,* trans. by Hugh G. Evelyn-White (New York: Dover Publications Inc., 2006).

Hill, Alan G., 'Three "Visions" of Judgement: Southey, Byron, and Newman', *The Review of English Studies* 41, no. 163 (1990), pp.334–50.

Hippolytus, 'The Refutation of All Heresies', http://www.valentino-salvato.com/Astrology/pdf/The_Refutation_of_All_Heresies.pdf [Accessed 3 May 2009].

Hodgson, David, 'Quantum Physics, Consciousness, and Free Will', In *The Oxford Handbook of Free Will* (Oxford: Oxford University Press, 2002), pp.85–110.

Hoefer, Carl, 'Causal Determinism', *The Stanford Encyclopedia of Philosophy* (2010). http://plato.stanford.edu/archives/spr2010/entries/determinism-causal/ [Accessed 10 Oct 2012].

Homer, *Iliad*, trans. by E.V. Rieu (London: The Penguin Classics, 1964).

———. *Iliad,* trans. by Samuel Butler (1898; Digireds.com Publishing, 2009).

Hone, Margaret E.,*The Modern Text-Book of Astrology*, 5th edn (1951; London: L.N. Fowler & Co. Ltd, 1973).

Hosny, May Ahmed, 'Fate in Ancient Egypt', *Journal of Association of Arab Universities for Tourism and Hospitality* 19, no. 3 (2020), pp.61–68.

Hume, David, *An Enquiry Concerning Human Understanding*, ed. by Eric Steinberg (Cambridge: Hackett Publishing Company, 1977).

———, *A Treatise of Human Nature* (New York: Dover Philosophical Classics, 2003).

Ibn Ezra, Abraham ben Meir, and Shlomo translator Sela. *Abraham Ibn Ezra Latinus on Nativities : A Parallel Latin-English Critical Edition of 'Liber Nativitatum' and 'Liber Abraham Iudei De Nativitatibus'*. [in Latin texts, translated from Hebrew, with English translations on facing pages; critcal matter in English.] (Leiden ; Boston: Koninklijke Brill NV, 2019).

Ibn Ezra, Rabbi Avraham, *The Book of Nativities and Revolutions*, trans. by Meira B. Epstein (ARHAT Publications, 2008).

Ince, Martin, *Dictionary of Astronomy* (Teddington: Peter Collins Publishing, 1997).

Ingold, Tim, 'The Temporality of the Landscape', *World Archaeology* 25, no. 2 (1993), pp.152–74.

Inwood, B., *Oxford Studies in Ancient Philosophy (*Oxford: Oxford University Press, 2008).

Jacques, Elliott, *The Form of Time* (London: Heinemann, 1982).

James, William, *The Will to Believe. Essays in Popular Philosophy* (London and New York: Longmans, Green and Co., 1912).

Jarrett, C.E., *Spinoza: A Guide for the Perplexed* (Continuum, 2007).

Jastrow, Morris, 'Astrology,' in *The Encyclopaedia Britannica* (Cambridge: Cambridge University Press, 1910).

Jerome, Lawrence E., 'Astrology and Modern Science: A Critical Analysis', *Leonardo* 6, no. 2 (1973), pp.121–30.

Johnston, Sarah Iles, and Peter T. Struck, eds, *Mantikê: Studies in Ancient Divination* (Leiden: Brill 2005).

Jung, C.G., *Symbols of Transformation*, trans. by R.F.C. Hull, Vol. 5 (1956; Princeton, NJ: Princeton University, 1990).

Kane, Robert, *A Contemporary Introduction to Free Will* (New York and Oxford: Oxford University Press, 2005).

Kant, Immanuel, *Kritik Der Urteilskraft*, ed. by G. Lehmann (Stuttgart: Reclam, 1971).

———, *Critique of Pure Reason*, trans. by Paul Guyer and Allen W. Wood (Cambridge: Cambridge University Press, 1998).

Karshner, Edward L., 'Thought, Utterance, Power: Toward a Rhetoric of Magic', *Philosophy & Rhetoric* 44 (2011), pp.52–71.

Klima, Gyula, Fritz Allhoff, and Anand Vaidya, *Medieval Philosophy: Essential Readings with Commentary* (Oxford: Blackwell, 2007).

Kulas, John T, Alicia A Stachowski, and Brad A Haynes, 'Middle Response Functioning in Likert-Responses to Personality Items', *Journal of Business and Psychology* 22, no. 3 (2008), pp.251–59.

Laëtius, Diogenes, 'Physics', trans. by Brad Inwood, in *The Stoics Reader*, ed. by Brad Inwood and Lloyd P. Gerson (Cambridge, MA: Hackett Publishing Company, Inc., 2008), pp.51–112.

Laplace, Pierre-Simon, *A Philosophical Essay on Probabilities* (1812; New York :Cosmio, 2007).

Larson, Edward J., *Evolution: The Remarkable History of a Scientific Theory* (New York: Modern Library, 2004).

Leenhardt, Maurice, *The Preface of the Notebooks on Primitive Mentality by Lucien Lévy-Bruhl*, trans. by Peter Riviére (San Francisco, CA: Harper & Row Publishers, 1975).

Lehoux, Daryn, 'Tomorrow's News Today: Astrology, Fate, and the Way Out', *Representations* Summer (2006), pp.105–22.

Leo, Alan, *Astrology for All*, 4th edn (Fowler, 1969, 1974).

———. *Astrology for All*. The Works of Alan Leo, Astrology Cd No. 1. 1998 edn, Vol. 2007, London, UK (1910).

———. *The Progressed Horoscope* (1905; London: L.N. Fowler, 1929).

Levental, Orr, Udi Carmi, and Assaf Lev, 'Jinx, Control, and the Necessity of Adjustment: Superstitions among Football Fans', *Frontiers in Psychology* 12 (2021), pp.1–10.

Lévy-Bruhl, Lucien, *The Notebooks on Primitive Mentality*, trans. by Peter Riviére (San Francisco, CA: Harper & Row Publishers, 1975).

Light, Church of, http://www.light.org/zain1.php3 [Accessed 3 April 2009].

Lilly, William, *Christian Astrology*, 3rd edn (1647; London: Regulus Publishing, 1985).

Lin, Martin, 'Teleology and Human Action in Spinoza', *The Philosophical Review* 115, no. 3 (2006), pp.317–54.

Long, A.A., 'Review: Calcidius', *The Classical Review* 25, no. 1 (1975), pp.52–54.

———, 'Soul and Body in Stoicism', *Phronesis* 27, no. 1 (1982), pp.34–57.

Long, A.A., and D.N. Sedley, *The Hellenistic Philosophers*, Vol. 1 (Cambridge: Cambridge University Press, 1987, 2007).

Loux, Michael J., *Metaphysics a Contemporary Introduction* (London and New York: Routledge, 2006).

Lucas, J.R., *The Freedom of the Will* (Oxford: Clarendon, 1970).

Lucretius, *De Rerum Natura*, trans. by W.H.D. Rouse, Loeb Classical Library (Harvard University Press, 1975).

Luisi, Pier Luigi, 'Contingency and Determinism', *Philosophical Transactions: Mathematical, Physical and Engineering Sciences* 361, no. 1807 (2003), pp.1141–47.

Markus, Hazel Rose, and Shinobu Kitayama, 'Culture and the Self. Implications for Cognition, Emotion, and Motivation', *Psychological Review* 98, no. 2 (1991), pp.244–53.

Marmura, Michael E., 'Some Aspects of Avicenna's Theory of God's Knowledge of Particulars', *Journal of the American Oriental Society* 82, no. 3 (1962), pp.299–312.

Martin, Clare, *Mapping the Psyche, an Introduction to Pyschological Astrology. Volume 1, the Planets and the Zodiac Signs* (London: Centre for Psychological Astrology Press, 2005).

Martin, John Levi, '"The Authoritarian Personality", 50 Years Later: What Lessons Are There for Political Psychology?', *Political Psychology* 22, no. 1 (2001), pp.1–26.

Mason, Jennifer, 'Linking Qualitative and Quantitative Data Analysis', In *Analyzing Qualitative Data*, ed. by Alan Bryman and Robert G. Burgess (London: Routledge, 1994), pp.89–109.

Massie, Pascal, *Contingency, Time and Possibility, an Essay on Aristotle and Duns Scotus* (Maryland: Lexington Books, 2011).

Matthews, Sarah H., 'Crafting Qualitative Research Articles on Marriages and Families', *Journal of Marriage and Family* 67, no. 4 (2005), pp.799–808.

Mayer, Michael, *The Mystery of Personal Identity* (San Diego, CA: ACS Publications, 1984).

McGilvary, Evander Bradley, 'Freedom and Necessity in Human Affairs', *International Journal of Ethics* 45, no. 4 (July 1935), pp.379–98.

McKenna, Michael, and Derk Pereboom, *Free Will : A Contemporary Introduction* (London: Routledge, 2016).

Melton, Gordon J., 'The Emergence of New Religions in Eastern Europe since 1989', In *New Religions and New Religiosity*, ed. by Eileen Baker and Margot Warburg (Aarhus: Aarhus University Press, 2001), pp.45–66.

Meštrović, Stjepan G., 'Rethinking the Will and Idea of Sociology in the Light of Schopenhauer's Philosophy', *The British Journal of Sociology* 40, no. 2 (1989), pp.271–93.

Mirti, Grazia, 'Galileo's Correspondence', trans. by Julianne Evans, in *Galileo's Astrology*, ed. by Nicholas Campion and Nick Kollerstrom (Bristol: Cinnabar Books, 2003), pp.73–96.

Mitchell, David, *Cloud Atlas: A Novel* (London: Random House, 2004).

Mo, Weimin, and Wang Wie, 'Cogito: From Descartes to Sartre', *Frontiers of Philosophy in China* 2, no. 2 (2007), pp.247–64.

Moreschini, C., ed., *St Gregory of Nazianzus, Poemata Arcana* (Oxford: Oxford University Press, 1997).

Morin, Jean-Baptiste, *The Morinus System of Horoscope Interpretation*, trans. by Richard S Baldwin, Astrologica Gallica Book Twenty One (1661; Washington, DC: AFA Inc., 1974).

Nederman, Cary J., and James Wray Goulding, 'Popular Occultism and Critical Social Theory: Exploring Some Themes in Adorno's Critique of Astrology and the Occult', *Sociological Analysis* 42, no. 4 (1981), pp.325–32.

Newton, Isaac, *Principia*, trans. by Motte-Cajori (Berkeley, CA: University of California Press, 1966).

———, *Newton's Principia, the Mathematical Principles of Natural Philosophy*, trans. Andrew Motte (New York: Daniel Adees, 1846).

Nichols, Shaun, 'Folk Intuitions on Free Will', http://www.ucl.ac.uk/~uctytho/dfwNichols.html [Accessed 7 July 2010].

Nichols, Shaun, and Joshua Knobe, 'Moral Responsibility and Determinism: The Cognitive Science of Folk Intuitions', *Nous* 41 (2007), pp.663–85.

Norton, John, 'The Dome: An Unexpectedly Simple Failure of Determinism', *Philosophy of Science* (2008), pp.786–98.

O'Connor, T., and H.Y. Wong, *Emergent Properties*, in E. N. Zalta, ed., *The Stanford Encyclopedia of Philosophy* (Fall 2015 Edition), https://plato.stanford.edu/entries/properties-emergent/

Oken, Alan, *Soul-Centered Astrology* (New York and London: Bantam, 1990).

Onians, Richard Broxton, *The Origins of European Thought About the Body, the Mind, the Soul, the World, Time and Fate* (1951; London: Cambridge University Press, 1954).

The Oxford Classical Dictionary, ed. by M.Cary, J.D. Denniston, J. Wright Duff, A.D. Nock, W.D. Ross and H.H.Scullard (Oxford: Clarendon Press, 1957).

Parpola, Simo, *Letters from Assyrian Scholars to the Kings Esarhaddon and Assurbanipal Part 1* (Germany: Butzon and Kevelaer, 1970).

Pereboom, Derk, 'Hard Incompatibilism', In *Four Views on Free Will*, ed. by John Martin Fischer (Oxford: Blackwell Publishing, 2007), pp.85–125.

———. 'Living without Fee Will: The Case for Hard Incompatibilism', In *The Oxford Handbook of Free Will* (Oxford: Oxford University Press, 2002), pp.477–88.

Peric, Zheljana, 'The Decline of Astrology: A Symbol of Man's Disconnection with Nature, Self and the Cosmos', Paper presented at the Proceedings of the 53rd Annual Meeting of the International Society for the Systems Sciences, University of Queensland, Brisbane, Australia July 12–17, 2009.

Pfeffer, Michelle, 'Reassessing the Marginalization of Astrology in the Early Modern World', *The Historical Journal* 66, no. 5 (2023), pp.1152–76.

Pingree, David, 'Astrology', In *Dictionary of the History of Ideas*, ed. by Philip P Weiner (New York: Charles Scribner's Sons, 1969).

Plato, *Alcibiades I*, trans. by D.S. Hutchinson, *Plato Complete Works*, ed. by John M. Cooper (Cambridge: Hackett Publishing Company, 1997).

———, *Laws*, trans. by Trevor J. Saunders, *Plato, Complete Works* (Cambridge: Hackett Publishing Company, 1997).

———, *Phaedo*, trans. by G.M.A Grube, *Plato Complete Works*, ed. by John M. Cooper (Cambridge: Hackett Publishing Company, 1997).

———, *Phaedrus*, trans. by Alexander Nehamas and Alexander Woodruff, *Plato Complete Works*, ed. by John M. Cooper (Cambridge: Hackett Publishing Company, 1997).

———, *Republic*, trans. by G.M.A Grube, rev. by C.D.C. Reeve, *Plato Complete Works*, ed. by John M. Cooper (Cambridge: Hackett Publishing Company, 1997).

———, *Timaeus*. trans. by Donald J. Zeyl, *Plato Complete Works*, ed. by John M. Cooper (Cambridge: Hackett Publishing Company, 1997).

Plotinus, *The Enneads*, trans. by Stephen MacKenna (New York: Larson Publications, 1992).

Poincaré, Henri Jules, *Science and Method* (London: T- Nelson, 1914).

Poppi, Antonino, 'On Trial for Astral Fatalism: Galileo Faces the Inquisition', In *Galileo's Astrology*, ed. by Nicholas Campion and Nick Kollerstrom (Bristol: Cinnabar Books, 2003), pp.49–58.

Potter, David, *Prophets and Emperors: Human and Divine Authority from Augustus to Theodosius* (Cambridge, MA: Harvard University Press, 1994).

Pritchard, James B., ed., *Ancient near Eastern Texts* (Princeton, NJ: Princeton University Press, 1969).

Proclus, *On Providence*, trans. by Carlos Steel (London: Bloomsbury Academic, 2014).

Project, Focus, 'First Light - Preliminary Findings from the Astrologer's Survey Questionnaire in the United States', In *U.A.C. '95*. (Monterey, CA: 1995).

Ptolemy, Claudius, *The Tetrabiblos*, trans. by J.M. Ashmand (Mokelumne Hill, CA: Health Research, 1969).

———, *Tetrabiblos Book I*, trans. by Robert Schmidt (Berkeley Springs, WV: The Golden Hind Press, 1994).

Quinn, Patrick, *St. Thomas Aquinas's Concept of the Human Soul and the Influence of Platonism* (New York: Brill, 2009).

Randall, Gerald H., 'Immanence, Stoic and Christian', *The Harvard Theological Review* 14, no. 1 (1921), pp.1–14.

Ray, John J., 'Why the F Scale Predicts Racism: A Critical Review', *Political Psychology* 9, no. 4 (1988), pp.671–79.

Rayner, Sheila, Clare Rayner, and Rob Newell, *Dane Rudhyar, an Interview*. Oral History of the Arts Archive (Long Beach, CA: University of California Press, 1977).

Rescher, Nicholas, *Process Metaphysics, an Introduction to Process Philosophy* (New York: State University of New York, 1996).

Rethy, Robert, 'The Teaching of Nature and the Nature of Man in Descartes' "Passions De L'ame"', *The Review of Metaphysics* 53, no. 3 (2000), pp.657–83.

Rochberg, Francesca, 'Fate and Divination in Mesopotamia', *Archiv für Orientforschung, Beiheft*, no. 19 (1982), pp.363–71.

———, *The Heavenly Writing, Divination, Horoscopy, and Astronomy in Mesopotamian Culture* (Cambridge, UK: Cambridge University Press, 2004).

Ross, W. D., *Aristotle*, 6th edn, with a new introduction by John L. Ackrill, ed. (London: Routledge, 1995).

Roth, Ann Macy, and Catharine H. Roehrig, 'Magical Bricks and the Bricks of Birth', *The Journal of Egyptian Archaeology* 88 (2002), pp.121–39.

Rudhyar, Dane, *Astrological Signs the Pulse of Life* (Boulder, CO, and London: Shambhala, 1978).

Schippers, Michaela, and Paul A.M. Van Lange, 'The Psychological Benefits of Superstitious Rituals in Top Sport: A Study among Top Sportspersons', *Jourrnal of Applied Social Psychology* 36, no. 10 (2006), pp.2532–53.

Schopenhauer, Arthur, ed., *Prize Essay on the Freedom of the Will* (Cambridge: Cambridge University Press, 1960).

———, *The World as Will and Idea* (1818; New York: Dover Press, 1969).

Scruton, Roger, 'Spinoza', in *The Great Philosophers, from Socrates to Turing*, ed. by Ray Monk and Frederic Raphael (London: Phoenix Paperback, 2000). pp.135–74.

Sela, Shlomo, ed., *Abraham Ibn Ezra's Introduction to Astrology* (Leiden and Boston, MA: Brill, 2017).

Sharp, Hasana, 'The Force of Ideas in Spinoza', *Political Theory* 35, no. 6 (2007), pp.732–55.

Shaw, Patricia, *Changing Conversations in Organizations: A Complexity Approach to Change* (London and New York: Routledge, 2002).

Simmel, Georg, *Schopenhauer and Nietzsche* (1907; Amherst, MA: University of Massachusetts Press, 1986).

Sklenář, R. ,'Seneca, Oedipus 980-94: How Stoic a Chorus?'. *The Classical Journal* 103, no. 2 (2007), pp.183–94.

Smith, Norman Kemp, 'The Naturalism of Hume (I)', *Mind* (1905), pp.149–73.

Smith, Steven B., 'What Kind of Democrat Was Spinoza?', *Political Theory* 33, no. 1 (2005), pp.6–27.

Sobel, Dava, *Galileo's Daughter* (London: Fourth Estate, 1999).

Solomon, Robert, 'On Fate and Fatalism', *Philosophy East and West* 53, no. 4 (October 2003), pp.435–54.

Sophocles, *Oedipus the King*, trans. by F. Storr (Cambridge, MA: Harvard University Press, 1912).

Soontiëns, F.J.K., 'Evolution: Teleology or Chance?'. *Journal for General Philosophy of Science / Zeitschrift für allgemeine Wissenschaftstheorie* 22, no. 1 (1991), pp.133–41.

Spinoza, Baruch de, *On the Improvement of the Understanding*. trans. by R.H.M. Elwes (MobileReference.com, 2008).

———, *The Ethics*, trans. by R.H.M. Elwes (1883; Forgotten Books, 2008).

Spinoza, Baruch de, S .Barbone, L .Rice, and L. Meijer *[Renati Des Cartes Principia: Philosophiae. English], The Principles of Cartesian Philosophy* (Hackett Pub., 1998).

Stent, Gunther S., 'Epistemic Dualism of Mind and Body', *Proceedings of the American Philosophical Society* 142, no. 4 (1998), pp.578–88.

Subbotsky, Eugene, *Magic and the Mind: Mechanisms, Functions, and Development of Magical Thinking and Behavior* (Oxford University Press, 2010).

Taylor, Bron, *Introducing Religion and Dark Green Religion* (Oakland, CA: University of California Press, 2010).

Thomas, Aquinas Saint, and Timothy McDermott, *Summa Theologiae* (Methuen: 1991).

Thorndike, Lynn, *A History of Magic and Experimental Science*, 8 vols (New York: Macmillan, 1958).

———, *The History of Magic and Experimental Science*, Vol. II (New York: MacMillan, 1923).

———, *History of Magic and Experimental Science Part 1* (New York and London: Columbia University Press, 1923).

Tiberias, Omar of, *Three Books on Nativities*, trans. by Robert Hand (Berkeley Springs, WV: Golden Hind Press, 1997).

Tilley, Christopher, *A Phenomenology of Landscape* (Oxford: Berg, 1994).

Tompkins, Sue, *The Contemporary Astrologer's Handbook* (London: Flare Publications, 2006).

Tyson, G.A., 'People Who Consult Astrologers: A Profile', *Personality and Individual Differences* 3 (1982), pp.119–26.

Urmson, J.O., *The Greek Philosophical Vocabulary* (London: Duckworth, 1990).

Valens, Vettius, 'The Anthologies', trans. by Mark Riley (2010). https://www.csus.edu/indiv/r/rileymt/Vettius%20Valens%20entire.pdf accessed 12 Sep 2009.

———. *The Anthology Book V & Vi*, trans. by Robert Schmidt (Berkeley Springs, WV: The Golden Hind Press, 1997).

Vargas, Manuel, 'Revisionism', In *Four Views on Free Will* (Oxford: Blackwell Publishing, 2007). pp.126–65.

Voltaire, 'The Ignorant Philosopher', in *The Best Known Works of Voltaire* (London: Blue Ribbon Books, 1932).

Vyse, Stuart A., *Superstition: A Very Short Introduction*, 1st edn (Oxford: Oxford University Press, 2019).

Ward, Margaret, 'Butterflies and Bifurcations: Can Chaos Theory Contribute to Our Understanding of Family Systems?', *Journal of Marriage and the Family* 57, no. 3 (1995), pp.629–38.

Waring, Philippa, *The Dictionary of Omens and Superstitions* (London: Treasure Press, 1978).

Watson, Gary, 'Free Action and Free Will', *Mind* 96, no. 382 (1987), pp.145–72.

——, 'Free Agency', *The Journal of Philosophy* 72, no. 8 (1975), pp.205–20.

——, 'Soft Libertarianism and Hard Compatibilism', *The Journal of Ethics* 3, no. 4 (1999), pp.351–65.

Watters, Barbara H., *Horary Astrology and the Judgment of Events* (Washington: Valhalla, 1973).

Wedel, Theodore Otto, *The Mediaeval Attitude toward Astrology, Particularly in England* (Oxford: University Press, 1920).

Weil, Simone, 'The Iliad, or the Poem of Force', *Chicago Review* 18, no. 2 (1965), pp.5–30.

Whitehead, Alfred North, *Adventures of Ideas* (Harmondsworth: Pelican Books, 1933, 1942).

Wolf, Susan, 'Asymmetrical Freedom', *The Journal of Philosophy* 77, no. 3 (1980), pp.151–66.

——. *Freedom within Reason* (New York and Oxford: Oxford University Press, 1990).

Wolfson, Elliot, 'Structure, Innovation, and Diremptive Temporality: The Use of Models to Study Continuity and Discontinuity in Kabbalistic Tradition', *Journal for the Study of Religions and Ideologies* 6, no. 18 (2007), pp.143–67.

Woodroff, John, Neil Bone, and Storm Dunlop, *Philip's Astronomy Dictionary* (London: George Philip Ltd, 1995).

Wuthnow, Robert, 'Astrology and Marginality', *Journal for the Scientific Study of Religion* 15, no. 2 (1976), pp.157–68.

Zain, C.C., *Delineating the Horoscope* (1922; Whitefish, MT: Kessinger Publishing, 2004).

Zucconi, L.M., 'Medicine and Religion in Ancient Egypt', *Religion Compass* 1, no. 1 (2007), pp.26–37.

INDEX

Abū Ma'shar, 40–41, 105
Adorno, Theodor, 80–83, 98,100
Akkadian, 10
Al-Ghazālī, 39, 46, 64
Almagest, 25
almutens, 40, 56
Ambient, 36, 37
Anankē, 17
antecedent causes, 2, 23, 24, 31, 59
Apollo, 12, 52
Aquinas, Saint Thomas, 43–44, 46, 49, 51, 60, 127
arbitrium brutum, 70
arbitrium sensitivum, 70
Aristotelian, 25–28, 33, 39, 43, 44, 45, 58–59, 91
Aristotle, 18–20, 29, 30, 31, 33, 36, 39, 42, 54, 89, 123, 127, 146
Ash'arite, 39, 40
Assyrian, 5, 11, 75
Astrologica nonnulla, 56
astrology, Aquinas, 44, 46
astrology, Arabic, 39, 42, 43, 45, 46, 56, 61
astrology, as divine force, 77
astrology, as magic, 77
astrology, definitions of, 23–24, 45, 75 (modern)
astrology, horary, *see* horary astrology.
astrology, medicine, 42, 44–46, 55
astrology, Morin, 57–58
astrology, purpose of, 93
astrology, reform, 57
Augustine, Saint, 33–35, 41, 46, 49, 60, 79
Avicenna, 38–39, 42
Big Bang, 63–64

Bonatti, Guido, 45–47, 87
Brenzoni, Ottavio, 56
Calcidius, 35–38, 46, 59, 69, 87, 116, 123, 140, 142
causal chain, 36–37, 39
causal-determinist, 4
causation, Aristotle's theory of, 36
causation, chain of, 20, 69, 70
causation, linear, 22, 51
causation, secondary, 39, 40
causation, theory of, 18, 19
cause, creator of, 44
causes, chain of, 34, 35
causes, secondary, 19, 33, 39–40, 44
ceteris paribus, 72
chains, internal that bound one, 53
Chaldeans, 23
Chance, 23
chaos theory, 71
Christian Astrology, 59
Christianity, 33, 43, 46, 51
chronos, 98
Chrysippus, 20, 21, 22
Cicero, Marcus Tullius, 20, 22–25, 31, 74, 75, 78, 79, 81, 106, 145,
Clark, Brian, 128, 129, 139, 140, 143
Coffin Texts, 10
comingLings, 26, 28, 29, 40
compatibilism, 22, 66, 70–71, 74, 97; see also incompatibilist.
compatibilism, definition, 66
compatibilist, 74, 85, 96, 97, 98, 99 ,102, 115, 126, 137, 140, 142
conatus, 53, 55, 60, 129
concurrentism, 44, 49
concurrentism, defination, 44

conflagration, 21, 22, 113
contingency/-ies, 18, 19, 36, 38, 43, 46, 47, 52
contingent/-s, 19, 36–38, 52
Cossar, Faye, 137, 138
cyclical, 21, 114, 148
Dante Alighieri, 45
Darwin, Charles, 65
Dawkins, Richard, 82, 98
deism, 44, 49, 50, 60
Demiurge, 15, 29
Democritus, 35
Descartes, René, 49–51, 55, 58, 60
desires, second-order, 70
destinies, argument of common 79
destinies, argument of different 79
Destiny, Tablets of, 10
determinism and fate, 72–73, 79, 142
determinism and the horoscope, 78
determinism as Necessity, 24, 78
determinism, celestial mechanics, 96
determinism, causal, 2, 38, 70
determinism, causal definition, 65
determinism, claims, 66
determinism, hard incompatibilism. See incompatibilism
determinism, Laplacian, 65
determinism, linear causation, 51
determinism, logical, 19, 31
determinism, moral, 17
determinism, moral responsibility, 68
determinism, not universal,

203

68–69
determinism, psychological, 125
determinism, universal, 38, 63, 65, 67, 68, 69, 71–73, 150
Diogenes, 20
divination, 25, 76–78, 84, 96, 146
dome, the, 72
Dominus Geniturae, 56
dualism/-ist, 16–18, 23, 30–31, 34, 42–44, 46, 49–51, 60, 67, 69, 90, 106, 117, 120, 131–32, 136, 143
Dunn, Barbara, 141, 142
Dykes, Ben, 124, 126
Egypt/-ian, 5, 7–10, 154
elements, Aristotelian, 25, 44
elements, comingling, 26, 44
elements, the four, 18, 19, 25, 26, 30, 39, 40, 43–45, 146
emergent, 65, 92, 94, 113, 114, 132, 143, 148–50,
Enūma Eliš, 10
Epictetus, 21, 27, 87, 109
fatalism, 2, 3, 22, 34, 35, 82, 83, 92, 103
fatalism, theological, 34
fatalistic, 22, 56
Fate as story, 149–50
fate creator, 46, 59, 141
fate, hybrid, 98, 102, 135
fate, negotiable, 96, 97, 98, 99, 102
Fate, theories of, 29–31, 89–92, 96, 106, 114, 116, 120, 143, 153
Fate, theory of, Stoic, 92
figure-flingers, astrologers, 80
fractals, 148
free will problem, 51, 66
freedom, delusion of, 35
F-Scale, 80
futilism, 29, 108
Galileo Galilei, 55–57, 59, 61
Garden of Eden, 36
Gellius, Aulus, 22
George, Demetra, 124, 126, 131
Gillett, Roy, 126
God's providence, 3, 29, 30, 33–36, 39, 41, 44, 46, 52, 64, 92, 103
Goethe, Johann Wolfgang von, 63, 64
Greene, Liz, 85, 124, 126–129,

131–32, 136, 143
Hamaker-Zondag, Karen, 133
Hammurabi, Code of, 10
Hand, Robert, 26, 45, 77, 133, 134
Hector, 11–13, 52
Heka, 9–10
Heraclitus, 146
Homer, 11–14, 16, 52
horary astrology, 58–59, 140, 141, 142, 157
horoscope, a Spinozian approach, 55
horoscope, inevitable, 78, 79, 83
human agency, 4, 7, 15, 24, 25, 33, 44, 49
Hume, David, 63, 66–68, 70, 73, 142
Ibn Ezra, Abraham, 41–42, 46
Iliad, 11–14, 52
immanent, 15, 20, 22, 37, 54, 90, 124, 151
incompatibilism, 55, 60, 66, 69, 74, 78, 92, 99, 101 105, 106
incompatibilism, definition, 66
incompatibilism, hard, 55, 60, 78, 92, 9, 101, 104–6
indeterminism, 72, 73, 147
indigenous astronomy, 85
inevitable future, 98 105
inevitable horoscope, 78, 79, 83; non-inevitable horoscope, 133
James, William, 65, 117, 118
jinxes, 38, 146
kairos, 98
Kant, Immanuel, 63, 64, 70
Laplace, Marquis Pierre Simon, 64, 65, 71
Leo, Alan, 83, 106–7, 113, 117, 130, 131
Lévy-Bruhl, Lucien, 146–47, 149, 151
libertarian/-ism, 37, 68, 69, 74, 78, 85, 86, 96, 99, 103, 108, 117, 140, 142
libertarian, definition, 68
libertarian, non-causal, 69, 74, 79
libertarianism, agent causal, 69
libertarianism, causal, 69
Lilly, William, 55, 58–59, 61, 77, 135, 140, 141

Lucretius, Titus, 68
maat, 7–9
magic, 9, 10, 24, 77
Mandelbrot, Benoit, 148
Marduk, 10
Martin, Clare, 127, 133, 134
Maternus, Firmicus, 105
matter, passive, 60
mental self-agency, 22, 24
Meskhenet, Egyptian deity, 8, 13
Mesopotamian/-s, 5, 7, 11, 13, 17, 24
miracles, 39, 67
Moirai, 11, 13, 15, 16, 17, 24
monist, 19, 22, 30, 31, 51
moral responsibility, 13, 15, 20, 22, 24, 30, 31, 35–37, 66–68, 70, 72–74, 78, 87, 99, 101, 106, 116, 131, 142
Morin, Jean-Baptiste, 55, 57–58, 59, 61
Moses, 36
mystical mind, 147
Myth of Er, 16
nam-tar, Akkadian fate, 10
necessity, 11–12, 13, 15–17, 22, 24–25, 27, 28, 31, 34, 36–37, 43, 46, 47, 49, 52, 54, 60, 63, 78, 106, 116, 160,
Newton, Isaac, 26, 60, 63–64, 65, 71
Nyssa, Saint Gregory of, 79
occasionalism, 39, 40, 44, 49, 64
Oedipus, 12, 13, 15, 22
Oedipus Rex, 12, 13, 15, 22
Oken, Alan, 125–26, 129–30, 135–39, 143
Omar of Tiberias, 40, 41
Oracle of Delphi, 12
participation, 103, 114, 151
particulars, 36, 38–39, 40, 41
Plato, 10, 13, 14, 15–18, 20, 21, 23, 26, 28, 29, 31, 34, 35, 36, 39, 50, 51, 53, 54, 65, 70, 87, 89 106–7, 123, 127, 129, 135, 146,
Platonic theory of fate, 90
Platonist, model, 22, 30
Plotinus, 123, 130
Pneuma, 20, 30, 146
Poincaré, Jules Henri, 71
predestination, 3, 39

prime mover, 18, 37
proper place, 19, 60, 146
providence, 27, 29, 39, 41; *see also* God's providence.
Ptahhotep, Instructions of, 7–8
Ptolemy, Claudius, 20, 25–29, 31, 42, 96, 108, 115, 120
reincarnation, 17, 21, 35–36, 83, 121, 150
Reinhart, Melanie, 136
Renenet, Egyptian deity, 8, 9, 13
res cogitans, 50, 60
res extensa, 50, 60
Rudhyar, Dane, 77, 91, 113, 117, 120, 134, 142
Schlegel, Friedrich von, 63, 64
Schopenhauer, Arthur, 132
sea battle, 19, 31
self-agency, 4, 37, 44, 63, 116, 142
self-identity, 1, 151–52
self-similarity, 148, 149, 150
Seven Hathors, 9, 13
Shai, Egyptian deity, 8, 9, 13
šīmtu, Akkadian fate, 10
Skinner, Christeen, 132–34
Sophocles, 12–14, 15, 16, 22
soul, 7, 8, 15–20, 21, 22, 23, 24, 26, 27, 28, 30, 31, 37, 38, 39, 42, 43, 44, 46–7, 50, 51, 55, 60, 67, 79, 87, 91–92, 104, 106–7, 109, 117, 118, 121, 123, 124, 126, 127–133, 142, 146, 161
soul, Thomist, 43
specie durationis, 54
Spindle of Necessity, 16, 17, 24, 31
Spinoza, Baruch de, 49, 51–55, 60, 66, 67, 71, 78, 109, 111, 150
Stoic, 7, 20–24, 25, 26, 27–29, 30, 31, 33, 34, 53–54, 60, 67, 87, 91, 92, 96, 99, 108, 109, 111, 112–15, 123, 124, 125, 126, 131, 136, 142, 149
sub specie aeternitatis, 53, 54, 55, 60, 140, 152
sublunar, 19, 25, 39, 40, 42, 45, 46, 56
sumpatheia, 20, 30, 146, 149
superstition/-s, 3, 4, 38, 61, 75, 76, 80, 146
sympathetic, 20, 22, 27, 28, 30, 33, 60, 90, 92, 96, 108, 112, 118, 121, 122, 123, 124, 126, 129, 140, 142, 143, 146, 149, 150, 154
sympathy, 20, 31, 40, 60, 146,
synchronicities, 146, 149, 154
Tale of the Doomed Prince, 9
Tatian, freedom of the will, 21
teleology/-ical, 94, 95, 149
Tetrabiblos, 25, 26, 28
Thoth, 8, 9
Three Bodies problem, 71
Tiamat, 10
Tompkins, Sue, 138–39, 143
transcendent, 15, 20, 54, 90
Tyche, 23, 31, 36
universals, 38, 39, 41, 46
Valens, 28, 29, 30, 31
Ward, Sue, 135, 136
weighing of the heart, 8, 9 (*image*), 154
Whitehead, Alfred, 60, 94, 113
World Soul, 15, 17, 20, 22, 30, 123, 126, 127, 146
Zain, C.C., 119–20
Zeno of Citium, 20
Zoller, Robert, 105

www.ingramcontent.com/pod-product-compliance
Lightning Source LLC
Chambersburg PA
CBHW061227070526
44584CB00029B/4026